By Robert L. Heilbroner

The Worldly Philosophers

*The Lives, Times, and Ideas of
the Great Economic Thinkers*

ROBERT L. HEILBRONER

A CLARION BOOK
Published by
SIMON AND SCHUSTER

THIRD EDITION, NEWLY REVISED—THIRD PRINTING
FOURTH PAPERBACK PRINTING
SBN 671-20151-4
LIBRARY OF CONGRESS CATALOG CARD NUMBER: 53-10871
MANUFACTURED IN THE UNITED STATES OF AMERICA
PRINTED BY THE MURRAY PTG. CO., FORGE VILLAGE, MASS.

TO

ADOLPH LOWE

WITH DEEPEST RESPECT

AND TO

JOAN

WITH DEEPEST LOVE

CONTENTS

PREFACE TO THE
THIRD REVISED EDITION

This is the third time I have revised The Worldly Philosophers
*—which is to say, the third time I have read the book cover to
cover since I wrote it. Each reading has come as a surprise,
partly pleasurable and partly not. It is very satisfying when I
find that I still agree with myself over the years. It is not when
I don't.*

*Some of these disagreements are simply the fruit of new knowl-
edge about the past—knowledge that rarely changes the main
outlines of our conception of economic thought and history, but
that requires alterations in detail and emphasis. These are scattered here and there throughout the book and will be unnoticeable except to the eye of an expert.*

*More important are the disagreements when the book turns to
the interpretation of the present or the prognosis for the future.
In the sections on imperialism, Marxism, the population problem, and current American problems, I have been forced to throw
out paragraphs, and even pages, to give voice to an increasing
disquietude I have felt since the last edition was published. The
central theme of this book is, after all, the evolution of capitalism, and whereas I am, if anything, more sanguine about the
long-term evolutionary possibilities for America, I am also much
more concerned about the chances for short-run miscalculation
and tragedy. All this is, however, in the background of the book;
the purpose of these pages remains, as before, to propound the
views of the Worldly Philosophers and not my own.*

9

Finally, I should like to thank the many readers, especially students and instructors, who have been kind enough to write to me, instead of making the usual exclamation marks in the margins of their books, when they objected to my prose, or caught me out in some fact, or quarreled with my interpretation of ideas. I have repaired a lot of prose, have altered some facts, and have at least thought hard about the ideas in question, even if I have not always changed them. In my Acknowledgments I have said that this book owes its existence in large part to my teachers. I am happy that I can now number so many readers and students among those teachers.

ROBERT L. HEILBRONER

March 1967

I

Introduction

THIS is a book about a handful of men with a curious claim to fame. By all the rules of schoolboy history books, they were nonentities: they commanded no armies, sent no men to their deaths, ruled no empires, took little part in history-making decisions. A few of them achieved renown, but none was ever a national hero; a few were roundly abused, but none was ever quite a national villain. Yet what they did was more decisive for history than many acts of statesmen who basked in brighter glory, often more profoundly disturbing than the shuttling of armies back and forth across frontiers, more powerful for good and bad than the edicts of kings and legislatures. It was this: they shaped and swayed men's minds.

And because he who enlists a man's mind wields a power even greater than the sword or the scepter, these men shaped and swayed the world. Few of them ever lifted a finger in action; they worked, in the main, as scholars—quietly, inconspicuously, and without much regard for what the world had to say about them. But they left in their train shattered empires and exploded continents, they buttressed and undermined political regimes, they set class against class and even nation against nation—not because they plotted mischief, but because of the extraordinary power of their ideas.

Who were these men? We know them as the Great Economists. But what is strange is how little we know about them. One would think that in a world torn by economic problems, a world that constantly worries about economic affairs and talks of economic issues, the great economists would be as familiar as the great philosophers or statesmen. Instead they are only shadowy figures of the past, and the matters they so passionately debated are regarded with a kind of distant awe. Economics, it is said, is undeniably important, but it is cold and difficult, and best left to those who are at home in abstruse realms of thought.

Nothing could be further from the truth. A man who thinks that economics is only a matter for professors forgets that this is the science that has sent men to the barricades. A man who has looked into an economics textbook and concluded that economics is boring is like a man who has read a primer on logistics and decided that the study of warfare must be dull.

No, the great economists pursued an inquiry as exciting—and as dangerous—as any the world has ever known. The ideas they dealt with, unlike the ideas of the great philosophers, did not make little difference to our daily working lives; the experiments they urged could not, unlike the scientists', be carried out in the isolation of a laboratory. The notions of the great economists were world-shaking, and their mistakes nothing short of calamitous.

"The ideas of economists and political philosophers," wrote Lord Keynes, himself a great economist, "both when they are right and when they are wrong, are more powerful than is commonly understood. Indeed the world is ruled by little else. Practical men, who believe themselves to be quite exempt from any intellectual influences, are usually the slaves of some defunct economist. Madmen in authority, who hear voices in the air, are distilling their frenzy from some academic scribbler of a few years back. I am sure that the power of vested interests is vastly exaggerated compared with the gradual encroachment of ideas."

To be sure, not all the economists were such titans. Thousands of them wrote texts, some of them monuments of dullness, and explored minutiae with all the zeal of medieval scholars. If economics today has little glamour, if its sense of great adventure is often lacking, it has no one to blame but its own practitioners. For the Great Economists were no mere intellectual fusspots. They took the whole world as their subject, and portrayed that world in a dozen bold attitudes: angry, desperate, hopeful. The evolution of their heretical opinions into common sense, and their exposure of common sense as superstition, constitute nothing less than the gradual construction of the architecture of contemporary life.

An odder group of men—one less apparently destined to remake the world—could scarcely be imagined.

There were among them a philosopher and a madman, a parson and a stockbroker, a revolutionary and a nobleman, an aesthete, a skeptic, and a tramp. They were of every nationality, of every walk of life, of every turn of temperament. Some were brilliant, some were bores; some ingratiating, some impossible. At least three made their own fortunes, but as many could never master the elementary economics of their personal finances. Two were eminent businessmen, one was never much more than a traveling salesman, another frittered away his fortune.

Their viewpoints toward the world were as varied as their fortunes—there was never such a quarrelsome group of thinkers. One was a lifelong advocate of women's rights; another insisted that women were demonstrably inferior to men. One held that "gentlemen" were only barbarians, whereas another maintained that non-gentlemen were savages. One of them—who was very rich—urged the abolition of riches; another—quite poor—disapproved of charity. Several of them claimed that with all its shortcomings, this was the best of all possible worlds; several others devoted their lives to proving that it wasn't.

All of them wrote books, but a more varied library was never seen. One or two wrote best sellers that reached to the mud huts of Asia; others had to pay to have their obscure works published and never touched an audience beyond the most restricted circles. A few wrote in language that stirred the pulse of millions; others —no less important to the world—wrote in a prose which then, as now, fogs the brain.

It was neither their personalities, their careers, their biases, nor even their ideas which bound them together. Their common denominator was something else: a common curiosity. They were all fascinated by the world about them, by its complexity and its seeming disorder, by the cruelty which it so often masked in sanctimony and the successes of which it was so often unaware.

They were all of them absorbed in the behavior of their fellow man, first as he created material wealth, and then as he trod on the toes of his neighbor to gain a share of it.

Hence they can be called the worldly philosophers, for they sought to embrace in a scheme of philosophy the most worldly of all of man's activities—his drive for wealth. It is not, perhaps, the most elegant kind of philosophy, but there is no more intriguing or more important one. Who would think to look for Order and Design in a pauper family and a speculator breathlessly awaiting ruin, or seek Consistent Laws and Principles in a mob marching in a street and a greengrocer smiling at his customers? Yet it was the faith of the great economists that just such seemingly unrelated threads could be woven into a single tapestry, that at a sufficient distance the milling world could be seen as an orderly progression, and the tumult resolved into a chord.

A large order of faith, indeed! And yet, astonishingly enough, it turned out to be justified. For once the economists had unfolded their patterns before the eyes of their generations, the pauper and the speculator, the greengrocer and the mob were no longer incongruous actors inexplicably thrown together on a stage; but each was understood to play a role, happy or otherwise, which was essential for the advancement of the human drama itself. When the economists were done, what had been only a humdrum or a chaotic world became an ordered society with a meaningful life history of its own.

It is this search for the order and meaning of social history that lies at the heart of economics. Hence it is the central theme of this book. We are embarked not on a lecture tour of principles, but on a journey through history-shaping ideas. We will meet not only pedagogues on our way, but many paupers, many speculators both ruined and triumphant, many mobs, even here and there a grocer. We shall be going back to rediscover the roots of our own society in the welter of social patterns which the great economists discerned, and in so doing we shall come to know the great economists themselves—not merely because their personalities were often colorful but because their ideas bore the stamp of their originators.

It would be convenient if we could begin straight oft with the first of the great economists—Adam Smith himself. But Adam Smith lived at the time of the American Revolution and we must account for the perplexing fact that six thousand years of recorded history had rolled by and no *worldly* philosopher had yet come to dominate the scene. An odd fact: man had struggled with the economic problem since long before the time of the Pharaohs, and in these centuries he had produced philosophers by the score, scientists, political thinkers, historians, artists by the gross, statesmen by the hundred dozen. Why, then, were there no economists?

It will take us a chapter to find out. Until we have probed the nature of an earlier and far longer-lasting world than our own—a world in which an economist would have been not only unnecessary but impossible—we cannot set the stage on which the great economists may take their places. Our main concern will be with the handful of men who lived in the last two centuries. First, however, we must understand the world which preceded their entrance and we must watch that earlier world give birth to the modern age—the age of the economists—amid all the upheaval and agony of a major revolution.

II
The Economic Revolution

SINCE he came down from the trees, man has faced the problem of survival, not as an individual but as a member of a social group. His continued existence is testimony to the fact that he has succeeded in solving the problem; but the continued existence of want and misery, even in the richest of nations, is evidence that his solution has been, at best, a partial one.

Yet man is not to be too severely censured for his failure to achieve a paradise on earth. It is hard to wring a livelihood from the surface of this planet. It staggers the imagination to think of the endless efforts that must have been expended in the first domestication of animals, in the discovery of planting seed, in the first working of surface ores. It is only because man is a socially cooperative creature that he has succeeded in perpetuating himself at all.

But the very fact that he has had to depend on his fellow man has made the problem of survival extraordinarily difficult. Man is not an ant, conveniently equipped with an inborn pattern of social instincts. On the contrary, he seems to be stubbornly endowed with a fiercely self-centered nature. If his relatively weak physique forces him to seek cooperation, his untamed inner drives constantly threaten to disrupt his social working partnerships.

In primitive society, the struggle between aggression and cooperation is taken care of by the environment; when the specter of starvation looks a community in the face every day—as with the Eskimos or the African hunting tribes—the pure need for self-preservation pushes society to the cooperative completion of its daily tasks. But in an advanced community, this tangible pressure of the environment is lacking. When men no longer work shoulder to shoulder in tasks directly related to survival—indeed when half or more of the population never touches the earth, enters the mines, builds with its hands, or even enters a factory—the perpetuation of the human animal becomes a remarkable social feat.

So remarkable, in fact, that society's existence hangs by a hair. A modern community is at the mercy of a thousand dangers: if its farmers should fail to plant enough crops, if its railroad men should take it into their heads to become bookkeepers or its bookkeepers should decide to become railroad men; if too few should offer their services as miners, puddlers of steel, candidates for engineering degrees—in a word, if any of a thousand intertwined tasks of society should fail to get done—industrial life would soon become hopelessly disorganized. Every day the community faces the possibility of breakdown—not from the forces of nature, but from sheer human unpredictability.

Over the centuries man has found only three ways of guarding against this calamity.

He has ensured his continuity by organizing his society around tradition, by handing down the varied and necessary tasks from generation to generation according to custom and usage: son follows father and a pattern is preserved. In ancient Egypt, says Adam Smith, "every man was bound by a principle of religion to follow the occupation of his father, and was supposed to commit the most horrible sacrilege if he changed it for another." Similarly, in India, until recently, certain occupations were traditionally assigned by caste; in fact, in much of the unindustrialized world, one is still born to one's métier.

Or society can solve the problem differently. It can use the whip of central authoritarian rule to see that its tasks get done. The pyramids of ancient Egypt did not get built because some enterprising contractor took it into his head to build them, nor do the Five Year Plans of the Soviet Union get carried out because they happen to accord with hand-me-down custom or individual self-interest. Both Russia and Egypt are authoritarian societies; politics aside, they have ensured their *economic survival* by the edict of one authority and by the penalties that supreme authority sees fit to issue.

For countless centuries man dealt with the problem of survival according to one or the other of these solutions. And as long as the problem was handled by tradition or command, it never gave rise to that special field of study called economics. Although the societies of history have shown the most astonishing economic diversity, although they have exalted kings and commissars, used dried codfish and immovable stones for money, distributed their goods in the simplest communistic patterns or in the most highly ritualistic fashion, so long as they ran by custom or command, they needed no economists to make them comprehensible. Theologians, political theorists, statesmen, philosophers, historians, yes—but, strange as it may seem, economists, no.

For the economists waited upon the invention of a third solution to the problem of survival. They waited upon the development of an astonishing game in which society assured its own continuance by allowing each individual to do exactly as he saw fit—provided he followed a central guiding rule. The game was called the "market system," and the rule was deceptively simple: each should do what was to his best monetary advantage. In the market system the lure of gain, not the pull of tradition or the whip of authority, steered each man to his task. And yet, although each was free to go wherever his acquisitive nose directed him, the interplay of one man against another resulted in the necessary tasks of society getting done.

It was this paradoxical, subtle, and difficult solution to the problem of survival that called forth the economist. For unlike the simplicity of custom and command, it was not at all obvious that with each man out only for his own gain, society could in fact endure. It was by no means clear that all the jobs of society— the dirty ones as well as the plush ones—would be done if custom and command no longer ran the world. When society no longer obeyed one man's dictates, who was to say where it would end?

It was the economists who undertook to explain this puzzle. But until the idea of the market system itself had gained acceptance, there was no puzzle to explain. And until a very few centuries ago, men were not at all sure that the market system was not to be viewed with suspicion, distaste, and distrust. The world

had gotten along for centuries in the comfortable rut of tradition and command; to abandon this security for the dubious and
perplexing security of the market system, nothing short of a revolution was required.

It was the most important revolution, from the point of view
of shaping modern society, that ever took place—fundamentally
more disturbing by far than the French, American, or even the
Russian Revolutions. To appreciate its magnitude, to understand
the wrenching which it gave society, we must immerse ourselves
in that earlier and long-forgotten world from which our own
society finally sprang. Only then will it be clear why the economists had so long to wait.

First stop: France. The year, 1305.

It is a fair we visit. The traveling merchants have arrived that
morning with their armed guard, have set up their gaily striped
tents, and are trading among themselves and with the local population. A variety of exotic goods is for sale: silks and taffetas,
spices and perfumes, hides and furs. Some have been transported
from the Levant, some from Scandinavia, some from only a few
hundred miles away. Along with the common people, local lords
and ladies frequent the stalls, eager to relieve the tedium of their
boring, draughty, manorial lives; along with the strange goods
from Araby they are eagerly acquiring new words from that incredibly distant land: divan, syrup, tariff, artichoke, spinach, jar.

But inside the tents we meet with a strange sight. Books of
business, open on the table, are sometimes no more than note-
books of transactions; a sample extract from one merchant reads:
"Owed ten gulden by a man since Whitsuntide. I forgot his
name." Calculations are made largely in Roman numerals and
sums are often wrong; long division is reckoned as something of
a mystery and the use of zero is not clearly understood. And for
all the gaudiness of the display and the excitement of the people,
the fair is a small thing. The total amount of goods which comes
into France in a year over the Saint Gothard pass (on the first sus-
pension bridge in history) would not fill a modern freight train;
the total amount of merchandise carried in the great Venetian
fleet would not fill one modern steel freighter.

Next stop: Germany. The year, 1550 odd.

Andreas Ryff, a merchant, bearded and fur-coated, is coming back to his home in Baden; he writes in a letter to his wife that he has visited thirty markets and is troubled with saddle-burn. He is even more troubled by the nuisances of the times; as he travels he is stopped approximately once every six miles to pay a customs toll; between Basle and Cologne he pays thirty-one levies.

And that is not all. Each community he visits has its own money, its own rules and regulations, its own law and order. In the area around Baden alone there are 112 different measures of length, 92 different square measures, 65 different dry measures, 163 different measures for cereals and 123 for liquids, 63 special measures for liquor, and 80 different pound weights.

We move on: we are in Boston in the year 1644.

A trial is in progress; one Robert Keayne, "an ancient professor of the gospel, a man of eminent parts, wealthy and having but one child, and having come over for conscience' sake and for the advancement of the gospel," is charged with a heinous crime: he has made over sixpence profit on the shilling, an outrageous gain. The court is debating whether to excommunicate him for his sin, but in view of his spotless past it finally relents and dismisses him with a fine of two hundred pounds. But poor Mr. Keayne is so upset that before the elders of the Church he does "with tears acknowledge his covetous and corrupt heart." The minister of Boston cannot resist this golden opportunity to profit from the living example of a wayward sinner and he uses the example of Keayne's avarice to thunder forth in his Sunday sermon on some false principles of trade. Among them are these:

"I. That a man might sell as dear as he can, and buy as cheap as he can.

"II. If a man lose by casualty of sea, etc., in some of his commodities, he may raise the price of the rest.

"III. That he may sell as he bought, though he paid too dear. . . ."

All false, false, false, cries the minister; to seek riches for riches' sake is to fall into the sin of avarice.

We turn back to England and France.

In England a great trading organization, The Merchant Adventurers Company, has drawn up its articles of incorporation; among them are these rules for the participating merchants: no indecent language, no quarrels among the brethren, no card playing, no keeping of hunting dogs. No one is to carry unsightly bundles in the streets. This is indeed an odd business firm; it sounds more nearly like a fraternal lodge.

In France there has been entirely too much initiative displayed of late by the weaving industry, and a *règlement* has been promulgated by Colbert in 1666 to get away from this dangerous and disruptive tendency. Henceforth the fabrics of Dijon and Selangey are to contain 1,408 threads including selvages, neither more nor less. At Auxerre, Avallon, and two other manufacturing towns, the threads are to number 1,376; at Châtillon, 1,216. Any cloth found to be objectionable is to be pilloried. If it is found three times to be objectionable, the merchant is to be pilloried instead.

There is something common to all these scattered fragments of bygone worlds. It is this: first, the idea of the propriety (not to say the necessity) of a system organized on the basis of *personal gain* has not yet taken root. Second, a separate, self-contained economic world has not yet lifted itself from its social context. The world of practical affairs is inextricably mixed up with the world of political, social, and religious life. Until the two worlds separate, there will be nothing that resembles the tempo and the feeling of modern life. And for the two to separate, a long and bitter struggle must take place.

It may strike us as odd that the idea of gain is a relatively modern one; we are schooled to believe that man is essentially an acquisitive creature and that left to himself he will behave as any self-respecting businessman would. The profit motive, we are constantly being told, is as old as man himself.

But it is not. The profit motive as we know it is only as old as "modern man." Even today the notion of gain for gain's sake is foreign to a large portion of the world's population, and it has been conspicuous by its absence over most of recorded history. Sir William Petty, an astonishing seventeenth-century character (who was in his lifetime cabin boy, hawker, clothier, physician, professor of music, and founder of a school named Political

Arithmetick), claimed that when wages were good, labor was "scarce to be had at all, so licentious are they who labor only to eat, or rather to drink." And Sir William was not merely venting the bourgeois prejudices of his day. He was observing a fact which can still be remarked among the unindustrialized peoples of the world: a raw working force, unused to wagework, uncomfortable in factory life, unschooled to the idea of an ever-rising standard of living, will not work harder if wages rise; it will simply take more time off. The idea of gain, the idea that each man not only may but should constantly strive to better his material lot, is an idea which was quite foreign to the great lower and middle strata of Egyptian, Greek, Roman, and medieval cultures, only scattered throughout Renaissance and Reformation times, and largely absent in the majority of Eastern civilizations. As a ubiquitous characteristic of society, it is as modern an invention as printing.

Not only is the idea of gain by no means as universal as we sometimes suppose, but the social sanction of gain is an even more modern and restricted development. In the Middle Ages the Church taught that "No Christian ought to be a merchant," and behind that dictum lay the thought that merchants were a disturbing yeast in the leaven of society. In Shakespeare's time the object of life for the ordinary citizen, for everybody, in fact, except the gentility, was not to advance his station in life, but to maintain it. Even to our Pilgrim forefathers, the idea that gain might be a tolerable—even a useful—goal in life would have appeared as nothing short of a doctrine of the devil.

Wealth, of course, there has always been, and covetousness is at least as old as the Biblical tales. But there is a vast deal of difference between the envy inspired by the wealth of a few mighty personages and a general struggle for wealth diffused throughout society. Merchant adventurers have existed as far back as the Phoenician sailors, and can be seen all through history, in the speculators of Rome, the trading Venetians, the Hanseatic League, and the great Portuguese and Spanish voyagers who sought a route to the Indies and to their personal fortunes. But the adventures of a few are a far different thing from an entire society moved by the venture spirit.

Take, for example, the extraordinary family of the Fuggers,

the great bankers of the sixteenth century. At their height, the Fuggers owned gold and silver mines, trade concessions, and even the right to coin their own money; their credit was far greater than the wealth of the kings and emperors whose wars (and household expenses) they financed. But when old Anton Fugger died, his eldest nephew, Hans Jacob, refused to take over the banking empire on the ground that the business of the city and his own affairs gave him too much to do; Hans Jacob's brother, George, said he would rather live in peace; a third nephew, Christopher, was equally uninterested. None of the potential heirs to a kingdom of wealth apparently thought it was worth the bother.

Apart from kings (those that were solvent) and a scattering of families like the Fuggers, the early capitalists were not the pillars of society, but often its outcasts and *déracinés*. Here and there an enterprising lad like Saint Godric of Finchale would start as a beachcomber, gather enough wares from the wrecks of ships to become a merchant, and after making his fortune, retire in sanctity as a hermit. But such men were few. As long as the paramount idea was that life on earth was only a trying preamble to Life Eternal, the business spirit was neither encouraged nor did it find spontaneous nourishment. Kings wanted treasure and for that they fought wars; the nobility wanted land and since no self-respecting nobleman would willingly sell his ancestral estates, that entailed conquest, too. But most people—serfs, village craftsmen, even the masters of the manufacturing guilds—wanted to be left alone to live as their fathers had and as their sons would in turn.

The absence of the idea of gain as a normal guide for daily life —in fact the positive disrepute with which the idea was held by the Church—constituted one enormous difference between the strange world of the tenth to sixteenth centuries and the world that began, a century or two before Adam Smith, to resemble our own. But there was an even more fundamental difference. The idea of "making a living" had not yet come into being. Economic life and social life were one and the same thing. Work was not yet a means to an end—the end being money and the things it buys. Work was an end in itself, encompassing, of course, money and commodities, but engaged in as a part of a tradition, as a natural way of life. In a word, the great social invention of "the market" had not yet been made.

Markets, of course, have existed as far back as history goes. The Tablets of Tell-el-Amarna tell of lively trade between the Pharaohs and the Levantine kings in 1400 B.C.: gold and war chariots were swapped for slaves and horses. But while the idea of exchange must be very nearly as old as man, as with the idea of gain, we must not make the mistake of assuming that all the world has the bargaining propensities of a twentieth-century American schoolboy. Purely by way of curious illustration, it is reported that among the New Zealand Maoris you cannot ask how much food a bonito-hook is worth, for such a trade is never made and the question would be regarded as ridiculous. By way of turnabouts, however, in some African communities it is perfectly legitimate to inquire how many oxen a woman is worth—an exchange which we look upon as the Maoris do swapping food and fishhooks (although where dowries still exist, they narrow the gap between us and the Africans.)

But markets, whether they be exchanges between primitive tribes where objects are casually dropped on the ground or the exciting traveling fairs of the Middle Ages, are not the same as the market system. For the market system is not just a means of exchanging goods; *it is a mechanism for sustaining and maintaining an entire society.*

And that mechanism was far from clear to the minds of the medieval world. The concept of widespread gain was blasphemous enough, as we have seen. The broader notion that a general struggle for gain might actually bind together a community would have been held as little short of madness.

There was a reason for this blindness. The Middle Ages, the Renaissance, the Reformation—indeed the whole world until the sixteenth or seventeenth centuries—could not envisage the market system for the thoroughly sound reason that Land, Labor, and Capital—the basic agents of production which the market system allocates—did not yet exist. Land, labor, and capital in the sense of soil, human beings, and tools are of course coexistent with society itself. But the idea of abstract land or abstract labor did not immediately suggest itself to the human mind, any more than did the idea of abstract energy or matter. Land, labor, and capital as "agents" of production, as impersonal, dehumanized economic entities, are as much modern conceptions as the calculus. Indeed, they are not much older.

Take, for example, land. As late as the fourteenth or fifteenth century there was no land, at least in the modern sense of freely salable, rent-producing property. There were lands, of course—estates, manors, and principalities—but these were emphatically not real estate to be bought and sold as the occasion warranted. Such lands formed the core of social life, provided the basis for prestige and status, and constituted the foundation for the military, judicial, and administrative organization of society. Although land was salable under certain conditions (with many strings attached), it was not generally *for sale*. A medieval nobleman in good standing would no more have thought of selling his land than the governor of Connecticut would think of selling a few counties to the governor of Rhode Island.

And the same lack of salability was true for labor. When we talk of the labor market today, we mean the endless bargaining process in which individuals sell their services to the highest bidder. There simply was no such process in the precapitalist world. There was a vast hodgepodge of serfs, apprentices, and journeymen who labored, but most of this labor never entered a market to be bought and sold. In the country, the peasant lived tied to his lord's estate; he baked at the lord's oven and ground at the lord's mill, tilled the lord's fields and served his lord in war, but he was rarely if ever paid for any of his services: these were his *duties* as a serf, not the "labor" of a freely contracting agent. In the towns the apprentice entered the service of a master; the length of his apprenticeship, the number of his colleagues, his rate of pay, his hours of work, the very methods he used were all regulated by a guild. There was little or no bargaining between servant and master except for sporadic strikes when conditions became intolerable. This was no more of a labor market than is provided by interns in a hospital.

Or take capital. Certainly capital existed in the precapitalist world, in the sense of private wealth. But although the funds existed, there was no impetus to put them to new and aggressive use. Instead of risk and change, the motto was safety first. Not the shortest and most efficient, but the longest and most labor-consuming process was the preferred technique of production. Advertising was forbidden and the idea that one master guilds-man might produce a better product than his colleagues was re-garded as treasonable. In sixteenth-century England, when mass production in the weaving trade first reared its ugly head, the guilds protested to the king. The wonderworkshop—two hundred looms and a service staff including butchers and bakers to take care of the working force—was thereupon outlawed by His Maj-esty: such efficiency and concentration of wealth would set a bad precedent.

Hence the fact that the medieval world could not conceive the market system rested on the good and sufficient reason that it had not yet conceived the abstract elements of production itself. Lacking land, labor, and capital, the Middle Ages lacked the market; and lacking the market (despite its colorful local marts and traveling fairs), society ran by custom and tradition. The lords gave orders and production waxed and waned accordingly. Where no orders were given, life went on in its established groove. Had Adam Smith lived in the years before 1400 he would have felt no need to construct a theory of political economy. There was no mystery to penetrate in understanding what made the Middle Ages hang together and no veil to pierce to discover both order and design. Ethics and politics, yes; there was much to be explained and rationalized in the relations of lower lords to higher lords and higher lords to kings, and a great deal to be puzzled over in the conflict between the teachings of the Church and the incorrigible tendencies of the merchant class. But eco-nomics, no. Who would look for abstract laws of supply and de-mand, or cost, or value, when the explanation of the world lay like an open book in the laws of the manor and the Church and the customs of a lifetime? Adam Smith might have been a great moral philosopher in that earlier age, but he could never have been a great economist; there would have been nothing for him to do.

There would be nothing for any economist to do for several centuries—until this great self-reproducing, self-sufficient world erupted into the bustling, scurrying, free-for-all of the eighteenth century. "Erupted" is perhaps too dramatic a word, for the change would take place over centuries rather than in a single violent spasm. But the change, long drawn out though it was, was not a peaceful evolution; it was an agonized convulsion of society, a revolution.

Just to commercialize the land—to convert the hierarchy of social relationships into so many vacant lots and advantageous sites—required nothing less than the uprooting of an entrenched feudal way of life. To make "workers" out of the sheltered serfs and apprentices—no matter how exploitative the cloak of paternalism may have been—required the creation of a frightened disoriented class called the proletariat. To make capitalists out of guild masters meant that the laws of the jungle had to be taught to the timid denizens of the barnyard.

Hardly a peaceful prospect, any of this. Nobody *wanted* this commercialization of life. How bitterly it was resisted can only be appreciated if we take one last journey back to watch the economic revolution taking place.

We are back in France; the year, 1666.

The capitalists of the day face a disturbing challenge which the widening market mechanism has inevitably brought in its wake: change.

The question has come up whether a guild master of the weaving industry should be allowed to try an innovation in his product. The verdict: "If a cloth weaver intends to process a piece according to his own invention, he must not set it on the loom, but should obtain permission from the judges of the town to employ the number and length of threads that he desires, after the question has been considered by four of the oldest merchants and four of the oldest weavers of the guild." One can imagine how many suggestions for change were tolerated.

Shortly after the matter of cloth weaving has been disposed of, the button-makers guild raises a cry of outrage; the tailors are beginning to make buttons out of cloth, an unheard-of thing. The government, indignant that an innovation should threaten a settled industry, imposes a fine on the cloth-button makers and even on those who wear cloth buttons. But the wardens of the button guild are not yet satisfied. They demand the right to search people's homes and wardrobes and even to arrest them on the streets if they are seen wearing these subversive goods.

And this dread of change and innovation is not just the comic resistance of a few frightened merchants. Capital is fighting in earnest against change, and no holds are barred. In England a revolutionary patent for a stocking frame is not only denied in 1623, but the Privy Council orders the dangerous contraption abolished. In France the importation of printed calicoes is threatening to undermine the clothing industry. It is met with measures which cost the lives of sixteen thousand people! In Valence alone on one occasion 77 persons are sentenced to be hanged, 58 broken on the wheel, 631 sent to the galleys, and one lone and lucky individual set free for the crime of dealing in forbidden calico wares.

But capital is not the only agent of production which is frantically seeking to avoid the dangers of the market way of life. What is happening to labor is still more desperate.

Let us turn back to England.

It is the end of the sixteenth century, the great era of English expansion and adventure. Queen Elizabeth has made a triumphal tour of her kingdom. But she returns with a strange plaint. "Paupers are everywhere!" she cries. This is a strange observation, for only a hundred years before, the English countryside consisted in large part of peasant proprietors tilling their own lands, the yeoman, the pride of England, the largest body of independent, free, and prosperous citizens in the world. Now, "Paupers are everywhere!" What has happened in the interim?

What has happened has been an enormous movement of expropriation—or, rather, the beginning of such a movement, for it was then only in its inception. Wool has become a new, profitable commodity, and wool demands grazing pastures for the wool producer. The pastures are made by enclosing the common land; the patchwork crazy quilt of small scattered holdings (unfenced and recognizable only by a tree here and a rock there dividing one man's land from another) and the common lands on which all might graze their cattle or gather peat, are suddenly declared to be all the property of the lord of the manor and no longer available to the whole parish. Where before was a kind of communality of ownership, now there is private property. Where there were yeomen, now there are sheep. One John Hales in 1549 wrote: ". . . where XL persons had their lyvings, now one man and his shepherd hath all. . . . Yes, those shepe is the cause of all theise meschieves, for they have driven husbandrie out of the countries, by the which was encreased before all kynde of victuall, and now altogether shepe, shepe."

It is almost impossible to imagine the scope and impact of the process of enclosure. As early as the middle of the sixteenth century riots had broken out against it: in one such uprising, 3,500 people were killed. By the mid-eighteenth century, the process was still in full swing; not until the mid-nineteenth would it run its terrible historic course. Thus in 1820, nearly fifty years after the American Revolution, the Duchess of Sutherland dispossessed 15,000 tenants from 794,000 acres of land, replaced them with 131,000 sheep, and by way of compensation rented her evicted families an average of two acres of submarginal land each.

But it was not merely the wholesale land-grabbing that warrants attention. The tragedy is what happened to the peasant. Deprived of the right to use the common land, he could no longer maintain himself as a "farmer." Since no factories were available, he could not—even if he had wanted to—metamorphose into a factory worker. Instead, he became that most miserable of all social classes, an agricultural proletarian, and where agricultural work was lacking, a beggar, sometimes a robber, usually a pauper. Terrified at the alarming increase in pauperism throughout the country, the English Parliament tried to deal with the problem by localizing it. It tied paupers to their parishes for a pittance of relief and dealt with wanderers by whipping, branding, and mutilation. A social reformer of the time of Adam Smith seriously proposed to deal with the migrant pauper by confining him to institutions for which he candidly suggested the name Houses of Terror. But what was worst of all was that the very measures which the country took to protect itself from the pauper—tying him to his local parish where he could be kept alive on poor relief—prevented the only possible solution to the problem. It was not that the English ruling classes were utterly heartless and cruel. Rather, they failed to understand the concept of a fluid, mobile labor force which would seek work wherever work was to be found according to the dictates of the market. At

every step, the commercialization of labor, like the commercialization of capital, was feared, fought, and misconceived.

The market system with its essential components of land, labor,
and capital was born in agony—an agony that began in the thirteenth century and did not run its course until well into the
nineteenth. Never was a revolution less well understood, less wel-
comed, less planned. But the great market-making forces would
not be denied. Insidiously they ripped apart the mold of custom,
insolently they tore away the usages of tradition. For all the
clamor of the button makers, cloth buttons won the day. For all
the action of the Privy Council, the stocking frame became so
valuable that in another seventy years the same Privy Council
would forbid its exportation. For all the breakings on the wheel,
the trade in calicoes increased apace. Over last-ditch opposition
from the Old Guard, economic land was created out of ancestral
estates, and over the wails of protest from employees and masters
alike, economic labor was ground out of unemployed apprentices
and dispossessed farm laborers.

The great chariot of society, which for so long had run down
the gentle slope of tradition, now found itself powered by an
internal combustion machine. Transactions, transactions, transactions and gain, gain, gain provided a new and startlingly powerful motive force.

What forces could have been sufficiently powerful to smash a
comfortable and established world and institute in its place this
new unwanted society?

There was no single massive cause. The new way of life grew
inside the old, like a butterfly inside a chrysalis, and when the
stir of life was strong enough it burst the old structure asunder.
It was not great events, single adventures, individual laws, or
powerful personalities which brought about the economic revolution. It was a process of internal growth.

First, there was the gradual emergence of national political
units in Europe. Under the blows of peasant wars and kingly
conquest, the isolated existence of early feudalism gave way to
centralized monarchies. And with monarchies came the growth
of the national spirit; in turn this meant royal patronage for
favored industries, such as the great French tapestry works, and

the development of armadas and armies with all their necessary satellite industries. The infinity of rules and regulations which plagued Andreas Ryff and his fellow sixteenth-century traveling merchants gave way to common laws, common measurements, common currency.

An aspect of the political change which was revolutionizing Europe was the encouragement of foreign adventure and exploration. In the thirteenth century, the brothers Polo went as unprotected merchants on their daring journey into the land of the great Khan; in the fifteenth century Columbus sailed for what he hoped would be the same destination under the royal auspices of Isabella. The change from private to national exploration was part and parcel of the change from private to national life. And in turn the great national adventures of the English and Spanish and Portuguese sailor-capitalists brought a flood of treasure and treasure-consciousness back to Europe. "Gold," Christopher Columbus had said, "is a wonderful thing! Whoever possesses it is master of everything he desires. With gold one can even get souls into heaven." The sentiments of Christopher Columbus were the sentiments of an age and hastened the advent of a society oriented toward gain and chance and activated by the chase after money. Be it noted, in passing, that the treasures of the East were truly fabulous. With the share received as a stockholder in Sir Francis Drake's voyage of the *Golden Hynd,* Queen Elizabeth paid off all England's foreign debts, balanced its budget, and invested abroad a sum large enough, at compound interest, to account for Britain's entire overseas wealth in 1930!

A second great current of change was to be found in the slow decay of the religious spirit under the impact of the skeptical, inquiring, humanist views of the Italian Renaissance. The world of Today elbowed aside the world of Tomorrow, and as life on earth became more important, so did the notion of material standards and ordinary comforts. Behind the change in religious tolerance was the rise of Protestantism, which hastened a new attitude toward work and wealth. The Church of Rome had always regarded the merchant with a dubious eye and had not hesitated to call usury a sin. But now that this merchant was every day climbing in society, now that he was no longer a mere useful appendage but an integral part of a new kind of world, some re-evaluation of his function became necessary. The Protestant leaders paved the way for an amalgamation of spiritual and temporal life. Far from eulogizing the life of poverty and spiritual contemplation, as separate from worldly life, it became the part of positive piety to make the most of one's God-given talents in daily business. Acquisitiveness became a recognized virtue—not immediately for one's private enjoyment, but for the greater glory of God. From here it was only a step to the identification of riches with spiritual excellence, and of rich men with saintly ones.

In the twelfth century a local folk tale tells of a usurer about to be married who was crushed by a falling statue as he was entering the church. On examination, the statue was also of a usurer, thus revealing God's displeasure with dealers in money. Even in the mid-1600's, as we may remember, poor Robert Keayne collided head on with the Puritan religious authorities because of his business practices. In such an atmosphere of hostility, it was not easy for the market system to expand. Hence the gradual acceptance by the spiritual leaders of the innocuousness, indeed the benefits, of the market way was essential for the full growth of the system.

Still another deep current lies in the slow social changes that eventually made the market system possible. We are accustomed to thinking of the Middle Ages as a time of stagnation and lack of progress. Yet in five hundred years, the medievalists fathered one thousand towns (an immense achievement), connected them with rudimentary but usable roads, and maintained their populations with food brought from the countryside. All this developed the familiarity with money and markets and the buying and selling way of life.

Progress was not only a matter of this slow urbanization. There was technical progress, too, of a vastly important sort. The commercial revolution could not begin until some form of rational money-accounting had developed: although the Venetians of the twelfth century were already using sophisticated accounting devices, the merchants in Europe were little better than schoolboys in their accounting ignorance. It took time for a recognition of the need for bookkeeping to spread; not until the seventeenth century was double entry a standard practice. And not until money was rationally accounted for could large-scale business operation run successfully.

Perhaps most important of all in the pervasiveness of its effect was a rise in scientific curiosity. Although the world would wait until the age of Adam Smith for its cataclysmic burst of technology, the Industrial Revolution could not have taken place had not the ground been prepared by a succession of basic subindustrial discoveries. The precapitalist era saw the birth of the printing press, the paper mill, the windmill, the mechanical clock, the map, and a host of other inventions. The idea of invention itself took hold; experimentation and innovation were looked on for the first time with a friendly eye.

No single one of these currents, acting by itself, could have turned society upside down. Indeed, many of them may have been as much the effects as the causes of a great convulsion in human organization. History turns no sharp corners, and the whole vast upheaval sprawled out over time. Evidences of the market way of life sprang up side by side with older traditional ways, and remnants of the former day persisted long after the market had for all practical purposes taken over as the guiding principle of economic organization. Thus guilds and feudal privileges were not finally abolished in France until 1790, and the Statute of Artificers which regulated guild practices in England was not repealed until 1813.

But by the year 1700, twenty-three years before Adam Smith was born, the world which had tried Robert Keayne, prohibited merchants from carrying unsightly bundles, worried over "just" prices, and fought for the privilege of carrying on in its fathers' footsteps was on the wane. In its place society has begun to heed a new set of "self-evident" dicta. Some of them are:

"Every man is naturally covetous of lucre."

"No laws are prevalent against gaine."

"Gaine is the Centre of the Circle of Commerce."

A new idea has come into being: "economic man"—a pale wraith of a creature who follows his adding-machine brain wherever it leads him. The textbooks will soon come to talk of Robinson Crusoes on desert isles who will organize their affairs as if they were so many penny-pinching accountants.

In the world of affairs a new fever of wealth and speculation has gripped Europe. In France in 1718 a Scottish adventurer named John Law organized a wild blue-sky venture known as the Mississippi Company, selling shares in an enterprise which would mine the mountains of gold in America. Men and women fought in the streets for the privilege of winning shares, murders were committed, fortunes made overnight. One hotel waiter netted thirty million *livres*. When the company was about to topple with frightful losses for all investors, the government sought to stave off disaster by rounding up a thousand beggars, arming them with picks and shovels, and marching them through the streets of Paris as a band of miners off for the Land of Eldorado. Of course the structure collapsed. But what a change from the timid capitalists of a hundred years ago to the get-rich-quick mobs jostling in the Rue de Quincampoix; what a money-hungry public this must have been to swallow such a bare-faced fraud!

No mistake about it, the travail was over and the market system had been born. The problem of survival was henceforth to be solved neither by custom nor by command, but by the free action of profit-seeking men bound together only by the market itself. The system was to be called capitalism. And the idea of gain which underlay it was so firmly rooted that men would soon vigorously affirm that it was an eternal and omnipresent attitude.

The idea needed a philosophy.

The human animal, it is repeatedly said, is distinguished above all by his self-consciousness. This seems to mean that, having set up his society, he is not content to let things be; he must tell himself that the particular society in which he lives is the best of all possible societies, and that the arrangements within it mirror in their own small way the arrangements which providence has made outside. Hence every age breeds its philosophers, apologists, critics, and reformers.

But the questions with which the earliest social philosophers concerned themselves were focused on the political rather than the economic side of life. As long as custom and command ruled the world, the problem of riches and poverty hardly struck the earlier philosophers at all, other than to be accepted with a sigh or railed at as another sign of man's inner worthlessness. As long as men, like bees, were born to be drones, no one much worried over the rationale of the laboring poor—the vagaries of queens were infinitely more elevating and exciting.

"From the hour of their birth," wrote Aristotle, "some are marked out for subjection and some for command," and in that comment was summed up not so much the contempt as the disinterest with which the early philosophers looked at the workaday world. The existence of a vast laboring substratum was simply taken for granted, and money and market matters were not only too sweaty but too vulgar to engage the consideration of a gentleman and a scholar. It was the rights of kings, divine and otherwise, and the great questions of power temporal and power spiritual which provided the arena for the contest of ideas—not the pretensions of pushy merchants. Although personal riches had their role to play in making the world go round, until the struggle for riches became general, ubiquitous, and patently vital to society, there was no need for a general philosophy of riches.

But one might ignore the nasty struggling aspect of the marketplace world for just so long; then one might fulminate against it. Finally when it penetrated to the very sanctums of the philosophers themselves, it was better to ask whether even here the evidences of some master pattern might not yet be seen. To this end, for two hundred years before Adam Smith, the philosophers spun their theories of daily life.

But into what a strange succession of molds they cast the world as they sought to penetrate to its underlying purposes!

At first the wretched struggle for existence found its be-all and end-all in the accumulation of gold. Christopher Columbus, Cortez, or Francis Drake were not only state adventurers; they were thought to be the agents of *economic progress* as well. To the Bullionists, as the sixteenth- and seventeenth-century philosophers called themselves, it was quite self-evident that gold was the natural mainspring and the proper object of all mundane affairs. Theirs was a philosophy of great armadas and adventures, kingly wealth and national stinginess, and an overriding belief that if all went well in the search for treasure, a nation could scarcely fail to prosper.

But by the eighteenth century, the Bullionists were already looked upon as a trifle naïve. A new school had grown up—the school of Political Arithmetick—and for the political arithmeticians, the great unifying principle of society was not treasure but commerce itself. Hence the philosophical question to which they addressed themselves was not how to corner the gold market, but how to create ever more and more wealth by assisting the rising merchant class in the furtherance of its tasks.

The new philosophy brought with it a new social problem: how to keep the poor poor. It was generally admitted that unless the poor were poor, they could not be counted upon to do an honest day's toil without asking for exorbitant wages. "To make society happy," wrote a leading moralist in 1723, "it is necessary that great numbers should be wretched as well as poor." So the political arithmeticians looked on the cheap agricultural and industrial labor of England and gravely nodded approval.

But gold and commerce were by no means the only ideas that superimposed some kind of order over the chaos of daily life. There were countless pamphleteers, parsons, cranks, and bigots who sought the justification—or the damnation—for society in a dozen different explanations. But the trouble was, all the models were so unsatisfactory. One man said a nation obviously must not buy more than it sells, while another as stoutly maintained that a nation was quite obviously better off if it took in more than it gave in exchange. Some insisted it was trade which made a nation rich and exalted the trader; others argued that trade was only a parasitical growth on the strong body of the farmer. Some said the poor were meant by God to be poor and even if they weren't, their poverty was essential to the wealth of the nation; others saw in pauperism a social evil and could not see how poverty could create wealth.

Out of the *mêlée* of contradictory rationalizations one thing alone stood clear: man insisted on some sort of intellectual ordering to help him understand the world in which he lived. The economic world loomed harsh and yet more and more important. No wonder Dr. Samuel Johnson himself said, "There is nothing which requires more to be illustrated by philosophy than trade does." In a word, the time for the economists had arrived.

Out of the *mêlée* came also a philosopher of astonishing scope. Adam Smith published his *Inquiry into the Nature and Causes of the Wealth of Nations* in 1776, thereby adding a second revo-

lutionary event to that fateful year. A political democracy was
born on one side of the ocean; an economic blueprint was unfolded on the other. But while not all of Europe followed America's political lead, after Smith had displayed the first true tableau
of modern society, all of the Western World became the world
of Adam Smith: his vision became the prescription for the spec-
tacles of generations. Adam Smith would never have thought of
himself as a revolutionist; he was only explaining what to him
was very clear, sensible, and conservative. But he gave the world
the image of itself for which it had been searching. After the
Wealth of Nations, men began to see the world about themselves
with new eyes; they saw how the tasks they did fitted into the
whole of society, and they saw that society as a whole was proceeding at a majestic pace toward a distant but clearly visible
goal.

III

The Wonderful World
of Adam Smith

A VISITOR to England in the 1760's would quite probably have learned of a certain Dr. Smith of the University of Glasgow. Dr. Smith was a well-known, if not a famous, man; Voltaire had heard of him, David Hume was his intimate, students had traveled all the way from Russia to hear his labored but enthusiastic discourse. In addition to his scholastic accomplishments, Dr. Smith was known as a rather remarkable personality. He was, for example, notoriously absent-minded: once he had fallen into a tanning pit walking along in earnest disquisition with a friend, and it was said that he had brewed himself a beverage of bread and butter and pronounced it the worst cup of tea he had ever tasted. But his personal quirks, which were many, did not interfere with his intellectual abilities. Dr. Smith was among the foremost philosophers of his age.

At Glasgow Dr. Smith lectured on problems of Moral Philosophy, a discipline a great deal more broadly conceived in that day than in ours. Moral Philosophy covered Natural Theology, Ethics, Jurisprudence, and Political Economy: it thus ranged all the way from man's sublimest impulses toward order and harmony to his somewhat less orderly and harmonious activities in the grimmer business of gouging out a living for himself.

Natural theology—the search for design in the confusion of the cosmos—has been an object of the human rationalizing impulse from earliest times; our traveler would have felt quite at ease as Dr. Smith expounded the natural laws that underlay the seeming chaos of the universe. But when it came to the other end of the spectrum—the search for a grand architecture beneath the hurly-burly of daily life—our traveler might have felt that Dr. Smith was really stretching philosophy beyond its proper limits.

For if the English social scene of the late eighteenth century suggested anything, it was most emphatically not rational order nor moral purpose. As soon as one looked away from the elegant lives of the leisure classes, society presented itself as a brute struggle for existence in its meanest form. Outside the drawing rooms of London or the pleasant rich estates of the counties, all that one saw was rapacity, cruelty, and degradation mingled with the most irrational and bewildering customs and traditions of some still earlier and already anachronistic day. Rather than a carefully engineered machine where each part could be seen to contribute to the whole, the body social resembled one of James Watt's strange steam machines: black, noisy, inefficient, dangerous. How curious that Dr. Smith should have professed to see order, design, and purpose in all of this!

Suppose, for example, our visitor had gone to see the tin mines of Cornwall. There he would have watched miners lower themselves down the black shafts, and on reaching bottom draw a candle from their belts and stretch out for a sleep until the candle guttered. Then for two or three hours they would work the ore until the next traditional break, this time for as long as it took to smoke a pipe. A full half day was spent in lounging, half in picking at the seams. But had our visitor traveled up north and nerved himself against a descent into the pits of Durham or Northumberland, he would have seen something quite different. Here men and women worked together, stripped to the waist, and sometimes reduced from pure fatigue to a whimpering half-human state. The wildest and most brutish customs were practiced; sexual appetites aroused at a glance were gratified down some deserted shaftway; children of seven or ten who never saw daylight during the winter months were used and abused and paid a pittance by the miners to help drag away their tubs of coal; pregnant women drew coal cars like horses and even gave birth in the dark black caverns.

But it was not just in the mines that life appeared colorful, traditional, or ferocious. On the land, too, an observant traveler would have seen sights hardly more suggestive of order, harmony, and design. In many parts of the country bands of agricultural poor roamed in search of work. From the Welsh highlands, Companies of Ancient Britons (as they styled themselves) would come trooping down at harvest time; sometimes they had one horse, unsaddled and unbridled, for the entire company; sometimes they all simply walked. Not infrequently there would be only one of the lot who spoke English and so could serve as intermediary between the band and the gentlemen-farmers whose lands they asked permission to aid in harvesting. It is not surprising that wages were as low as sixpence a day.

And finally, had our visitor stopped at a manufacturing town, he would have seen still other remarkable sights—but again, not such as to betoken order to the uneducated eye. He might have marveled at the factory built by the brothers Lombe in 1742. It was a huge building (for those days), five hundred feet long and six stories high, and inside were machines described by Daniel Defoe as consisting of "26,586 Wheels and 97,746 Movements, which work 73,726 Yards of Silk-Thread every time the Water-Wheel goes round, which is three times in one minute." Equally worthy of note were the children who tended the machines round the clock for twelve or fourteen hours at a turn, cooked their meals on the grimly black boilers, and were boarded in shifts in barracks where, it was said, the beds were always warm.

A strange, cruel, haphazard world this must have appeared to eighteenth-century as well as to our modern eyes.

All the more remarkable, then, to find that it could be reconciled with a scheme of Moral Philosophy envisioned by Dr. Smith, and that that learned man actually claimed to fathom within it the clear-cut outlines of great purposeful laws fitting an overarching and meaningful whole.

What sort of man was this urbane philosopher?

"I am a beau in nothing but my books," was the way Adam Smith once described himself, proudly showing off his treasured library to a friend. He was certainly not a handsome man. A medallion profile shows us a protruding lower lip thrust up to meet a large aquiline nose and heavy bulging eyes looking out from heavy lids. All his life Smith was troubled with a nervous affliction; his head shook, and he had an odd and stumbling manner of speech.

In addition, there was his notorious absent-mindedness. In the 1780's when Smith was in his late fifties, the inhabitants of Edinburgh were regularly treated to the amusing spectacle of their most illustrious citizen, attired in a light-colored coat, knee breeches, white silk stockings, buckle shoes, flat broad-brimmed beaver hat, and cane, walking down the cobbled streets with his eyes fixed on infinity and his lips moving in silent discourse. Every pace or two he would hesitate as if to change his direction or even reverse it; his gait was described by a friend as "vermicular."

Accounts of his absence of mind were common. On one occasion he descended into his garden clad only in a dressing gown and, falling into a reverie, walked fifteen miles before coming to. Another time while walking with an eminent friend in Edinburgh, a guard presented his pike in salute. Smith, who had been thus honored on countless occasions, was suddenly hypnotized by the saluting soldier. He returned the honor with his cane and then further astonished his guest by following exactly in the guard's footsteps, duplicating with his cane every motion of the pike. When the spell was broken, Smith was standing at the head of a long flight of steps, cane held at the ready. Having no idea that he had done anything out of the ordinary, he grounded his stick and took up his conversation where he had left off.

This absent-minded professor was born in 1723 in the town of Kirkcaldy, County Fife, Scotland. Kirkcaldy boasted a population of fifteen hundred; at the time of Smith's birth, nails were still used as money by some of the local townspeople. When he was four years old, a most curious incident took place. Smith was kidnaped by a band of passing gypsies. Through the efforts of his uncle (his father had died before his birth), the gypsies were traced and pursued, and in their flight they abandoned young Adam by the roadside. "He would have made, I fear, a poor gypsy," says one of his biographers.

From his earliest days, Smith was an apt pupil, although even as a child given to fits of abstraction. He was obviously destined for teaching and so at seventeen he went to Oxford on a scholarship—making the journey on horseback—and there he remained for six years. But Oxford was not then the citadel of learning which it later became. Most of the public professors had long ago given up even a pretense of teaching. A foreign traveler recounts his astonishment over a public debate there in 1788. All four participants passed the allotted time in profound silence, each absorbed in reading a popular novel of the day. Since instruction was the exception rather than the rule, Smith spent the years largely untutored and untaught, reading as he saw fit. In fact he was once nearly expelled from the university because a copy of David Hume's *A Treatise of Human Nature* was found in his rooms—Hume was no fit reading matter, even for a would-be philosopher.

In 1751—he was then twenty-eight—Smith was offered the Chair of Logic at the University of Glasgow, and shortly thereafter he was given the Chair of Moral Philosophy. Unlike Oxford, Glasgow was a serious center of study, and boasted a galaxy of talent. But it still differed considerably from the modern conception of a university. The prim professorial group did not entirely appreciate a certain levity and enthusiasm in Smith's manner. He was accused of sometimes smiling during religious services (no doubt during a reverie), of being a firm friend of that outrageous Hume, of not holding Sunday classes on Christian Evidences, of petitioning the Senatus Academicus for permission to dispense with prayers on the opening of class, and of delivering prayers that smacked of a certain "natural religion." Perhaps this all fits into better perspective if we remember that Smith's own teacher, Hutcheson, broke new ground at Glasgow by refusing to lecture to his students in Latin!

But for all the inevitable academic rivalry, Smith was happy at Glasgow. In the evenings he played whist—his absent-mindedness made him a somewhat undependable player—attended learned societies, and lived a quiet and sheltered life. He was beloved of his students, noted as a lecturer—even Boswell came to hear him— and his odd gait and manner of speech gained the homage of imitation. Little busts of himself even appeared in booksellers' windows.

It was not merely his eccentric personality that gave him prestige. In 1759 he published a book which made an instant sensation. It was entitled *The Theory of Moral Sentiments,* and it catapulted Smith immediately into the forefront of English philosophers. The *Theory* was an inquiry into the origin of moral approbation and disapproval. How does it happen that man, who is a creature of self-interest, can form moral judgments in which self-interest seems to be held in abeyance or transmuted to a higher plane? Smith held that the answer lay in our ability to put ourselves in the position of a third person, an impartial observer, and in this way to form a sympathetic notion of the moral (as opposed to the selfish) merits of a case.

The book and its problems attracted widespread interest. In Germany *das Adam Smith Problem* became a favorite subject for debate. More importantly, from our point of view, the treatise met with the favor of an intriguing man named Charles Townshend.

Townshend is one of those wonderful figures with which the eighteenth century seems to abound. A witty and even learned man, Townshend was, in the words of Horace Walpole, "a man endowed with every great talent, who must have been the greatest man of his age, if only he had common sincerity, common steadiness, and common sense." Townshend's fickleness was notorious; a quip of the times put it that Mr. Townshend was ill of a pain in his side, but declined to specify which side. As evidence of his lack of common sense, it was Townshend, as Chancellor of the Exchequer, who helped precipitate the American Revolution, first by refusing the colonists the right to elect their own judges and then by imposing a heavy duty on American tea.

But his political shortsightedness notwithstanding, Townshend was a sincere student of philosophy and politics, and as such a devotee of Adam Smith. What is more important, he was in a position to make him an unusual offer. In 1754 Townshend had made a brilliant and lucrative marriage to the Countess of Dalkeith, the widow of the Duke of Buccleuch, and he now found himself casting about for a tutor for his wife's son. Education for a young man of the upper classes consisted largely of the Grand Tour, a stay in Europe where one might acquire that polished finish so highly praised by Lord Chesterfield. Dr. Adam Smith would be an ideal companion for the young duke, thought Townshend, and accordingly he offered him three hundred pounds a year plus expenses and a pension of three hundred pounds a year for life. It was too good an offer to be declined. At best Smith never realized more than one hundred seventy pounds from the fees which, in those days, professors collected directly from their students. It is pleasant to note that his pupils refused to accept a refund from Dr. Smith when he left, saying that they had already been more than recompensed.

The tutor and His young Grace left for France in 1764. For eighteen months they stayed in Toulouse where a combination of abominably boring company and Smith's execrable French made his sedate life at Glasgow look like dissipation. Then they moved on to the south of France (where he met and worshiped Voltaire and repulsed the attentions of an amorous marquise), thence to Geneva, and finally to Paris. To relieve the tedium of the provinces, Smith began work on a treatise of political economy, a subject on which he had lectured at Glasgow, debated many evenings at the Select Society in Edinburgh, and discussed at length with his beloved friend David Hume. The book was to be the *Wealth of Nations,* but it would be twelve years before it was finished.

Paris was better going. By this time Smith's French, although dreadful, was good enough to enable him to talk at length with the foremost economic thinker in France. This was a M. Quesnay, a physician in the court of Louis XV and personal doctor to Mme. Pompadour. Quesnay had propounded a school of economics known as Physiocracy and devised a chart of the economy called a *tableau économique.* The *tableau* was truly a physician's insight: in contradistinction to the ideas of the day which still held that wealth was the solid stuff of gold and silver, Quesnay insisted that wealth sprang from production and that it flowed through the nation, from hand to hand, replenishing the body social like the circulation of blood. The *tableau* made a vast impression—Mirabeau the elder characterized it as an invention deserving of equal rank with writing and money. But the trouble with Physiocracy was that it insisted that only the agricultural classes produced true "wealth" and that the manufacturing and commercial classes merely manipulated it in a sterile way. Hence Quesnay's system had but limited usefulness for practical policy. True, it advocated a policy of *laissez faire*—a radical departure for the times. But in denigrating the industrial side of life it flew against the sense of history, for the whole development of

capitalism unmistakably pointed to the emergence of the industrial classes to a position of superiority over the landed classes.

This was not a congenial philosophy to Adam Smith. The notion of the circulation of wealth he gladly accepted and acknowledged, but the idea that industry was somehow sterile and barren
struck him as a peculiar construction of the world. After all, had
he not grown up in Kirkcaldy and Glasgow where one could see
wealth being created at every hand in the workshops and factories of craftsmen? But despite his rejection of the agricultural
orientation of the Physiocrat cult (M. Quesnay's followers, like
Mirabeau, were nothing if not adulatory), Smith had a profound
personal admiration for the French doctor. Had it not been for
Quesnay's death, the *Wealth of Nations* would have been dedicated to him.

In 1766 the tour was brought to an abrupt halt when the duke's
younger brother, who had joined them, was murdered in the
streets of Paris. His Grace returned to his estates at Dalkeith,
and Smith went first to London, and then to Kirkcaldy. Despite
Hume's entreaties, there he stayed, for the better part of the next
ten years, while the great treatise took shape. Most of it he dictated, standing against his fireplace and nervously rubbing his
head against the wall until his pomade had made a dark streak
on the paneling. Occasionally he would visit his former charge
on his estates at Dalkeith, and once in a while he would go to
London to discuss his ideas with the literati of the day. One of
them was Dr. Samuel Johnson, to whose select club Smith belonged, although he and the venerable lexicographer had hardly
met under the most amiable of circumstances. Sir Walter Scott
tells us that Johnson, on first seeing Smith, attacked him for some
statement he had made. Smith vindicated the truth of his contention. "What did Johnson say?" was the universal inquiry. "Why,
he said," said Smith, with the deepest impression of resentment,
"he said, 'You lie!' " "And what did you reply?" "I said, 'You are
a son of a —!' " On such terms, says Scott, did these two great
moralists first meet and part and such was the classical dialogue
between two great teachers of philosophy.

Smith met as well a charming and intelligent American, one
Benjamin Franklin, who provided him with a wealth of facts
about the American colonies and a deep appreciation of the

role which they might someday play. It is undoubtedly due to
Franklin's influence that Smith subsequently wrote of the colonies that they constituted a nation "which, indeed, seems very
likely to become one of the greatest and most formidable that
ever was in the world."

In 1776, *Wealth of Nations* was published. Two years later
Smith was appointed Commissioner of Customs for Edinburgh, a
sinecure worth six hundred pounds a year. With his mother, who
lived until she was ninety, Smith lived out his bachelor's life in
peace and quiet; serene, content, and absent-minded to the end.

And the book?

It has been called "the outpouring not only of a great mind,
but of a whole epoch." Yet it is not, in the strict sense of the
word, an "original" book. There is a long line of observers before Smith who have approached his understanding of the world:
Locke, Stewart, Law, Mandeville, Petty, Cantillon, not to mention Quesnay and Hume again. Smith took from all of them:
there are over a hundred authors mentioned by name in his
treatise. But where others had fished here and there, Smith spread
his net wide; where others had clarified this and that issue,
Smith illuminated the entire landscape. The *Wealth of Nations*
is not a wholly original book, but it is unquestionably a masterpiece.

It is, first of all, a huge panorama. It opens with a famous
passage describing the minute specialization of labor in the manufacture of pins, and covers, before it is done, such a variety of
subjects as "the late disturbances in the American colonies" (evidently Smith thought the Revolutionary War would be over by
the time his book reached the press), the wastefulness of the student's life at Oxford, and the statistics on the herring catch since
1771.

A glance at the index compiled for a later edition by Cannan
shows the range of Smith's references and thoughts. Here are a
dozen entries from the letter A:

> Abassides, opulence of Saracen empire under
> Abraham, weighed shekels
> Abyssinia, salt money
> Actors, public, paid for the contempt attending their profession

In fine print the index goes on for sixty-three pages: before it ends it has touched on everything: "Riches, the chief enjoyment of, consists in the parade of; Poverty, sometimes urges nation to inhuman customs; Stomach, desire for food bounded by narrow capacity of the; Butcher, brutal and odious business." When we have finished the nine hundred pages of the book we have a living picture of England in the 1770's, of apprentices and journeymen and rising capitalists, of landlords and clergymen and kings, of factories and farms and foreign trade.

The book is heavy going. It moves with all the deliberation of an encyclopedic mind, but not with the precision of an orderly one. This was an age when authors did not stop to qualify their ideas with ifs, ands, and buts, and it was an era when it was quite possible for a man of Smith's intellectual stature virtually to embrace the great body of knowledge of his times. Hence the book ducks nothing, minimizes nothing, fears nothing. What an exasperating book! Again and again it refuses to wrap up in a concise sentence a conclusion it has laboriously arrived at over fifty pages. The argument is so full of detail and observation that one constantly has to chip away the ornamentation to find the steel structure which holds it together underneath. Coming to silver, Smith detours for seventy-five pages to write a "diversion" on it; coming to religion, he wanders off in a chapter on the sociology of morality. But for all its weightiness, the text is shot through with insights, observations, and well-turned phrases that imbue this great lecture with life. It was Smith who first called England "a nation of shopkeepers"; it was Smith who wrote, "By nature a philosopher is not in genius and disposition half so different from a street porter, as a mastiff is from a greyhound." And of the East India Company, which was then ravaging the East, he wrote: "It is a very singular government in which every member of the administration wishes to get out of the country . . .

as soon as he can, and to whose interest, the day after he has left it and carried his whole fortune with him, it is perfectly indifferent though the whole country was swallowed up by an earthquake."

The *Wealth of Nations* is in no sense a textbook. Adam Smith is writing to his age, not to his classroom; he is expounding a doctrine which is meant to be of importance in running an empire, not an abstract treatise for scholastic distribution. The dragons which he slays (such as the Mercantile System, which takes over two hundred pages to die) were alive and panting, if a little tired, in his day.

And finally, the book is a revolutionary one. To be sure, Smith would hardly have countenanced an upheaval which disordered the gentlemanly classes and enthroned the common poor. But the import of the *Wealth of Nations* is revolutionary, nonetheless. Smith is not, as is commonly supposed, an apologist for the up-and-coming bourgeois; as we shall see, he is an admirer of their work but suspicious of their motives, and mindful of the needs of the great laboring mass. But it is not his aim to espouse the interests of any class. He is concerned with promoting the wealth of the entire nation. And wealth, to Adam Smith, consists of the goods which *all* the people of society consume; note *all*— this is a democratic, and hence radical, philosophy of wealth. Gone is the notion of gold, treasures, kingly hoards; gone the prerogatives of merchants or farmers or working guilds. We are in the modern world where the flow of goods and services consumed by everyone constitutes the ultimate aim and end of economic life.

And now, what of the lessons of the text?

Two great problems absorb Adam Smith's attention. First, he is interested in laying bare the mechanism by which society hangs together. How is it possible for a community in which everyone is busily following his self-interest not to fly apart from sheer centrifugal force? What is it which guides each individual's private business so that it conforms to the needs of the group? With no central planning authority and no steadying influence of age-old tradition, how does society manage to get those tasks done which are necessary for survival?

These questions lead Smith to a formulation of the laws of the market. What he sought was "the invisible hand," as he called it, whereby "the private interests and passions of men" are led in the direction "which is most agreeable to the interest of the whole society."

But the laws of the market will be only a part of Smith's inquiry. There is another question which interests him: whither society? The laws of the market are like the laws which explain how a spinning top stays upright; but there is also the question of whether the top, by virtue of its spinning, will be moved along the table.

To Smith and the great economists who followed him, society is not conceived as a static achievement of mankind which will go on reproducing itself, unchanged and unchanging, from one generation to the next. On the contrary, society is seen as an organism which has its own life history. To discover the shape of things to come, to isolate the forces which impel society along its path—this is the grand objective of economic science.

But until we have followed Smith's unraveling of the laws of the market, we cannot rush to this larger and more fascinating problem. For the laws of the market themselves will be an integral part of the larger laws which cause society to prosper or decay. The mechanism by which the heedless individual is kept in line with everybody else will affect the mechanism by which society itself changes over the years.

Hence we begin with a look at the market mechanism. It is not the stuff that excites the imagination or stirs the pulse. Yet, for all its dryness, it has an immediacy which should lead us to consider it with a respectful eye. Not only are the laws of the market essential to an understanding of the world of Adam Smith, but these same laws will underlie the very different world of Karl Marx, and the still different world in which we live today. Since we are all, knowingly or otherwise, under their sovereignty, it behooves us to scrutinize them rather carefully.

Adam Smith's laws of the market are basically simple. They tell us that the outcome of a certain kind of behavior in a certain social framework will bring about perfectly definite and foreseeable results. Specifically they show us how the drive of individual self-interest in an environment of similarly motivated individuals will result in competition; and they further demonstrate how competition will result in the provision of those goods that society wants, in the quantities that society desires, and at the prices society is prepared to pay. Let us see how this comes about.

It comes about in the first place because self-interest acts as a driving power to guide men to whatever work society is willing to pay for. "It is not from the benevolence of the butcher, the brewer, or the baker that we expect our dinner," says Smith, "but from their regard to their self-interest. We address ourselves, not to their humanity, but to their self-love, and never talk to them of our necessities, but of their advantages."

But self-interest is only half the picture. It drives men to action. Something else must prevent the pushing of profit-hungry individuals from holding society up to exorbitant ransom: a community activated only by self-interest would be a community of ruthless profiteers. This regulator is competition, the socially beneficial consequence of the conflicting self-interests of all the members of society. For each man, out to do his best for himself with no thought of social cost, is faced with a flock of similarly motivated individuals who are in exactly the same boat. Each is only too eager to take advantage of his neighbor's greed if it urges him to exceed a common denominator of acceptable behavior. A man who permits his self-interest to run away with him will find that competitors have slipped in to take his trade away; if he charges too much for his wares or if he refuses to pay as much as everybody else for his workers, he will find himself without buyers in the one case and without employees in the other. Thus very much as in the *Theory of Moral Sentiments,* the selfish motives of men are transmuted by interaction to yield the most unexpected of results: social harmony.

Consider, for example, the problem of high prices. Suppose we have one hundred manufacturers of gloves. The self-interest of each one will cause him to wish to raise his price above his cost of production and thereby to realize an extra profit. But he cannot. If he raises his price, his competitors will step in and take his market away from him by underselling him. Only if all glove manufacturers combine and agree to maintain a solid front will an unduly high price be charged. And in this case, the collusive coalition could be broken by an enterprising manufacturer from another field—say, shoe-making—who decided to move his capital into glove manufacture where he could steal away the market by shading his price.

But the laws of the market not only impose a competitive price on products. They also see to it that the producers of society heed society's demands for the *quantities* of goods it wants. Let us suppose that consumers decide they want more gloves than are being turned out, and fewer shoes. Accordingly the public will scramble for the stock of gloves on the market, and the shoe business will be dull. As a result glove prices will tend to rise as consumers try to buy more of them than there are ready at hand, and shoe prices will tend to fall as the public passes the shoe stores by. But as glove prices rise, profits in the glove industry will rise, too; and as shoe prices fall, profits in shoe manufacturing will slump. Again self-interest will step in to right the balance. Workers will be released from the shoe business as shoe factories contract their output; they will move to the glove business where business is booming. The result is quite obvious: glove production will rise and shoe production fall.

And this is exactly what society wanted in the first place. As more gloves come on the market to meet demand, glove prices will fall back into line. As fewer shoes are produced, the surplus of shoes will soon disappear and shoe prices will again rise up to normal. Through the mechanism of the market, society will have changed the allocation of its elements of production to fit its new desires. Yet no one has issued a dictum, and no planning authority has established schedules of output. Self-interest and competition, acting one against the other, have accomplished the transition.

And one final accomplishment. Just as the market regulates both prices and quantities of *goods* according to the final arbiter of public demand, so it also regulates the *incomes* of those who cooperate to produce those goods. If profits in one line of business are unduly large, there will be a rush of other businessmen into that field until competition has lowered surpluses. If wages are out of line in one kind of work, there will be a rush of men into the favored occupation until it pays no more than comparable jobs of that degree of skill and training. Conversely, if profits or wages are too low in one trade area, there will be an exodus of capital and labor until the supply is better adjusted to the demand.

All this may seem somewhat elementary. But consider what Adam Smith has done, with his impetus of self-interest and his regulator of competition. First, he has explained how prices are kept from ranging arbitrarily away from the actual cost of producing a good. Second, he has explained how society can induce its producers of commodities to provide it with what it wants. Third, he has pointed out why high prices are a self-curing disease, for they cause production in those lines to increase. And finally, he has accounted for a basic similarity of incomes at each level of the great producing strata of the nation. In a word, he has found in the mechanism of the market a self-regulating system for society's orderly provisioning.

Note "self-regulating." The beautiful consequence of the market is that it is its own guardian. If output or prices or certain kinds of remuneration stray away from their socially ordained levels, forces are set into motion to bring them back to the fold. It is a curious paradox which thus ensues: the market, which is the acme of individual economic freedom, is the strictest taskmaster of all. One may appeal the ruling of a planning board or win the dispensation of a minister; but there is no appeal, no dispensation, from the anonymous pressures of the market mechanism. Economic freedom is thus more illusory than at first appears. One can do as one pleases in the market. But if one pleases to do what the market disapproves, the price of individual freedom is economic ruination.

Does the world really work this way? To a very real degree it did in the days of Adam Smith. Even in his time, of course, there were already factors which acted as restraints against the free operation of the market system. There were combinations of manufacturers who rigged prices artifically high and associations of journeymen who resisted the pressures of competition when it acted to lower their wages. And already there were more disquieting signs to be read. The Lombe brothers' factory was more than a mere marvel of engineering and a source of wonderment to the visitor: it betokened the coming of large-scale industry and the emergence of employers who were immensely powerful individual actors in the market. The children in the cotton mills could surely not be considered market factors of equal power with the employers who bedded, boarded, and exploited them. But for all its ominous portents, eighteenth-century England approached, even if it did not wholly conform to, the model which Adam Smith had in mind. Business *was* competitive, the average factory *was* small, prices *did* rise and fall as demand ebbed and rose, and prices *did* invoke changes in output and occupation. The world of Adam Smith has been called a world of atomistic competition; a world in which no part of the productive mechanism, laborer or capitalist, was large enough to interfere with or to resist the pressures of competition. It was a world in which each agent was forced to scurry after his self-interest in a vast social free-for-all.

And today? Does the competitive market mechanism still operate?

This is not a question to which it is possible to give a simple answer. The nature of the market has changed vastly since the eighteenth century. We no longer live in a world of atomistic competition in which no man can afford to swim against the current. Today's market mechanism is characterized by the huge size of its participants: giant corporations and equally giant labor unions obviously do not behave as if they were individual proprietors and workers. Their very bulk enables them to stand out against the pressures of competition, to disregard price signals, and to consider what their self-interest shall be in the long run rather than in the immediate press of each day's buying and selling.

Then, in addition, the growth of government intervention has altered the scope of the market mechanism. Like a medieval lord, the government does not recognize its master in the market; more often than not it *sets* the market rather than abiding by it. That all these factors have weakened the primary guiding function of the market is apparent: later we will be concerned with what contemporary economists have to say about this problem. But it would seem, nonetheless, that for all the new quality of twentieth-century industrial society, the great principles of self-interest and competition, however watered down or hedged about, still provide basic rules of behavior which no economic participant can afford to disregard entirely. It is not the neat world of

Adam Smith in which we live, but the laws of the market can still be discerned in it if we look beneath the surface.

But the laws of the market are only a description of the behavior which gives society its cohesiveness. Something else must make it go. Ninety years after the *Wealth of Nations,* Karl Marx was to make the portentous announcement that he had unearthed "laws of motion" which described how capitalism proceeded slowly, unwillingly, but ineluctably to its doom. But the *Wealth of Nations* already had its own laws of motion. However, quite unlike the Marxist prognosis, Adam Smith's world went slowly, quite willingly, and more or less inevitably to Valhalla.

Valhalla would have been the last destination that most observers would have predicted. Sir John Byng, touring the North Country in 1792, looked from his coach window and wrote: "Why, here now, is a great flaring mill . . . all the Vale is disturb'd. . . . Sir Richard Arkwright may have introduced Much Wealth into his Family and into his Country, but, as a Tourist, I execrate his Schemes, which having crept into every Pastoral Vale, have destroyed the course, and the Beauty of Nature." "Oh! What a dog's hole is Manchester," said Sir John on arriving there.

In truth, much of England was a dog's hole. The three centuries of turmoil which had prodded land, labor, and capital into existence seemed to have been only a preparation for still further upheaval, for the recently freed agents of production began to be combined in a new and ugly form: the factory. And with the factory came new problems. Twenty years before Sir John's tour, Richard Arkwright, who had gotten together a little capital peddling women's hair to make wigs, invented (or stole) the spinning throstle. But having constructed his machine, he found it was not so easy to staff it. Local labor could not keep up with the "regular celerity" of the process—wagework was still generally despised and some capitalists found their new-built factories burned to the ground out of sheer blind malice. Arkwright was forced to turn to children—"their small fingers being active." Furthermore, since they were unused to the independent life of farming or crafts, children adapted themselves more readily to the discipline of factory life. The move was hailed as a philan-

thropic gesture—would not the employment of children help to
alleviate the condition of the "unprofitable poor"?

For if any problem absorbed the public mind, besides its mixed
admiration of and horror at the factory, it was this omnipresent
problem of the unprofitable poor. In 1720 England was crowded
with a million and a half of them—a staggering figure when we
realize that her total population was only twelve or thirteen million. Hence the air was full of schemes for their disposition.
Despairing schemes, mostly. For the common complaint was the
ineradicable sloth of the pauper, and this was mixed with consternation at the way in which the lower orders aped their betters.
Workpeople were actually drinking tea! The common folk
seemed to prefer wheaten bread to their traditional loaf of rye
or barley! Where would all this lead to, asked the thinkers of the
day; were not the wants of the poor ("which it would be prudence to relieve, but folly to cure," as a contemporary pamphlet
expressed it) essential for the welfare of the state? What would
happen to Society if the indispensable gradations of society were
allowed to disappear?

But if consternation described the prevalent attitude of the day
toward the great amorphous mass of working England, it certainly
did not describe Adam Smith's philosophy. "No society can surely
be flourishing and happy, of which by far the greater part of the
numbers are poor and miserable," he said. And not only did he
have the temerity to make so radical a statement, but he proceeded to demonstrate that society was in fact constantly improving; that it was being propelled, willy-nilly, toward a positive
goal. It was not moving because anyone willed it to, or because
Parliament might pass laws, or England win a battle. It moved
because there was a concealed dynamic beneath the surface of
things which powered the social whole like an enormous engine.

For one salient fact struck Adam Smith as he looked at the
English scene. This was the tremendous gain in productivity
which sprang from the minute division and specialization of
labor. Going into a pin factory, this is what Smith saw: "One man
draws out the wire, another straights it, a third cuts it, a fourth
points it, a fifth grinds it at the top for receiving the head; to
make the head requires two or three distinct operations; to put
it on is a peculiar business; to whiten it is another; it is even a

trade by itself to put them into paper. . . . I have seen a small manufactory of this kind where ten men only were employed and where some of them consequently performed two or three distinct operations. But though they were very poor, and therefore but indifferently accommodated with the necessary machinery, they could, when they exerted themselves, make among them about twelve pounds of pins in a day. There are in a pound upwards of four thousand pins of a middling size. Those ten persons, therefore, could make among them upwards of forty-eight thousand pins in a day. . . . But if they had all wrought separately and independently . . . they certainly could not each of them make twenty, perhaps not one pin a day. . . ."

There is hardly any need to point out how infinitely more complex present-day production methods are from those of the eighteenth century. Smith, for all his disclaimers, was sufficiently impressed with a small factory of ten people to comment on it; what would he have thought of one employing ten thousand! But the great gift of the division of labor is not its complexity—indeed it simplifies most toil. Its advantage lies in its capacity to increase what Smith calls "that universal opulence which extends itself to the lowest ranks of the people." That universal opulence of the eighteenth century looks like a grim existence from our modern vantage point. But if we view the matter in its historical perspective, if we compare the lot of the workingman in eighteenth-century England to his predecessor a century or two before, it is clear that mean as his existence was, it constituted a considerable advance. Smith makes the point vividly:

Observe the accommodation of the most common artificer or day labourer in a civilized and thriving country, and you will perceive that the number of people of whose industry a part, though but a small part, has been employed in procuring him this accommodation, exceeds all computation. The woollen coat, for example, which covers the day-labourer, as coarse and rough as it may seem, is the produce of the joint labour of a great multitude of workmen. The shepherd, the sorter of the wool, the wool-comber or carder, the dyer, the scribbler, the spinner, the weaver, the fuller, the dresser, with many others, must all join their different arts in order to complete even this homely production. How many merchants and carriers, besides, must have been employed . . . how much commerce and navigation . . . how many ship-builders, sailors, sail-makers, rope makers . . .

Were we to examine, in the same manner, all the different parts of his dress and household furniture, the coarse linen shirt which he wears next to his skin, the shoes which cover his feet, the bed which he lies on . . . the kitchen-grate at which he prepares his victuals, the coals which he makes use of for that purpose, dug from the bowels of the earth, and brought to him perhaps by a long sea and a long land carriage, all the other utensils of his kitchen, all the furniture of his table, the knives and forks, the earthen or pewter plates upon which he serves up and divides his victuals, the different hands employed in preparing his bread and his beer, the glass window which lets in the heat and the light, and keeps out the wind and the rain, with all the knowledge and art requisite for preparing that beautiful and happy invention . . . ; if we examine, I say, all those things . . . we shall be sensible that without the assistance and cooperation of many thousands, the very meanest person in a civilized country could not be provided, even according to what we very falsely imagine, the easy and simple manner in which he is commonly accommodated. Compared indeed with the more extravagant luxury of the great, his accommodation must no doubt appear extremely simple and easy; and yet it may be true, perhaps, that the accommodation of a European prince does not always so much exceed that of an industrious and frugal peasant, as the accommodation of the latter exceeds that of many an African king, the absolute master of the lives and liberties of ten thousand naked savages.

What is it that drives society to this wonderful multiplication of wealth and riches? Partly it is the market mechanism itself, for the market harnesses man's creative powers in a milieu which encourages him, even forces him, to invent, innovate, expand, take risks. But there are more fundamental pressures behind the restless activity of the market. In fact, Smith sees deep-seated laws of evolution which propel the market system in an ascending spiral of productivity.

The first of these is the Law of Accumulation.

Let us remember that Adam Smith lived at a time when the rising industrial capitalist could and did realize a fortune from his investments. Richard Arkwright, apprenticed to a barber as a young man, died in 1792 leaving an estate of £500,000. Samuel Walker, who started a forge going in an old nailshop in Rotherham, left a steel foundry on that site worth £200,000. Josiah Wedgwood, who stumped about his pottery factory on a wooden leg scrawling "This won't do for Jos. Wedgwood" wherever he saw evidence of careless work, left an estate of £240,000 and much landed property. The Industrial Revolution in its early stages provided a veritable grab bag of riches for whoever was quick enough, shrewd enough, industrious enough to ride with its current.

And the object of the great majority of the rising capitalists was first, last, and always, to accumulate their savings. At the beginning of the nineteenth century, £2,500 was collected in Manchester for the foundation of Sunday schools. The sum total contributed to this worthy cause by the single largest employers in the district, the cotton spinners, was £90. The young industrial aristocracy had better things to do with its money than contribute to unproductive charities—it had to accumulate, and Adam Smith approved wholeheartedly. Woe to him who did not accumulate. And as for one who encroached on his capital—"like him who perverts the revenues of some pious foundation to profane purposes, he pays the wages of idleness with those funds which the frugality of his forefathers had, as it were, consecrated to the maintenance of industry."

But Adam Smith did not approve of accumulation for accumulation's sake. He was, after all, a philosopher, with a philosopher's disdain for the vanity of riches. Rather, in the accumulation of capital Smith saw a vast benefit to society. For capital—if put to use in machinery—provided just that wonderful division of labor which multiplies man's productive energy. Hence accumulation becomes another of Smith's two-edged swords: the avarice of private greed again redounding to the welfare of the community. Smith is not worried over the problem which will face twentieth-century economists: will private accumulations actually find their way back into more employment? For him the world is capable of indefinite improvement and the size of the market is limited only by its geographical extent. Accumulate and the world will benefit, says Smith. And certainly in the lusty atmosphere of his time there was no evidence of any unwillingness to accumulate on the part of those who were in a position to do so.

But—and here is a difficulty—accumulation would soon lead to a situation where further accumulation would be impossible. For accumulation meant more machinery and more machinery meant more demand for workmen. And this in turn would sooner or later lead to higher and higher wages, until profits—the source of accumulation—were eaten away. How is this hurdle surmounted?

It is surmounted by the second great law of the system: the Law of Population.

To Adam Smith, laborers, like any other commodity, could be produced according to the demand. If wages were high, the number of workpeople would multiply; if wages fell, the numbers of the working class would decrease.

Nor is this quite so naïve a conception as it appears at first blush. In Smith's day infant mortality among the lower classes was shockingly high. "It is not uncommon," says Smith, ". . . in the Highlands of Scotland for a mother who has borne twenty children not to have two alive." In many places in England, half the children died before they were four, and almost everywhere half the children only lived to the age of nine or ten. Malnutrition, evil living conditions, cold, and disease took a horrendous toll among the poorer element. Hence although higher wages may have affected the birth rate only slightly, it could be expected to have a considerable influence on the number of children who would grow to working age.

Hence if the first effect of accumulation would be to raise the wages of the working class, this in turn would bring about an increase in the number of workers. And now the market mechanism takes over. Just as higher prices on the market will bring about a larger production of gloves and the larger number of gloves in turn press down the higher prices of gloves, so higher wages will bring about a larger number of workers, and the increase in their numbers will set up a reverse pressure on the level of their wages. Population, like glove production, is a self-curing disease—as far as wages are concerned.

And this meant that accumulation might go safely on. The rise in wages which it caused and which threatened to make further accumulation unprofitable is tempered by the rise in population. Accumulation leads to its own undoing, and then is rescued in the nick of time. The obstacle of higher wages is undone by the growth in population which those very higher wages made feasible. There is something fascinating in this automatic process of aggravation and cure, stimulus and response, in which the very factor which seems to be leading the system to its doom is also slyly bringing about the conditions necessary for its further health.

And now observe that Smith has constructed for society a giant endless chain. As regularly and as inevitably as a series of interlocked mathematical propositions, society is started on an upward march. From any starting point the probing mechanism of the market first equalizes the returns to labor and capital in all its different uses, sees to it that those commodities demanded are produced in the right quantities, and further ensures that prices for commodities are constantly competed down to their costs of production. But further than this, society is dynamic. From its starting point accumulation of wealth will take place, and this accumulation will result in increased facilities for production and in a greater division of labor. So far, all to the good. But accumulation will also raise wages as capitalists bid for workers to man the new factories. As wages rise further accumulation begins to look unprofitable. The system threatens to level off. But meanwhile workmen will have used their higher wages to rear their children with fewer mortalities. Hence the supply of workmen will increase. As population swells, the competition among workmen will press down on wages again. And so accumulation will continue, and another spiral in the ascent of society will begin.

This is no business cycle which Smith describes. It is a long-term process, a secular evolution. And it is wonderfully certain. Provided only that the market mechanism is not tampered with, everything is inexorably determined by the preceding link. A vast reciprocating machinery is set up with all of society inside it: only the tastes of the public—to guide producers—and the actual physical resources of the nation are outside the chain of cause and effect.

And observe, furthermore, that what is foreseen is a constantly improving state of affairs. True, the rise in the working population will always force wages back toward a subsistence level. But *toward* is not *to;* as long as the accumulation process continues— and Smith sees no reason why it should cease—there is virtually endless opportunity for society to improve its lot. Smith did not imply that this was the best of all possible worlds: he had read Voltaire's *Candide* and was no Dr. Pangloss himself. But there was no reason why the world should not *move* in the direction of improvement and progress. Indeed, if one left the market mechanism alone and allowed it and the great social laws to work themselves out, it was inevitable that progress would result.

In the very long run, well beyond the horizon, one could just discern the final destination for society. By then the "natural" level of wages would have risen considerably (for Smith assumed that basic subsistence wages were a sociological phenomenon rather than a brute animal fact). The landlord would also have fared well, for population would be large and pressing on what was, after all, a God-given and fixed supply of land. The capitalist alone would have suffered a difficult fate; since riches would have multiplied almost beyond calculation, the capitalist would realize the wages of management, but precious little profit beyond that: he would be a hard-working, well-remunerated, but certainly not luxuriously rich person. A strange paradise of hard work, much real wealth, and little leisure this would be.

But the road to society's eventual resting place was long and there was too much to be done between the world of Adam Smith and that final campground to warrant spending much time on its detail. The *Wealth of Nations* is a program for action, not a blueprint for Utopia.

The book took hold only slowly. It was to be almost eight years before it was quoted in Parliament, the first to do so being Charles James Fox, the most powerful member of Commons (who admitted later that he had never actually *read* the book). Then, when recognition came—as it did—it was from an unexpected ally. The rising capitalists—and let us remember that this sturdy, upstart class of parvenus was not bothered with twentieth-century ideas about equality or economic justice—found in Smith's treatise the perfect theoretical justification for their own opposition to factory legislation. The fact that Smith had written of "the mean rapacity, the monopolizing spirit of the merchants and manufacturers" and that he had said they "neither are, nor ought to be, the rulers of mankind"— all this was ignored in favor of the great point which Smith drew from his inquiry: *let the market alone.*

What Smith had meant by this was one thing; what his proponents made him out to mean was another. Smith, as we have said, was not the proponent of any one class. He was a slave to his system. His whole economic philosophy stemmed from his unquestioning faith in the ability of the market to guide the system to its point of highest return. The market—that wonderful social machine—would take care of society's needs *if it was left alone,* so that the laws of evolution might take over to lift society toward its promised reward. Smith was neither antilabor nor anticapital; if he had any bias it was in favor of the consumer. "Consumption is the sole end and purpose of all production," he wrote, and then proceeded to castigate those systems which placed the interest of the producer over that of the consuming public.

But in Smith's panegyric of a free and unfettered market the rising industrialists found the theoretical justification they needed to block the first government attempts to remedy the scandalous conditions of the times. For Smith's theory does unquestionably lead to a doctrine of *laissez faire.* To Adam Smith the least government is certainly the best: governments are spendthrift, irresponsible, and unproductive. And yet Adam Smith is not necessarily opposed—as his posthumous admirers made him out to be— to *all* government action which has as its end the promotion of the general welfare. He warns, for example, of the stultifying effect of mass production, which robs men of their creative natural powers, and prophesies a decline in the manly virtues of the laborer, "unless the government takes some pains to prevent it." Similarly he is in favor of public education to raise the citizenry above the level of mere uncomprehending cogs in a vast machine.

What Smith *is* against is the meddling of the government with the market mechanism. He is against restraints on imports and bounties on exports, against government laws which shelter industry from competition, and against government spending for unproductive ends. Notice that these activities of the government largely have the interest of the *merchant* class at heart. Smith never faced the problem—which was to cause such intellectual agony for later generations—of whether the government is weakening or strengthening the market mechanism when it steps in with welfare legislation. Aside from poor relief, there was virtually no welfare legislation in Smith's day—the government was the unabashed ally of the governing classes, and the great tussle within the government was whether it should be the landowning or the industrial classes who should most benefit. The question of whether the working class should have a voice in the direction of economic affairs simply did not enter any respectable person's mind.

The great enemy to Adam Smith's system is not so much government per se as monopoly—in any form. "People of the same trade seldom meet together," says Adam Smith, "but the conversation ends in a conspiracy against the public, or in some diversion to raise prices." And the trouble with such goings on is not so much that they are morally reprehensible in themselves —they are, after all, only the inevitable consequence of man's self-interest—as that they impede the fluid working of the market. And of course Smith is right. If the working of the market is trusted to produce the greatest number of goods at the lowest possible prices, anything that interferes with the market necessarily lowers social welfare. If, as in Smith's time, no master hatter anywhere in England could employ more than two apprentices or no master cutler in Sheffield more than one, the market system cannot possibly yield its full benefits. If, as in Smith's time, paupers are tied to their local parishes and prevented from seeking work where work might be found, the market cannot attract labor where labor is wanted. If, as in Smith's time, great companies are given monopolies of foreign trade, the public cannot realize the full benefits of cheaper foreign produce.

Hence, says Smith, all these impediments must go. The market must be left free to find its own natural levels of prices and wages and profits and production; whatever interferes with the market does so only at the expense of the true wealth of the nation. But because any act of the government—even such laws as those requiring the whitewashing of factories or preventing the shackling of children to machines—could be interpreted as hampering the free operation of the market, the *Wealth of Nations* was liberally quoted to oppose the first humanitarian legislation. Thus by a strange injustice the man who warned that the grasping eighteenth-century industrialists "generally have an interest to deceive and even to oppress the public" came to be regarded as their economic patron saint. Even today—in blithe disregard of his actual philosophy—Smith is generally regarded as a *conservative* economist, whereas in fact, he was more avowedly hostile to the *motives* of businessmen than most New Deal economists.

In a sense the whole wonderful world of Adam Smith is a testimony to the eighteenth-century belief in the inevitable triumph of rationality and order over arbitrariness and chaos. Don't try to do good, says Smith. Let good emerge as the by-product of selfishness. How like the philosopher to place such faith in a vast social machinery and to rationalize selfish instincts into social virtues! There is nothing halfhearted about Smith's abiding trust in the consequence of his philosophical beliefs. He urges that judges should be paid by the litigants rather than by the state, since in that way their self-interest will lead them to expedite the cases brought before them. He sees little future for the newly emerging business organizations called corporations since it seems highly improbable that such impersonal bodies could muster the necessary self-interest to pursue complex and arduous undertakings. Even the greatest humanitarian movements, such as the abolition of slavery, are defended in his own terms; best abolish slavery, says Adam Smith, since to do so will probably be cheaper in the end.

The whole complex irrational world is reduced to a kind of rational scheme where human particles are nicely magnetized in a simple polarity toward profit and away from loss. The great system works, not because man directs it, but because self-interest and competition line up the filings in the proper way; the most that man can do is to help this natural social magnetism along, to remove whatever barriers stand before the free working out of this social physics, and to cease his misguided efforts to escape from its thralldom.

And yet for all its eighteenth-century flavor, its belief in rationality, natural law, and the mechanized chain of human action and reaction, the world of Adam Smith is not without its warmer values. Do not forget that the great beneficiary of the system was the consumer—not the producer. For the first time in the philosophy of everyday life, the consumer is king.

Of the whole, what has survived?

Not the great scheme of evolution. We shall see that profoundly altered by the great economists to follow. But let us not regard the world of Adam Smith as merely a primitive attempt to arrive at formulations which were beyond his grasp. Smith was the economist of preindustrial capitalism; he did not live to see the market system threatened by enormous enterprises or his laws of accumulation and population upset by sociological developments fifty years off. When Smith lived and wrote there had not yet been a recognizable phenomenon which might be called a "business cycle." The world he wrote about actually existed, and his systematization of it, mechanical though it was, provides as good an explanation as any.

Yet something must have been missing from Smith's conception. For although he saw an evolution for society, he did not see a revolution—the Industrial Revolution. Smith did not see in the ugly factory system, in the newly tried corporate form of business organization, or in the weak attempts of journeymen to form protective organizations, the first appearance of new and disruptively powerful social forces. In a sense his system presupposes that eighteenth-century England will remain unchanged forever. Only in quantity will it grow: more people, more goods, more wealth; its quality will remain unchanged. His are the dynamics of a static community; it grows but it never matures.

But although the system of evolution has been discarded, the great panorama of the market remains as a major achievement. To be sure, Smith did not "discover" the market; others had preceded him in pointing out how the interaction of self-interest and competition brought about the provision of society. But Smith was the first to understand the full philosophy of action which such a conception demanded, the first to formulate the entire scheme in a wide and systematic fashion. He was the man who made England, and then the whole Western World, understand just how the market kept society together and the first to build an edifice of social order on the understanding he achieved. Later economists will embroider Smith's description of the market and will inquire anxiously into the defects which subsequently appeared in it. None will improve on the richness and life with which Smith imbued this aspect of the world.

For Smith's encyclopedic scope and knowledge there can be only admiration. It was only in the eighteenth century that so huge, all-embracing, secure, caustic, and profound a book could have been written. Smith anticipated Veblen by a hundred and fifty years when he wrote: "With the greater part of rich people, the chief enjoyment of riches consists in the parade of riches, which in their eye is never so complete as when they appear to possess those decisive marks of opulence which nobody can possess but themselves." He was a statesman ahead of his time when he wrote: "If any of the provinces of the British Empire cannot be made to contribute towards the support of the whole empire, it is surely time that Great Britain should free herself from the expence of defending those provinces in time of war, and of supporting any part of their civil or military establishments in time of peace, and endeavour to accommodate her future views and designs to the real mediocrity of her circumstances."

And perhaps no economist will ever again so utterly encompass his age as Adam Smith. Certainly none was ever so serene, so devoid of contumacy, so penetratingly critical without rancor, and so optimistic without being utopian. To be sure, he shared the beliefs of his day, in fact he helped to forge them. It was an age of humanism and reason, and while both could be perverted for the cruelest and most violent purposes, Smith was never chauvinist, apologist, or compromiser. "For to what purpose," he wrote in the *Theory of Moral Sentiments,* "is all the toil and bustle of this world? What is the end of avarice and ambition, of the pursuit of wealth, of power, and pre-eminence?" The *Wealth of Nations* provides his answer: all the grubby scrabbling for wealth and glory has its ultimate justification in the welfare of the common man.

At the end of his life, Smith was ripe with honors and respect. Burke traveled to Edinburgh to see him; he was elected Lord Rector at his old University of Glasgow; he saw the *Wealth of Nations* translated into Danish, French, German, Italian, Spanish. Only Oxford ignored him; it never deigned to give him an honorary degree. At one time Pitt the Younger, then Prime Minister, was meeting with Addington, Wilberforce, and Grenville, and Adam Smith had been invited to attend. As the old philosopher walked into the room, everyone rose. "Be seated, gentlemen," he said. "No," replied Pitt, "we will stand until you are first seated, for we are all your scholars."

In 1790 Smith died; he was sixty-seven. Curiously, his passing attracted relatively little notice; perhaps people were too busy worrying about the French Revolution and the repercussions it might have on the English countryside. He was buried in the Canongate churchyard with an unpretentious tombstone; it states that Adam Smith, author of *Wealth of Nations,* lies here. It would be hard to conceive of a more durable monument.

IV

The Gloomy Presentiments
of Parson Malthus
and David Ricardo

IN ADDITION to the omnipresent problem of poverty, a bothersome question worried England throughout most of the eighteenth century: the question of how many Englishmen there were. The worrisome aspect of the problem lay in the fact that England's natural enemies on the Continent bulged with what, to British eyes, must have appeared as a veritable flood of humanity, while England, with her slender resources, was convinced that her own population was on the decline.

Not that England was any too sure exactly how many Britishers there were; in hypochondriacal fashion, she preferred to worry in a factual vacuum. It would not be until 1801 that the first real census would be held and when it came it would be heralded as "totally subversive of the last remnants of English liberty." Hence, Britain's earlier knowledge about the state of her human resources depended on the efforts of amateur statisticians: Dr. Price, a Nonconformist minister; Houghton, an apothecary and dealer in coffee and tea; and Gregory King, by trade a maker of maps.

Drawing on records of hearth taxes and baptismal registers, in 1696 King reckoned up the number of souls in the British Isles as something near five and a half million—what seems to have been an extraordinarily accurate estimate. But King was concerned not only with the contemporary state of affairs. Looking into the future he wrote: "In all probability, the next doubling of the people of England will be in about six hundred years to come, or by the year of our Lord 2300. . . . The next doubling after that will be, in all probability, in less than twelve or thirteen hundred years, or by the year of our Lord 3500 or 3600. At which time the kingdom will have 22 million souls . . . in case," the map maker added circumspectly, "the world should last so long."

But by the time of Adam Smith, King's projection of a gently rising population had given way to another view. Comparing eighteenth-century records of hearth-money taxes with those of an earlier day, Dr. Richard Price proved conclusively that the population of England had *declined* by over thirty per cent since the Restoration. The validity of his computation was obviously dubious and other investigators hotly disputed his findings; nevertheless what Dr. Price believed to be so was taken as fact, and what with the political exigencies of the times, highly unpalatable fact. "The decay of population," moaned William Paley, the theologist reformer, "is the greatest evil the state can suffer, and the improvement of it the object which ought . . . to be aimed at, in preference to every other political purpose whatsoever." Paley was not alone in his belief; the younger Pitt, the Prime Minister, even introduced a new poor-relief bill for the specific purpose of boosting the population. The bill was to pay liberal allowances for children, since it was quite apparent to Pitt that by having children a man "enriched his country," even if his offspring should turn out to be paupers.

What is striking about the population question to our modern eyes is not whether England actually was or was not in danger of petering out as a nation. In retrospect, what is interesting is how harmonious either view of the population problem was with a philosophy which put its faith in natural law, reason, and progress. Was the population declining? Then it should be encouraged to grow, and grow it would under the august auspices of the laws which Adam Smith had shown to be the guiding principles of a free market economy. Was the population growing? All to the good, since everyone agreed that a growing population was a national source of wealth. No matter which way one cut the cake, the result was favorable to an optimistic prognosis for society; or to put it differently, there was nothing in the population question, as it was understood, to shake men's faith in their future.

Perhaps no one summed up this optimistic outlook so naïvely and completely as William Godwin. Godwin, a minister and pamphleteer, looked at the vulgar world about him and shrank back in dismay. But he looked into the future and what he saw was good. In 1793 he published *Political Justice*, a book which excoriated the present but which gave promise of a distant future in which "there would no longer be a handful of rich and a multitude of poor. . . . There will be no war, no crime, no administration of justice, as it is called, and no government. Besides this there will be no disease, anguish, melancholy, or resentment." What a wonderful vision! It was, of course, highly subversive, for Godwin's Utopia called for complete equality and for the most thoroughgoing anarchic communism: even the property contract of marriage would be abolished. But in view of the high price of the book (it sold for three guineas) the Privy Council decided not to prosecute the author, and it became the fashion of the day in the aristocratic salons to discuss Mr. Godwin's daring ideas.

One home in which this debate took place was Albury House, not far from Guildford, where there resided a curious old gentleman who was described by *Gentleman's Magazine* on his death in 1800 as "an eccentric character in the strictest sense of the term." This eccentric was Daniel Malthus, a friend of David Hume and a passionate admirer of Rousseau with whom he had gone on local botanizing walks and from whom he had received a herbarium and a set of books in one of the French philosopher's recurrent urges for self-dispossession. Like so many leisurely but inquiring gentlemen of his day, Daniel Malthus enjoyed nothing better than a stimulating intellectual dialogue, and for an opponent he usually turned to his gifted son, the Reverend Thomas Robert Malthus.

Quite naturally Godwin's paradise came up for consideration and as might perhaps be expected of an eccentric disciple of Rousseau, Malthus the elder felt sympathetically inclined toward the supremely rational Utopia. But young Malthus was not so hopeful as his father. In fact, as the argument progressed, he began to see an insurmountable barrier between human society as it existed and this lovely imaginary land of everlasting peace and plenty. To convince his father he wrote his objections down at length, and so impressed was Daniel Malthus with his son's ideas that he suggested the thesis be published and presented to the public.

It was. In 1798 an anonymous treatise of fifty thousand words appeared on the scene. It was entitled *An Essay on the Principle of Population as It Affects the Future Improvement of Society,* and with it perished at one blow all the fond hopes of a harmonious universe. In a few pages young Malthus pulled the carpet from under the feet of the complacent thinkers of the times, and what he offered them in place of progress was a prospect meager, dreary, and chilling.

For what the essay on population said was that there was a tendency in nature for population to outstrip all possible means of subsistence. Far from ascending to an ever higher level, society was caught in a hopeless trap in which the human reproductive urge would inevitably shove humanity to the sheer brink of the precipice of existence. Rather than headed for Utopia, the human lot was forever condemned to a losing struggle between ravenous and multiplying mouths and the eternally insufficient stock of Nature's cupboard, however diligently that cupboard might be searched.

No wonder that after he read Malthus, Carlyle called economics "the dismal science," and that poor Godwin complained that Malthus had converted friends of progress into reactionaries by the hundreds.

In one staggering intellectual blow Malthus undid all the roseate hopes of an age oriented toward self-satisfaction and a comfortable vista of progress. But as if this were not enough, at the same time a quite different kind of thinker was also preparing the *coup de grâce* for yet another of the lulling assumptions of the late eighteenth and early nineteenth centuries. David Ricardo, an astonishingly successful stockbroker, was soon to outline a theory of economics which, while less spectacular than Malthus' inundation of humanity, would be in its own quiet way just as devastating to the pleasant premises of the age of Adam Smith.

For what Ricardo foresaw was the end of a theory of society

in which everyone moved together up the escalator of progress
sketched out by Smith. On the contrary, Ricardo saw that the
escalator worked with different effects on different classes, that
some rode triumphantly to the top, while others were carried up
a few steps and then kicked back down to the bottom. Worse
yet, those who kept the escalator moving were not those who
rose with its motion, and those who got the full benefit of the
ride did nothing to earn their reward. And to carry the metaphor
one step further, if you looked carefully at those who were ascending to the top, you could see that all was not well here
either; there was a furious struggle going on for a secure place
on the stairs.

Society to Adam Smith was a great family; to Ricardo it was a
bitter contest for supremacy, and small wonder that he should
have seen it as such. In the forty years since the *Wealth of Nations* England had divided into two hostile camps: the rising
industrialists, busy with their factories and fighting for parliamentary representation and social prestige, and the great landowners, a rich, powerful, and entrenched aristocracy, who looked
resentfully at the encroachments of the brassy *nouveaux riches*.

It was not the fact that the capitalists were making money
which enraged the landowners. It was the damnable fact that
they kept insisting that food prices were too high. For what had
happened in the short space of time since Adam Smith was that
England, which had long been a grain-exporting nation, was now
being forced to buy foodstuffs from abroad. Despite the mutterings of Dr. Price who saw England's population rapidly dwindling away, the actual growth of population had caused the
demand for grain to exceed the supply and had *quadrupled* the
price of a bushel of wheat. And as prices rose, so did profits: on
a farm in East Lothian, Scotland, profits and rent together averaged fifty-six per cent of invested capital; on another farm of
three hundred acres owned by a Mr. Birkhead—a very typical
medium-sized establishment—profits were £88 in 1790, £121 in
1803, and £160 ten years later. And on the large estates of thousands of acres profits rose accordingly.

As grain soared, enterprising merchants began to buy wheat
and corn abroad and bring them into the country. Quite naturally, the landlord looked on this practice with dismay. Farming

was not merely a way of life for the aristocracy, it was a business
—a big business. On the Reevesby estate in Lincolnshire in 1799,
for instance, Sir Joshua Banks needed two rooms for his offices,
separated them with a fireproof wall and an iron door, and was
proud of the fact that it took a hundred and fifty-six drawers to
classify all the papers pertaining to the farm. Although such a
landlord lived on his land and loved the land, although he saw
his tenants daily, joined societies for the purpose of discussing
crop rotation and the virtues of competing fertilizers, he did not
lose sight of the fact that his income depended on the price at
which he sold his crop.

Hence the flow of inexpensive grain from overseas was hardly
viewed in a tolerant light. But fortunately for the landlord, the
means were readily at hand to combat this distressing development. Dominating Parliament, the landlord simply legislated
himself an ironclad system of protection. He passed the Corn
Laws, which imposed sliding duties on the importation of grain;
the lower the domestic price fell, the higher went the duty. In
effect a floor was established to keep low-priced wheat permanently out of the English market.

But by 1813 the situation had gotten out of hand. Bad crops
and the war with Napoleon conspired to bring about virtual
famine prices. Wheat sold at a price of 118 shillings a quarter—
approximately 14 shillings per bushel. Thus a bushel of wheat
sold for a price equal to nearly *twice* a workman's *whole weekly
wage*—to put this into perspective, compare the highest price ever
reached by American wheat: $3.50 per bushel in 1920 when
weekly wages averaged $26.00.

Patently, the price of grain was fantastic, and what to do about
it became a question of enormous moment to the country. Parliament studied the situation carefully—and came up with the solution that the duty on foreign grain should be raised still higher!
The rationale was that higher prices in the short run would act
to stimulate a larger production of English wheat in the long
run.

This was too much for the industrialists to take. Contrary to
the landed proprietors, the capitalists wanted cheap grain, for
the price of food largely determined the amount they would
have to pay for labor. It was not out of humanitarian motives

that the industrialist fought for cheaper food. A great London banker, Alexander Baring, declared in Parliament: ". . . the labourer has no interest in this question; whether the price be 84 shillings or 105 shillings a quarter, he will get dry bread in the one case and dry bread in the other." By this Baring meant that regardless of the price of bread, the laborer would get wages enough to buy his crust and no more. But from the point of view of those who met payrolls and sought after profits, it made a vast deal of difference whether grain—and wages—were cheap or dear.

The business interests organized; Parliament found itself flooded with more petitions than it had ever received before. In view of the temper of the country, it became obviously inexpedient to push through the new higher Corn Laws without some deliberation. New committees were appointed in Commons and in Lords, and the issue was temporarily shelved. Fortunately, the next year saw the defeat of Napoleon and grain prices subsided again toward more normal levels. But it is an index to the political power of the landholding class that thirty years would have to pass until the Corn Laws were finally wiped from the books and cheap grain permitted to come freely into Britain.

Writing in the midst of such a period of crisis, it is not difficult to understand why David Ricardo saw economics in a different and far more pessimistic light than Adam Smith. Smith had looked at the world and had seen in it a great concert; Ricardo saw a vicious conflict. To the author of the *Wealth of Nations* there was every reason to believe that everyone could share in the benefits of a benign providence; to the inquiring stockbroker writing about a half century later, society was not only rent into warring groups, but it seemed inescapably true that the rightful winner of the conflict—the hard-working industrialist—was bound to lose. For Ricardo believed that the only class that would benefit from the progress of society was the landlord—unless his hold on the price of grain could be broken.

"The interest of the landlords is always opposed to the interest of every other class in the community," he wrote in 1815, and with that unequivocal sentence an undeclared war became recognized civil strife. And with the open declaration of hostilities there perished the last forlorn hope that this might after all turn out to be the best of all possible worlds. Now it seemed that if society did not drown in the Malthusian swamp of humanity, it would tear itself to pieces in the fight to secure places on David Ricardo's treacherous moving stairs.

We must look more closely at the profoundly disturbing ideas of the gloomy parson and the skeptical stockbroker. But first let us look at the men themselves.

It would be hard to imagine two persons more widely separated in their backgrounds and careers than Thomas Robert Malthus and David Ricardo. Malthus, as we know, was the son of an eccentric member of the English upper middle class; Ricardo was the son of a Jewish merchant-banker who had immigrated from Holland. Malthus was tenderly tutored for a university under the guidance of a philosophically minded father (one of his tutors went to jail for expressing the wish that the French revolutionaries would invade and conquer England); Ricardo went to work for his father at the age of fourteen. Malthus spent his life in academic research; he was the first professional economist, teaching at the college founded in Haileybury by the East India Company to train its young administrators; Ricardo set up in business for himself at the age of twenty-two. Malthus was never well-to-do; by the time he was twenty-six, Ricardo—who had started with a capital of eight hundred pounds —was financially independent, and in 1814, at the age of forty-two, he retired with a fortune variously estimated to be worth between £500,000 and £1,600,000.

Yet oddly enough it was Malthus, the academician, who was interested in the facts of the real world, and Ricardo, the man of affairs, who was the theoretician; the businessman cared only for invisible "laws" and the professor worried whether these laws fitted the world before his eyes. And as a final contradiction, it was Malthus with his modest income who defended the wealthy landowner, and Ricardo, a man of wealth and later a landlord himself, who fought against their interests.

Different as they were in background, training, and career, so they were accorded utterly different receptions. As for poor Malthus, in the words of a biographer, James Bonar: "He was the best abused man of his age. Bonaparte himself was not a greater enemy of his species. Here was a man who defended small-pox, slavery, and child-murder—a man who denounced soup-kitchens, early marriages, and parish allowances—a man who 'had the impudence to marry after preaching against the evils of a family.' " "From the first," says Bonar, "Malthus was not ignored. For thirty years it rained refutations."

Such abuse was bound to befall a man who urged "moral restraint" on the world. And yet Malthus was neither a prude (by the standards of his times) nor, certainly, an ogre. It is true that he urged the abolition of poor relief and even opposed housing projects for the working classes. But all this was done with the sincerest interest of the poorer classes at heart—and indeed may be contrasted with the view of some contemporary social theorists who suggested blandly that the poor be allowed to die peacefully in the streets.

Hence Malthus' position was not so much a hardhearted as a supremely *logical* one. Since according to his theory the basic trouble with the world was that there were too many people in it, anything which tended to promote "early connections" only aggravated the sum of mankind's misery. A man for whom "at Nature's mighty feast there is no cover" might be kept alive by charity, but since he would then propagate, such charity was only cruelty in disguise.

But logic does not always win popularity, and a man who points out the gloomy end of society can hardly expect to gain popular esteem. No doctrine was ever so reviled: Godwin described his theory as "that black and terrible demon that is always ready to stifle the hopes of humanity." In the eyes of less sophisticated readers, the demon was not so much Malthus' theory as the figure of the Reverend himself.

Ricardo, on the other hand, was a man on whom Fortune smiled from the start. A Jew by birth, he had broken with his family and adopted Quakerism to marry a handsome Quaker girl with whom he had fallen in love; but in a day when tolerance was hardly the rule—his father had traded in a part of the Exchange known as the Jews Walk—Ricardo achieved both social status and widespread private respect. Later in life, when he was in Commons, he was called on to speak from both sides of the

House. "I have no hope," he said, "of conquering the alarm with which I am assailed the moment I hear the sound of my own voice." That voice was described by one witness as "harsh and screamy," by another as "sweet and pleasant" although "pitched extremely high"; but when it spoke, the House listened. With his earnest and brilliant expositions which ignored the toss of events and concentrated on the basic structure of society "as if he had dropped from another planet," Ricardo became known as the man who educated Commons. Even his radicalism—he was a strong supporter of freedom of speech and assembly, and an opponent of Parliamentary corruption and Catholic persecution—did not detract from the veneration in which he was held.

It is doubtful whether his admirers understood much of what they read, for there is no more difficult economist to understand than Ricardo. But although the text might have been complex and involved, its import was plain: the interests of the capitalists and the landlords were irrevocably opposed and the interests of the landlords were inimical to the community. Hence, whether they understood him or not, the industrialists made him their champion: political economy even became so popular with them that ladies who hired governesses inquired whether they could teach its principles to their children.

But while Ricardo, the economist, walked like a god (although he was a most modest and retiring person), Malthus was relegated to a lower status. His essay on population was read, admired, and then disproved again and again—the very vehemence of the disproofs a disquieting testimony to the strength of his thesis. And while Ricardo's ideas were avidly discussed, Malthus' contributions to economics—aside from his essay on population—were largely looked on with a kind of benevolent tolerance, or ignored. For Malthus had a sense that all was not well with the world, but he was utterly incapable of presenting his arguments in a clear-cut logical fashion: he was even heretical enough to suggest that depressions—"general gluts," he called them—might upset society, an idea which Ricardo had no trouble in proving to be absurd. How exasperating for a modern reader! Intuitive and fact-minded, Malthus had a nose for trouble, but his woolly-headed expositions had no chance against the incisive brilliance of the stockbroker who saw the world only as a great abstract mechanism.

Hence they argued about everything. When Malthus published his own *Principles of Political Economy* in 1820, Ricardo went to the trouble of taking some 220-odd pages of notes to point out the flaws in the Reverend's arguments, and Malthus positively went out of his way in his book to expose the fallacies he was sure were inherent in Ricardo's point of view.

Strangest of all, the two were the closest of friends. They met in 1809 after Ricardo had published a series of masterful letters to the *Morning Chronicle* on the question of the price of bullion, and then had demolished a Mr. Bosanquet, who was rash enough to venture an opposing view. First James Mill and then Malthus sought out the author of the letters and a friendship formed among all three which endured to the end of their lives. A stream of correspondence passed between them, and they visited each other endlessly. "They hunted together in search of the Truth," wrote Maria Edgeworth, a contemporary writer, in a charming diary, "and huzzaed when they found her, without caring who found her first."

It was not all serious discussion; these were very human beings. Malthus, whether out of deference to his theories or other reasons, had married late, but he was fond of social gatherings. After his death, someone who had known him mused on his life at East India College: "The subdued jests and external homage and occasional insurrections of the young men; the archery of the young ladies; the curious politeness of the Persian professor . . . and the somewhat old-fashioned courtesies of the summer evening parties are all over now."

The pamphleteers compared him with Satan, but Malthus was a tall and handsome man and a gentle soul: his students called him "Pop" behind his back. He had one odd defect: from his great-great-grandfather he had inherited a cleft palate and his speech was difficult to understand; *l* was his worst letter and there is an amusing account of his saying into the ear trumpet of a deaf and famous lady: "Would not you like to have a look at the lakes of Killarney?" This defect and the indissoluble association of his name with overpopulation led one acquaintance to write:

Philosopher Malthus was here last week. I got an agreeable party for him of unmarried people . . . he is a good-natured man and, if there are no signs of approaching fertility, is civil to every lady. . . . Malthus is a real moral philosopher, and I would almost consent to speak as inarticulately, if I could think and act as wisely.

Ricardo at home also loved to entertain; his breakfasts were famous, and he seems to have indulged in a fondness for charades. In her *Life and Letters,* Miss Edgeworth tells of one round:

> *coxcomb*—Mr. Smith, Mr. Ricardo, Fanny, Harriet, and Maria, *crowing.* Ditto, ditto, *combing* hair. Mr. Ricardo, solus strutting, a *coxcomb,* very droll.

He was extraordinarily gifted as a businessman. "The talent for obtaining wealth," wrote his brother, "is not held in much estimation, but perhaps in nothing did Mr. R. more evince his extraordinary powers than he did in business. His complete knowledge of all its intricacies—his surprising quickness at figures and calculation—his capability of getting through, without any apparent exertion, the immense transactions in which he was concerned—his coolness and judgment—enabled him to leave all his contemporaries at the Stock Exchange far behind." His son later declared that his father's success was based upon his observation that people in general exaggerated the importance of events. "If therefore, dealing as he dealt in stocks, there was reason for a small advance, he bought, because he was certain the unreasonable advance would enable him to realize; so when stocks were falling, he sold in the conviction that alarm and panic would produce a decline not warranted by circumstances."

It was a curiously upside-down arrangement: the theoretical stockbroker versus the practical divine—particularly curious since the theoretician was at home in the world of money whereas the man of facts and figures was utterly at sea.

During the Napoleonic Wars Ricardo was an underwriter in a syndicate which bought Government securities from the Treasury and then offered them to the subscribing public. Ricardo often did Malthus a favor and carried him for a small block of securities on which the parson made a modest profit. On the eve of Waterloo Malthus thus found himself a small "bull" on the Exchange and the strain was too much for his nerves. He wrote to Ricardo urging him "unless it is wrong or inconvenient . . . to take an early opportunity of realizing a small profit on the share you have been good enough to promise me." Ricardo did, but with the stronger staying power of the professional speculator bought himself into a maximum bull position. Wellington won; Ricardo made an immense killing, and poor Malthus could not help being discomfited. Ricardo, on the other hand, wrote casually to the Reverend, "This is as great an advantage as ever I expect or wish to make by a rise. I have been a considerable gainer by the loan. Now for a little of our old subject," and he plunges back into a discussion of the theoretical meaning of a rise in the price of commodities.

Their endless debate went on, by letter and visit, until 1823. In his last letter to Malthus, Ricardo wrote: "And now, my dear Malthus, I have done. Like other disputants, after much discussion, we each retain our own opinions. These discussions, however, never influence our friendship; I should not like you more than I do if you agreed in opinion with me." He died that year suddenly, at the age of fifty-one; Malthus was to go on until 1834. As for his opinion of David Ricardo: "I never loved anybody out of my own family so much."

Although Malthus and Ricardo disagreed on almost everything, they did not disagree about what Malthus had to say about population. For in his celebrated *Essay* in 1798 Malthus seemed not only to elucidate the question once for all but also to shed a great deal of light on the terrible and persistent poverty which haunted the English social scene. Others had vaguely felt that somehow population and poverty were related and a popular if apocryphal story of the day concerned an island off the coast of Chile where one Juan Fernandez landed two goats in case he should later wish to find meat there. On revisiting the island he found that the goats had multiplied beyond reason, so he then landed a pair of dogs who also multiplied and cut down the goats. "Thus," wrote the author, a Reverend James Townshend, "a new kind of balance was restored. The weakest of both species were the first to pay the debt of nature; the most active and vigorous preserved their lives." To which he added: "It is the quantity of food which regulates the number of the human species."

But while this paradigm recognized the balance that must be struck in nature, it still failed to draw the final devastating conclusions implicit in the problem. This was left for Malthus to do.

He began with a fascination in the sheer numerical possibilities contained in the idea of *doubling*. ". . . If any person will take the trouble to make the calculation," he wrote, "he will see that if the necessaries of life could be obtained without limit, and the number of people could be doubled every twenty-five years, the population which might have been produced from a single pair since the Christian era, would have been sufficient, not only to fill the earth quite full of people, so that four should stand in every square yard, but to fill all the planets of our solar system in the same way, and not only them but all the planets revolving around the stars which are visible to the naked eye, supposing each of them . . . to have as many planets belonging to it as our sun has."

And in this appreciation of the staggering multiplicative powers of reproduction, he is quite right. One biologist has calculated that a pair of animals, each pair producing ten pairs annually, would at the end of twenty years be responsible for 700,000,000,-000,000,000,000 offspring; and Havelock Ellis mentions a minute organism which, if unimpeded in its division, would produce from one single tiny being a mass a million times larger than the sun—in thirty days.

But such examples of the prolific power of nature are meaningless in themselves. The vital question is: how great is the normal reproductive power of a human being? Malthus made the assumption that the human animal would tend to double his numbers in twenty-five years. In the light of his times this was a relatively modest assumption. It necessitated an average family of six, two of them were presumed to die before reaching the age of marriage. Turning to America, Malthus pointed out that the population there had in fact doubled itself every twenty-five years for the preceding century and a half, and that in some backwoods areas where life was freer and healthier, it was doubling every fifteen years!

But against the multiplying tendencies of the human race—and it is inconsequential to the argument whether it tended to double in twenty-five years or in fifty—Malthus opposed the obdurate fact that land, unlike people, cannot be multiplied. Land can be added to laboriously, but the rate of progress is slow and hesitant; unlike population, land does not breed. Hence while the number of mouths grows geometrically, the amount of cultivable land grows only arithmetically.

And the result, of course, is as inevitable as a proposition in logic: the number of people is bound, sooner or later, to outstrip the amount of food. "Taking the whole earth," wrote Malthus in his *Essay*, ". . . and supposing the present population to be equal to a thousand millions, the human species would increase as the numbers 1, 2, 4, 8, 16, 32, 64, 128, 256, and subsistence as 1, 2, 3, 4, 5, 6, 7, 8, 9. In two centuries the population would be to the means of subsistence as 256 to 9; in three centuries as 4096 to 13, and in two thousand years the difference would be incalculable."

Such a dreadful view of the future would be enough to discourage any man: "The view," Malthus wrote, "has a melancholy hue." The troubled Reverend was driven to the conclusion that the incorrigible and irreconcilable divergence between mouths and food could have only one result: the larger portion of mankind would forever be subjected to some kind of misery or other. For somehow the huge and ever potentially widening gap must be sealed: population, after all, cannot exist without food. Hence among the primitives such customs as infanticide; hence war, hence disease, and above all, poverty.

And if these are not enough: "Famine seems to be the last, the most dreadful resource of nature. The power of population is so superior to the power of the earth to provide subsistence . . . that premature death must in some shape or other visit the human race. The vices of mankind are active and able ministers of depopulation. . . . But should they fail in this war of extermination, sickly seasons, epidemics, pestilence, and plague advance in terrific array and sweep off their thousands and tens of thousands. Should success still be incomplete, gigantic inevitable famine stalks in the rear, and with one mighty blow, levels the population with the food of the world."

No wonder poor Godwin complained that Malthus had converted friends of progress into reactionaries. For this is truly the doctrine of despair. Nothing, *nothing* can rescue mankind from the constant threat of drowning under its own weight but the frail reed of "moral restraint." And how dependable is moral restraint against the great passion of love?

The prospect that Malthus foresaw has come true. Recently the Foreign Policy Association wrote:

> The statistics are almost beyond belief. Each day about 10,000 people in the underdeveloped countries die as a result of illnesses caused by malnutrition. Of every 20 children born in these countries, 10 are likely to perish in infancy from hunger or from the effects of an improper diet. Another seven may suffer physical or mental retardation.

This Malthusian nightmare will worsen, not improve, over the coming decades. For population in the backward areas is growing faster than the output of food—growing at a rate that, in the opinion of the world's food authorities, portends a famine of unprecedented and unimaginable proportions before the end of this century. "As matters stand," writes J. J. Spengler, an expert on the population problem, "the prospect is definitely Malthusian, with man sitting on a demographic time bomb."

Can the bomb be defused? The date of the explosion can be delayed somewhat if we manage to increase the output of food. To feed (at present semistarvation levels) the three billion humans who will arrive on the planet before the year 2000 will require a doubling of world food output, and this may strain capabilities to the breaking point. But even if a miracle *quadrupled* the output of food, we should only be deferring the famine by perhaps a generation. And meanwhile, there are other strains—housing the prospective billions will require the construction, in the next forty years, of as much shelter as has been built since the beginning of civilization.

If the time bomb is to be defused, all agree that it must be done through population control. Throughout history birth control has been practiced by the upper classes of all societies—which is one reason for the adage that the rich got richer and the poor got children. Now the problem is to introduce a knowledge of birth control among hundreds of millions of peasants, most of whom cannot read, do not trust doctors, and are suspicious of outsiders telling them how to change their ways of life.

Can it be done, before famine begins? Perhaps. The techniques exist. More important, there is evidence from a few areas (South Korea and Taiwan) where the effort has been made that peasants *will* accept birth control, not to please the economic planners, but to escape from the miserable cycle of birth followed by premature death. What we still do not know is whether the enormous administrative and medical effort needed to bring birth control to remote villages and urban slums can be mounted in time, and (to a lesser extent) whether religious opposition in the advanced countries may hamper the dissemination of knowledge.

It is too early to answer these questions. We only know that in our own day we are witnessing a last stage of the fearful progression that Malthus foresaw in 1798—a progression in which the fertility of humanity finally outstrips that of the soil, enforcing a ghastly limit on the quantity of human life.

Malthus did not aim his shafts at the then largely ignored continents of the East and South. His warning was directed at the Western world. There, miraculously, he was wrong. Something happened in England, on the Continent, in the United States, to retard the flood of new mouths. In 1860, sixty-three per cent of the couples married in Great Britain had families of four or more children; by 1925 only twenty per cent had more than four. Over the same span of time, the number of families with only one or two children increased from ten per cent of the total to more than half.

Why? What saved the West from the Malthusian doubling and redoubling? We do not fully understand the reasons; the laws of population growth are not yet completely clear. Birth control, of course, played a part. Originally it was called Neo-Malthusianism, a name which would have made Malthus wince: he quite disapproved of the practice. But something else seems to have been equally important. The process of industrialization itself appears to have a tempering influence on the size of families.

Marriages tend to take place later in advanced countries (this is the "moral restraint" on which Malthus pinned his slim hopes). The status of women is elevated from mere childbearers to active and working members of society. There are competing pleasures and desires which make a large family seem less desirable than in a simpler way of life.

To be sure, population in the United States is growing—and in recent years has been growing fairly fast. We too face a population problem, although we will experience it first in terms of crowding rather than hunger. As our numbers mount—there will be 300 million Americans before the year 2000—space dwindles. Lines of traffic lengthen, national parks get more and more like vast picnic grounds, resources such as water get consumed dangerously fast. Yet nothing like famine threatens the United States, for advances in agricultural technology have raced out ahead of sheer numbers of mouths. Malthus did not see that the *yield* from cultivable land could grow much more rapidly than the *area* of land. Indeed, the problem in the United States is that agricultural productivity has been increasing too fast, that we have been threatened with uneatable surpluses of food.

Cannot the world follow our example? The problem is that American agriculture is productive because it is the beneficiary of enormous capital investments. The average American farmer works with a larger value of equipment than the average factory worker. It will be decades before sufficient capital can be accumulated in the backward lands. By then it will be too late.

None of this could be accurately foreseen in Malthus' day. In 1801 despite severe misgivings and rumors to the effect that this was merely a prelude to a military dictatorship, the first scientific census was undertaken in Great Britain. John Rickman, a civil servant and statistician, calculated that England's population had increased by twenty-five per cent in three decades. Although this was far from doubling, no one doubted that were it not for the disease and poverty of the masses, the population would have grown like an avalanche. No one saw the future slowing down of the birth rate; rather it seemed as if Britain was forever to face the mean poverty which sprang from an insatiably spawning humanity scrabbling for an insufficient supply of food. Poverty no longer seemed accidental, or an act of God, or the result even of human indifference. It seemed as though some malign providence had condemned the human race to eternal dolor, as if all of mankind's efforts toward self-improvement were made a farce through the stinginess of nature.

It was all very discouraging. Paley, who had urged a larger population "in preference to every other political purpose whatsoever," now became a convert to Malthus' banner; Pitt, who had wanted his country enriched with more children, now withdrew his bill for higher poor relief in deference to the parson's opinions. Coleridge summed up the doleful outlook. "Finally, behold this mighty nation," he wrote, "its rulers and wise men listening to—Paley and—to Malthus! It is mournful, mournful."

Anyone who was not sufficiently depressed by Malthus had only to turn to David Ricardo.

At first glimpse this was not a particularly terrifying world— at least not after the Malthusian. The universe of David Ricardo, set forth in his *Principles of Political Economy* in 1817, is dry, spare, and condensed; there is none of the life, the lively detail of Adam Smith. Here is nothing but principle, abstract principle, expounded by an intellect which is focused on something more permanent than the changing flux of daily life. This is as basic, bare, unadorned and architectural as Euclid, but, unlike a set of pure geometrical propositions, this system has human overtones: it is a *tragic* system.

To understand that tragedy, we must take a moment to introduce the main characters in the drama. They are not, as we have said, *people:* they are prototypes. Nor do these prototypes, in the everyday sense of the word, *live:* they follow "laws of behavior." There is none of the bustle of Adam Smith's world here; instead we watch a kind of model puppet show in which the protean aspects of the real world have been reduced to a kind of one-dimensional caricature; this is the world stripped of everything but its economic motivations.

Whom do we meet? First, there are the workers, undifferentiated units of economic energy, whose only human aspect is a hopeless addiction to what is euphemistically called "the delights of domestic society." Their incurable penchant for these delights results in every rise in wages promptly being met with an increase in population. The workers get their dry crust, as Alexander Baring put it, for without it they could not perpetuate themselves. But over the long run they are condemned by their own weakness to a life at the margin of subsistence. Like Malthus, Ricardo saw only "self-restraint" as a solution for the working masses and although he wished the workers well, he did not put too much faith in their powers of self-control.

Next we meet the capitalists. They are not Adam Smith's conniving merchants. They are a gray and uniform lot, whose entire purpose on earth is to accumulate—that is, to save their profits and to reinvest them by hiring still more men to work for them; and this they do with unvarying dependability. Perhaps Ricardo's training in the dispassionate world of international finance blinded him to the variety of motives besides money-making which motivated even a nineteenth-century industrialist; but for whatever reason, his capitalists are nothing but economic machines for self-aggrandizement. But the capitalists' lot is not an easy one. For one thing, by competing among themselves, they quickly erase any undue profits which might accrue to one lucky soul who invented a new process or found an unusually profitable channel of trade. For another thing, their profits depend largely on the wages they have to pay, and as we shall see, this leads them into considerable difficulties.

But so far, save for the lack of realistic detail, it is not a world too far removed from that of Adam Smith. It was when Ricardo came to the landlord that things were different.

For Ricardo saw the landlord as a unique beneficiary in the organization of society. The worker worked, and for this he was paid a wage; the capitalist ran the show, and for this he gained a profit. But the landlord benefited from the powers of the soil, and his income—rent—was not held in line by either competition or by the power of population. In fact, he gained at everyone else's expense.

We must pause for a moment to understand how Ricardo came to this conclusion, for his morbid outlook for society hangs on his definition of the landlord's rent. Rent, to Ricardo, was not just the price one paid for the use of the soil, much as interest was the price of capital, and wages the price of labor. Rent was a very special kind of return which had its origin in the demonstrable fact that not all land was equally productive.

Suppose, says Ricardo, there are two neighboring landlords. On one landlord's fields the soil is fertile, and with the labor of a hundred men and a given amount of equipment he can raise fifteen hundred bushels of grain. On the second landlord's fields, the soil is less fecund; the same men and their equipment will raise only one thousand bushels. This is merely a technical fact of nature, but it has an economic consequence: grain will be cheaper, per bushel, on the fortunate landlord's estate. Obviously since both landlords must pay out the same wages and capital costs, there will be an advantage to the man who secures five hundred more bushels than his competitor.

Now it is from this *difference* in costs that rent springs, according to Ricardo. For if the demand is high enough to warrant tilling the soil on the less productive farm, it will certainly be a very profitable operation to raise grain on the more productive farm. Indeed, the greater the difference between the two farms, the greater will be the differential rent. If, for example, it is just barely profitable to raise grain at a cost of $2.00 a bushel on very bad land, then certainly a fortunate landowner whose rich soil produces grain at a cost of only 50 cents a bushel will gain a large rent indeed. For *both* farms will sell their grain in the same market, and the owner of the better ground will pocket the difference of $1.50 in their costs.

All this seems innocuous enough. But now let us fit it into the world that Ricardo envisaged, and its unpleasant consequences will become quite clear.

To Ricardo, the economic world was constantly tending to expand. As capitalists accumulated, they built new shops and factories. Therefore, the demand for laborers increased. This boosted wages, at least temporarily, for better pay would soon tempt the incorrigible working orders to avail themselves of those treacherous delights of domestic society and so to undo their advantage by flooding the market with still more workers. But—and here is where the world of Ricardo turns sharply away from the hopeful prospects of Adam Smith—as population expanded, it would become necessary to push the margin of cultivation out further. More mouths would demand more grain, and more grain would demand more fields. And quite naturally, the new fields put into seed would not be so productive as those already in use, for it would be a foolish farmer who had not already used the best soil available to him.

Thus, as the growing population caused more and more land to be put into use, the cost of grain would rise. So of course would the selling price of grain, and so too would the rents of well-situated landlords. And not only rents, but wages would rise, as well. For as grain became more expensive to produce, the laborer would have to be paid more, just to enable him to buy his dry crust and stay alive.

And now see the tragedy. The capitalist—the man responsible for the progress of society in the first place—has been put in a double squeeze. First, the wages he has to pay are higher, since bread is dearer. Secondly, the landlords are much better off, since rents have been rising on good land, as worse and worse land has got pushed into use. And as the landlord's share in society's fruit increases, there is only one class that can get elbowed aside to make room for him—the capitalist.

What a different conclusion from Adam Smith's great pageant of progress! In Smith's world everybody gradually became better off as the division of labor increased and made the community more wealthy. In Ricardo's world, *only* the landlord stood to gain. The worker was forever condemned to the margin, for, poor fellow, he tended to chase after every wage rise with a flock of children and thereby to compete his wages right back down to subsistence. The capitalist, who worked and saved and invested, found that all his trouble was for nothing: his wage costs were higher, his profits smaller, and his landed opponent far richer than he. And the landlord, who did nothing but collect his rents, sat back and watched them increase.

No wonder that Ricardo fought against the Corn Laws and showed the advantages of free trade which would bring cheap grain into Britain. No wonder the landlords fought tooth and nail for thirty years to keep cheap grain out of the country. And how natural that in Ricardo's exposition the young industrialist class saw the theory which just fitted their needs. Were they responsible for low wages? No, since it was only the worker's own blindness which drove him to multiply his numbers. Were they responsible for the progress of society? Yes, and what did it avail them to expend their energies and save their profits for still further adventures in production? All they got for their pains was the dubious satisfaction of watching rents and money wages rise, and their own profits shrink. It was they who drove the economic machine, and the landlord, lolling in the back seat, who gained all the pleasure and reward. Indeed a sensible capitalist would really have to ask himself if the game were worth the candle.

Now who was to pop up and say that Ricardo was unfair to the landlords but Parson Malthus!

Let us remember that Malthus was not just an expert on the population question. He was first and foremost an economist, and he had, as a matter of fact, propounded the "Ricardian" theory of rent before it was taken up and refined by Ricardo himself. But Malthus did not draw the same conclusions from his theory as his friend. "Rents," said Malthus, in his *Principles of Political Economy,* which appeared three years after Ricardo's, "are the reward of present valour and wisdom, as well as of past strength and cunning. Every day lands are purchased with the fruits of industry and talent." "In fact," Malthus adds in a footnote, "Mr. Ricardo himself is a landlord and a good example of what I mean."

It was not a very convincing rebuttal. Ricardo did not paint the landlord as a machinating figure of evil. He merely showed how the forces of economic development placed him unwittingly in a position where he stood to benefit from society's growth.

But we cannot stop here to trace all the permutations of this debate. What is important is that the dire *implications* of rent envisioned by Ricardo never came to pass. For the industrialists finally did break the power of the landlords and they did finally secure the importation of cheap food. The bleak hillsides up which the wheatfields were ominously climbing in Ricardo's day were, within a few decades, returned to pasture. Equally important, the population never grew so fast as to swamp the resources of the country. For the Ricardian theory says that rent arises from the inequalities between the best land and the worst; obviously, if the population problem is under control, this difference will not develop to such a degree that rental returns assume socially alarming proportions. But consider for a moment the situation if Britain today were forced to feed her present population of fifty millions entirely from the produce of home-grown crops—suppose the old Corn Laws had never been repealed. Is there any doubt that Ricardo's picture of a landlord-dominated society would be a frightening reality? The problem of rent has become almost an academic side issue in the modern Western World. But this is not because Ricardo's analysis was faulty; we have been spared the Ricardian dilemma only because the tempo of industrial life has rescued us from the Malthusian plight: industrialism has not only given us a brake on births, but it has enormously increased our ability to raise food from the land at our disposal.

But while Malthus regarded the landlord as a valiant fellow who contributed to the wealth of nations (Ricardo said he contributed as a *capitalist,* making agricultural improvements, but not as a mere beneficiary from the property rights of soil), the parson found yet another cause for concern. He was worried over the possibility of what he called a "general glut"—a flood of commodities without buyers.

Such an idea is by no means foreign to us who have worried about depressions all our lives. But it appeared foolish beyond belief to Ricardo. England had had upsets in trade, but all of these appeared to be traceable to some specific cause—a bank failure, or a burst of unwarranted speculation, or a war. And more important, for Ricardo's mathematical mind, the concept could be shown to be *logically impossible.* Therefore, it could never happen.

Ricardo's proof had been discovered by a young Frenchman named J. B. Say. Say had two very simple propositions. First, he believed that the *desire* for commodities was infinite. The desire for food might be limited by the capacity of a man's stomach, as Adam Smith had said, but his desire for clothes, furniture, luxuries, and ornaments seemed incalculably large. But not only was demand infinitely large, said Ricardo and Say, but the *ability* to purchase was guaranteed as well. For every good that was produced cost something—and every cost was some man's income. Whether that cost was wages, rent, or profits, its sale price ac-

crued as *someone's* income. And so how could a general glut
ever occur? The goods existed, the demand for them existed, and
the incomes to buy them existed as well. Only pure perversity
could prevent the market from finding the buyers it needed to
clear its wares.

But although Ricardo accepted this as valid on the face of it,
Malthus did not. It was not an easy argument to puncture, for it
did seem logically watertight. But Malthus looked behind the
process of swapping commodities for incomes, and came up with
a strange idea. Was it not possible, he said, for the act of *saving*
to make the demand for goods too small for the supply?

Again, to the modern world, this seems like a disturbingly
fruitful line of inquiry. But Ricardo said it was plain and simple
nonsense. "Mr. Malthus never appears to remember that to save
is to spend, as surely, as what he exclusively calls spending,"
writes Ricardo in a reproving note. What he meant was that it
was inconceivable to him that a man would bother to save his
profits for any reason except to put them back into industry and
earn still more profits.

This put Malthus in a quandary. Like Ricardo, he believed
that saving meant spending—for industrial purposes, of course.
But still, there seemed to be *something* in his argument—if only
he could put his finger on it. He never could. He wrote, for example, to prove that accumulation was not *quite* so essential as
Ricardo thought:

> Many a merchant has made a large fortune although, dur-
> ing the acquisition of this fortune, there was perhaps hardly
> a single year in which he did not rather increase than dimin-
> ish his expenditure on objects of luxury, enjoyment, and
> liberality.

To which Ricardo penciled this annihilatory comment:

> True, but a brother merchant who avoided an increased
> expenditure on objects of luxury, enjoyment, and liberality
> with the same profits, would get rich faster than him.

Poor Malthus! He never came off best in the exchange. His
arguments *were* confused, and it was neither the fault of his gen-

eration that they failed to understand him nor his error that he failed to understand Ricardo. For Malthus was stumbling on a phenomenon which would not absorb the attention of economists for fifty years—the problem of booms and depressions, whereas Ricardo was entirely taken up with quite a different problem. For Malthus, the issue was the immensely important one of How Much Is There? For Ricardo it was the far more explosive question of Who Gets What? No wonder they disagreed so endlessly; they were talking about different things.

What was their contribution, when all the argument was over?

Ricardo's gift to the world was plain. Here was a world stripped to its essentials and laid open for everyone to examine: the watchworks were exposed. In its very unreality lay its strength, for not only did the bare structure of a greatly simplified world reveal the laws of rent, but it elucidated as well vital questions of foreign trade, money, taxation, and economic policy. By building a model world, Ricardo gave the powerful tool of abstraction to economics—a tool that is essential if the distraction of everyday life is to be pierced and its underlying mechanism understood.

Malthus was never so successful in building an abstract world, and so his long-lasting academic contribution is smaller. But he pointed out the appalling problem of population and for that reason alone, his name is still alive. And he sensed, even if he could not explain, the problem of general depression which would occupy economists a century after his book.

The main issues with which both men wrestled are, in a sense, dead. For the Western World, at least, the population question is no longer a source of immediate concern—although it is a burning issue in the East and South—and the landlord's domination over the economy is a textbook curiosity. But between them, Malthus and Ricardo did one astonishing thing. They changed the viewpoint of their age from optimism to pessimism. No longer was it possible to view the universe of mankind as an arena in which the natural forces of society would inevitably bring about a better life for everyone. On the contrary, those natural forces which once seemed teleologically designed to bring harmony and peace into the world now seemed malevolent and menacing. If humanity did not groan under a flood of hungry mouths, it seemed that it might suffer under a flood of commodities without takers. And in either event, the outcome of a long struggle for progress would be a gloomy state where the worker just barely subsisted, where the capitalist was cheated of his efforts, and where the landlord gloated over his unearned and constantly growing spoil.

It was no small achievement for two men to convince the world that it was living in a fool's paradise. But they did; and so convincing was their proof that men sought to find a way out for society, not within the framework of the supposed natural laws, but in defiance of them. Malthus and Ricardo had shown that, left to itself, society would proceed to a kind of barely living hell. No wonder that reformers said, if that is the case, we will put our efforts to fighting against the natural tendencies of society. If drifting will land us on the rocks, we will swim against the current; and so the Utopian Socialists broke away from the faithful trust in the essential rightness of the world as it was.

In a sense, Malthus and Ricardo were the last of a generation which pinned its faith on reason, order, and progress. They were not apologists, nor were they defenders of an order of which they disapproved. Rather, they were impartial; they stood away from and above the social flux and with an impersonal eye plotted the direction of its current. And if what they saw was unpleasant—well, they were not to blame for that.

For these were the most scrupulously honest of men, who tracked down their ideas, regardless of where they led. Perhaps we should quote that footnote in which Malthus points out that Ricardo, the enemy of landlords, is a landlord himself:

> It is somewhat singular that Mr. Ricardo, a considerable receiver of rents, should have so much underrated their national importance; while I, who have never received, nor expect to receive any, shall probably be accused of overrating their importance. Our different situations and opinions may serve at least to shew our mutual sincerity, and afford a strong presumption, that to whatever bias our minds may have been subjected in the doctrines we have laid down, it has not been that, against which perhaps it is most difficult to guard, the insensible bias of situation and interest.

After they were both gone, Sir James Mackintosh, the Scottish philosopher, paid them a wonderful tribute. "I have known," he said, "Adam Smith slightly, Ricardo well, and Malthus intimately. Is it not something to say for a science that its three greatest masters were about the three best men I ever knew?"

V

The Visions of the
Utopian Socialists

IT IS not difficult to understand why Malthus and Ricardo should have conceived of the world in gloomy terms. England in the 1820's was a gloomy place to live: it had emerged triumphant from a long struggle on the Continent, but now it seemed locked in an even worse struggle at home. For it was obvious to anyone who cared to look that the burgeoning factory system was piling up a social bill of dreadful proportions and that the day of reckoning on that bill could not be deferred forever.

Indeed, a recital of the conditions that prevailed in those early days of factory labor is so horrendous that it makes a modern reader's hair stand on end. In 1828, *The Lion,* a radical magazine of the times, published the incredible history of Robert Blincoe, one of eighty pauper-children sent off to a factory at Lowdham. The boys and girls—they were all about ten years old—were whipped day and night, not only for the slightest fault, but to stimulate their flagging industry. And compared with a factory at Litton where Blincoe was subsequently transferred, conditions at Lowdham were rather humane. At Litton the children scrambled with the pigs for the slops in a trough; they were kicked and punched and sexually abused; and their employer, one Ellice Needham, had the chilling habit of pinching the children's ears until his nails met through the flesh. The foreman of the plant was even worse. He hung Blincoe up by his wrists over a machine so that his knees were bent and then he piled heavy weights on his

shoulders. The child and his co-workers were almost naked in
the cold of winter and (seemingly as a purely gratuitous sadistic
flourish) their teeth were filed down!

Without a doubt such frightful brutality was the exception
rather than the rule; indeed we suspect a little of the reformer's
zeal has embellished the account. But with full discount for ex-
aggeration, the story was nonetheless all too illustrative of a social
climate in which practices of the most callous inhumanity were
accepted as the natural order of events and even more important,
as nobody's business. A sixteen-hour working day was not uncommon, with the working force tramping to the mills at six in
the morning and trudging home at ten at night. And as a crown-
ing indignity, many factory operators did not permit their workpeople to carry their own watches, and the single monitory factory clock showed a strange tendency to accelerate during the
scant few minutes allowed for meals. The richest and most far-
sighted of the industrialists may have deplored such excesses, but
their factory managers or hard-pressed competitors seem to have
regarded them with an indifferent eye.

And the horrors of working conditions were not the only cause
for unrest. Machinery was now the rage, and machinery meant
the displacement of laboring hands by uncomplaining steel. As
early as 1779 a mob of eight thousand workers had attacked a
mill and burned it to the ground in unreasoning defiance of its
cold implacable mechanical efficiency, and by 1811 such protests
against technology were sweeping England. Wrecked mills dotted
the countryside and in their wake the word went about that
"Ned Ludd had passed." The rumor was that a King Ludd or a
General Ludd was directing the activities of the mob. It was not
true, of course. The Luddites, as they were called, were fired by
a purely spontaneous hatred of the factories which they saw as
prisons and the wagework which they still despised.

But the disturbances raised a real apprehension in the country.
Ricardo almost alone among the respectable people admitted
that perhaps machinery did not always operate to the immediate benefit of the workman, and for this opinion he was regarded
as having slipped, for once, from his usual acumen. To most observers, the sentiment was less reflective: the lower orders were
getting out of hand and should be severely dealt with. And to

the gentler classes, the situation seemed to indicate the coming of a violent and terrifying Armageddon. Southey, the poet, wrote: "At this moment nothing but the Army preserves us from that most dreadful of all calamities, an insurrection of the poor against the rich, and how long the Army may be depended upon is a question which I scarcely dare ask myself"; and Walter Scott lamented, ". . . the country is mined beneath our feet."

Little wonder that Malthus and Ricardo were such prophets of gloom and strife!

But all through this dark and troubled period, one spot in Britain shone like a beacon through the storm. In the dour mountains of Scotland, a good day's post from Glasgow, in country so primitive that the tollgate keepers at first refused gold coins (never having seen them before), stood the gaunt seven-story brick mills of a little community called New Lanark. Over the hilly roads from Glasgow rode a constant stream of visitors—twenty thousand signed the guestbook at New Lanark between 1815 and 1825—and the visiting crowds included such dignitaries as the Grand Duke Nicholas, later to be Tsar Nicholas I of Russia, Princes John and Maximilian of Austria, and a whole covey of parish deputations, writers, reformers, sentimental ladies, and skeptical businessmen.

What they came to see was the living proof that the squalor and depravity of industrial life were not the only and inevitable social arrangement. Here at New Lanark were neat rows of workers' homes with *two* rooms in every house; here were streets with the garbage neatly piled up awaiting disposal instead of being strewn in filthy disarray. And in the factories a still more unusual sight greeted the visitors' eyes. Over each employee hung a little cube of wood with a different color painted on each side: black, blue, yellow, and white. From darkest to lightest, the colors stood for different grades of deportment: white was excellent; yellow, good; blue, indifferent; black, bad. At a glance the factory manager could see how his work force was faring. It was mainly yellow and white.

For another surprise there were no children in the factories—at least none under the age of ten or eleven—and those that did work toiled only a short ten-and-three-quarter-hour day. Further-

more they were never punished; no one in fact was punished, and
save for a few adult incorrigibles who had to be expelled for
chronic drunkenness or some such vice, discipline seemed to be
wielded by benignity rather than fear. The door of the factory
manager stood open and anyone could (and did) present his objections to any rule or regulation. Everyone could inspect the
book which contained the detailed report of his deportment and
thus served as referent for the assignment of his colored cube,
and he could appeal if he felt that he had been unjustly rated.

Most remarkable of all were the little children. Instead of running wild and fierce through the streets, the visitors found them
in a large schoolhouse, fast at work and play. The littlest were
learning the names of the rocks and trees they found about them;
the slightly older were learning grammar from a frieze where
General Noun contested with Colonel Adjective and Corporal
Adverb. Nor was it all work, delightful as the work seemed to be.
Regularly the children gathered to sing and dance under the
tutelage of young ladies who had been instructed that no child's
question was ever to go unanswered, that no child was ever bad
without reason, that punishment was never to be inflicted, and
that children would learn faster from the power of example than
from admonition.

It must have been a wonderful and, indeed, an inspiring sight.
And for the business-minded gentlemen who were less likely to
be carried away by the sight of happy children than the tender-
hearted ladies, there was the irrefutable fact that New Lanark
was profitable, marvelously profitable. This was an establishment
run not only by a saint but by an eminently practical one, at that.

It was not only a practical saint who was responsible for New
Lanark but a most improbable one. Like so many of the early
nineteenth-century reformers on whom we look back as the Utopian Socialists, Robert Owen, the "benevolent Mr. Owen of New
Lanark," was a strange mixture of practicality and naïveté,
achievement and fiasco, common sense and madness. Here was a
man who advocated the abandonment of the plow in favor of
the spade; a man who from scratch became a great capitalist and
from a great capitalist a violent opponent of private property; a

man who advocated benevolence because it would pay dividends, and who then urged the abolition of money.

It is hard to believe that one man's life could take so many twists. It began as a chapter straight from Horatio Alger. Born of poor parents in Wales in 1771, Robert Owen left school at the age of nine to become apprenticed to a linen draper with the unlikely name of McGuffog. He might have stayed a linen draper always and watched the store name change to McGuffog and Owen, but in true business-hero style, he chose to go to Manchester; and there, at the age of eighteen and on the strength of £100 borrowed from his brother, he set himself up as a tiny capitalist manufacturing textile machinery. But the best was yet to come. A Mr. Drinkwater, the owner of a large spinning establishment, found himself one morning without a factory manager and advertised in the local paper for applicants. Owen had no knowledge of spinning mills, but he got the post in a fashion which might have provided a test for countless writers on the virtues of Pluck and Luck. "I put on my hat," wrote Owen over a half century later, "and proceeded straight to Mr. Drinkwater's counting house. 'How old are you?' 'Twenty this May,' was my reply. 'How often do you get drunk in the week?' . . . 'I was never,' I said, 'drunk in my life,' blushing scarlet at this unexpected question. 'What salary do you ask?' 'Three hundred a year,' was my reply. 'What?' Mr. Drinkwater said, with some surprise, repeating the words, 'Three hundred a year! I have had this morning I know not how many seeking the situation and I do not think all their askings together would amount to what you require.' 'I cannot be governed by what others seek,' said I, 'and I cannot take less.' "

It was a characteristic Owen gesture and it succeeded. At twenty he became the boy wonder of the textile world—an engaging young man with a rather straight nose in a very long face, and with large, frank eyes that advertised his candor. Within six months Mr. Drinkwater offered him a quarter interest in the business. But this was still only the prelude to a fabulous career. Within a few years Owen had heard of a set of mills for sale in the squalid village of New Lanark—coincidentally they were owned by a man with whose daughter he had fallen in love. To acquire either the mills or the hand of the daughter looked like

an impossible feat: Mr. Dale, the mill-owner, was a fervid Presby-
terian who would never approve of Owen's radical free-thinking
ideas, and then there was the question of how to find the capital
to buy the mills. Nothing daunted, Owen marched up to Mr.
Dale as he had once marched up to Mr. Drinkwater and the impossible became done. He borrowed the money, bought the mills,
and won the hand of the daughter in the bargain.

Matters might well have rested there. Within a year Owen had
made New Lanark a changed community; within five years it
was unrecognizable; in ten years more it was world-famous. It
would have been accomplishment enough for most men, for in
addition to winning a European reputation for farsightedness
and benevolence, Robert Owen made a fortune of at least £60,000
for himself.

But matters did not rest there. Despite his meteoric rise, Owen
conceived of himself as a man of ideas rather than as a mere man
of action; New Lanark had never been for him an idle exercise of
philanthropy. Rather, it was an opportunity to test out theories
which he had evolved for the advancement of humanity as a
whole. For Owen was convinced that mankind was no better than
its environment and that if that environment were changed, a
real paradise on earth might be achieved. In New Lanark he
could, as it were, test his ideas in a laboratory, and since they
succeeded beyond all measure there seemed no reason why they
should not be given to the world.

He soon had his chance. The Napoleonic Wars subsided and
in their wake came trouble. A succession of what Malthus would
have called "general gluts" wracked the country; from 1816 to
1820 with the exception of a single year, business was very bad.
The misery threatened to explode: "bread and blood" riots broke
out and a kind of hysteria gripped the country. The Dukes of
York and Kent and a body of notables formed a committee to
look into the causes of the distress and purely as a matter of
course they called upon Mr. Owen, the philanthropist, to present
his views.

The committee was hardly prepared for what it got. It had
no doubt expected a plea for factory reform, for Mr. Owen was
widely known for his championship of a shorter working day and
the abolition of child labor. Instead the notables found them-

selves reading a blueprint for social reorganization on a sweeping scale.

What Owen suggested was that the solution to the problem of poverty lay in making the poor productive. To this end he advocated the formation of Villages of Cooperation in which eight hundred to twelve hundred souls would work together in farm and factory to form a self-sustaining unit. The families were to live in houses grouped in parallelograms—the word immediately caught the public eye—with each family in a private apartment but sharing common sitting rooms and reading rooms and kitchens. Children over the age of three were to be boarded separately so that they could be exposed to the kind of education which would best mold their characters for later life. Around the school were gardens to be tended by the slightly older children, and around them in turn would stretch out the fields where crops would be grown—needless to say with the aid of spades and without the use of plows. In the distance, away from the living areas, would be a factory unit; in effect this would be a planned garden city.

The committee of notables was considerably taken aback. It was hardly prepared to urge the adoption of planned social communities in a day of untrammeled *laissez faire*. Mr. Owen was thanked and Mr. Owen's ideas were carefully ignored. But Owen was nothing if not single-purposed. He insisted upon a review of the applicability of his plans and flooded Parliament with tracts expounding his views. Again his determination won the day. In 1819 a special committee (including David Ricardo) was put together for the purpose of trying to raise the necessary ninety-six thousand pounds to establish one full-fledged experimental Village of Cooperation.

Ricardo was skeptical although willing to give the plan a trial, but the country was not skeptical at all; it found the idea an abomination. One editorialist wrote: "Robert Owen, Esq., a benevolent cotton-spinner . . . conceives that all human beings are so many plants which have been out of the earth for a few thousand years, and require to be reset. He accordingly determines to dibble them in squares after a new fashion. . . . Everybody, I believe, is convinced of Mr. Owen's benevolence and that he proposes to do us much good. I ask him to *let us alone,* lest he do us much mischief." Another critic, William Cobbett, then in exile in America for his own radical ideas, was even more scornful. "This gentleman," he wrote, "is for establishing *communities* of paupers! . . . Wonderful peace, happiness, and national benefit are to be the result. How the little matters of black eyes, bloody noses, and pulling of caps are to be *settled,* I do not exactly see. Mr. Owen's scheme has, at any rate, the recommendation of perfect novelty, for of such a thing as a *community of paupers,* I believe no human being has ever before heard. . . . Adieu, Mr. Owen of Lanark."

Owen did not, of course, envision a community of paupers. He believed, on the contrary, that paupers could become the producers of great wealth if they were given a chance to work, and that their deplorable social habits could be easily transformed into virtuous ones under the influence of a decent environment. And it was not only paupers who were to be thus elevated. The Villages of Cooperation were to be so manifestly superior to the turmoil of industrial life that other communities would naturally follow suit.

But it was obvious that Owen held his views alone. Serious-minded people saw in Owen's scheme a disturbing threat to the established order of things, and radical-minded people saw in it only a farce. The necessary money for the trial Village was never raised, but now there was no stopping the indomitable philanthropist. He had been a humanist; now he became a professional humanitarian. He had made a fortune; now he dedicated it to the realization of his ideas. He sold his interest in New Lanark and in 1824 set about building his own community of the future. Not unnaturally he chose America for his milieu, for where better to build Utopia than in the midst of a people who had known political liberty for fifty years?

For a site he bought from a religious sect of Germans known as Rappites a tract of thirty thousand acres on the banks of the Wabash in Posey County, Indiana. On the Fourth of July, 1826, he dedicated it with a Declaration of Mental Independence—independence from Private Property, Irrational Religion, and Marriage—and then left it to shift for itself with its lovely wishful name of New Harmony.

It could not and did not succeed. Owen had envisioned a Uto-

pia sprung full-blown into the world and he was not prepared
to wean one from the imperfect environment of the old society.
There was no planning: eight hundred settlers poured in, helter-
skelter, within a few weeks. There was not even elementary pre-
caution against fraud. Owen was bilked by an associate who piled
insult upon injury by setting up a whiskey distillery on land that
he had unfairly taken. And since Owen was not there, rival communities sprang up: Macluria under one William McClure and
others under other dissidents. The pull of acquisitive habit was
too strong for the bond of ideas; in retrospect it is only astonishing that the community managed to exist for as long as it did.

By 1828 it was apparent that the enterprise was a failure. Owen
sold the land (he had lost four-fifths of his entire fortune in the
venture) and went off to talk about his schemes to President Jack-
son and then to Santa Ana in Mexico. Neither of these gentlemen expressed more than polite interest.

Owen now came back to England. He was still the benevolent
(if slightly cracked) Mr. Owen, and his career was about to take
its final unexpected twist. For while most opinion had mocked
at his Villages of Cooperation, his teachings had sunk deep into
one section of the country: the working classes. This was the
time of the first modern trade-unions, and the leaders of the
spinners and the potters and the builders had come to regard
Owen as a man who could speak for their interests—indeed, as
their leader. Unlike his peers, they took his teachings seriously—
while the Villages of Cooperation were being debated by committees of notables, real working cooperative societies based on
his tracts were springing up throughout the country on a more
modest scale: producers' cooperatives and consumers' cooperatives
and even a few ill-fated attempts to follow Mr. Owen's ideas to
the letter and do away with money.

Without exception, the producers' cooperatives failed and the
moneyless exchanges ended in moneyless but equally final bankruptcies. But one aspect of the cooperative movement took root.
Twenty-eight devoted men who called themselves the Rochdale
Pioneers began the *consumer* cooperative movement. To Owen
it was only of passing interest, but with time it grew to be one
of the great sources of strength of the Labour party in Great
Britain. Curiously, the movement in which he took least inter-

est was to survive all the projects into which he poured his heart and strength.

Owen had no time for cooperatives for a good reason; on his return from America he had conceived a huge moral crusade and he plunged into it with a typical vigorous abandon. The onetime poor boy, onetime capitalist, onetime social architect now drew around him the leaders of the working-class movement. He bestowed a properly impressive name on his project: the Grand National Moral Union of the Productive and Useful Classes. The name was soon shortened to the Grand National Consolidated Trades Union, and since that was still quite a mouthful, to the Grand National. Under its banner the trade-union leaders rallied, and in 1833 the English working-class movement was officially launched.

It was a nationwide union—the precursor of the industrial trade-unions of our day. Its membership was five hundred thousand—a mammoth figure for that time—and it embraced virtually every important union in all of England. But, unlike a modern union, its goals were not limited to hours and wages or even to management prerogatives. The Grand National was to be an instrument not only of social betterment but of social change. Hence while its program asked for better wages and working conditions, it went on to expound a fuzzy amalgam of Villages of Cooperation, the abolition of money, and a number of other ideas from the potpourri of Owen's writing.

Owen stumped the country for his final cause. It was a flat fiasco. England was no more prepared for a national trade-union than America for a local paradise. Local unions could not control their members and local strikes weakened the national body. Owen and his lieutenants fell out; they accused him of atheism, and he charged them with fomenting class hatred. The Government stepped in and with violence and vengeance did its best to disrupt the growing movement. The employing classes heard in the Grand National the knell of private property and called for prosecution under antiunion laws. No youthful movement could have withstood such an onslaught. Within two years the great union was dead, and Owen at the age of sixty-four had played his last historical role.

He continued for another twenty years, the grand old man of

labor, urging his cooperative ideas, his preference for the spade, his naïve distrust of money. In 1839 he had an audience with Queen Victoria despite the protests of a group of the best people known as the Society for Peaceably Repressing Infidelity. But he was finished. In his last years he found a refuge in spiritualism, in endless tracts endlessly the same, and in his wonderful *Auto-biography*. In 1858, eighty-seven years old and still hopeful, he died.

What a romantic and fantastic story! And looking back, it is his story rather than his ideas which interests us. Owen was never a truly original and certainly never a flexible thinker. "Robert Owen is not a man to think differently of a book for having read it," was the devastating way in which one contemporary writer characterized him, and Macaulay, who fled at the sound of his voice, called him "always a gentle bore."

He was not, by any stretch of the imagination, an economist. But he was more than that: he was an economic innovator who reshaped the raw data with which economists have to deal. Like all the Utopian Socialists, Owen wanted the world changed; but while others wrote, powerfully or otherwise, he went ahead and tried to change it.

And on second thought, perhaps he did leave one great idea behind him. It is charmingly illustrated in this anecdote from the biography of his son, Robert Dale Owen.

"When the child screams from temper, my dear Caroline," said his father (Robert Owen), "set him in the middle of the nursery floor and be sure you don't take him up until he stops crying." "But my dear, he'll go on crying by the hour." "Then let him cry." "It may hurt his little lungs, and perhaps throw him into spasms." "I think not. At all events, it will hurt him more if he grows into an ungovernable boy. Man is the creature of circumstances."

"Man is the creature of circumstances." And who makes the circumstances but man himself? The world is not inevitably good or bad, but to the extent that we make it so. In that thought Owen left behind him a philosophy of hope more powerful than all of his fanciful notions about spades and plows or money or Villages of Cooperation.

Robert Owen is certainly the most romantic of that group of nineteenth-century protesters against raw capitalism, but he is by no means the most peculiar. For sheer perversity of character, honor must go to Count Claude Henri de Rouvroy de Saint-Simon and for indisputable eccentricity of ideas there is no peer of Charles Fourier.

Saint-Simon, as his rolling name suggests, was an aristocrat; his family claimed descent from Charlemagne. Born in 1760, he was brought up to be conscious of the nobility of his ancestry and of the importance of maintaining the luster of his name; every morning, as a youth, he was awakened by his valet who would cry: "Arise, Monsieur le Comte, you have great things to do today."

The knowledge that one is a chosen vessel of history can do strange things to a man. In Saint-Simon's case, it provided the excuse for an extravagant self-indulgence. Even as a boy he confused a devotion to principle with sheer pigheadedness; it is said that when a passing wagon interfered with a childhood game, he threw himself down across the road and obstinately refused to budge—and who was to throw a young count into the ditch? Later this same obstinacy led him to refuse to go to Communion at his father's behest—but the father, perhaps more used to his son's intransigence and certainly less awed by it, promptly threw him in jail.

His self-indulgence might have turned him toward that most self-indulgent of all political groups, the court of Louis XVI. But it was redeemed by a love for a most uncourtly idea: democracy. In 1778 the young Count went to America and distinguished himself in the Revolutionary War. He fought in five campaigns, won the Order of Cincinnatus, and most important of all, became a passionate disciple of the new ideas of freedom and equality.

But this did not yet constitute Great Things. The Revolutionary War left him in Louisiana; thence he went to Mexico to urge the Viceroy to build a canal that would have preceded the Panama. That might have made his name, but the idea came to naught—it was, of course, nine-tenths idea and one-tenth plan—and the young revolutionary noble returned to France.

He was just in time for the Revolution there, and he threw himself into it with fervor. His townspeople of Falvy in Peronne asked him to be mayor and he refused, saying that the election of the old nobility would be a bad precedent; then when they chose him for the National Assembly anyway, he proposed the abolition of titles and renounced his own to become plain Citoyen Bonhomme. His democratic predilections were not a pose; Saint-Simon had a genuine feeling for his fellow man. Before the Revolution he had been posting to Versailles one day, in the height of style, when he came across a farmer's cart mired in the road. Saint-Simon got down from his carriage, put his elegantly clad shoulder to the wheel, and then found the farmer's conversation so interesting that he dismissed his own vehicle and rode to Orléans with his new-found peasant friend.

The Revolution dealt strangely with him. On the one hand he speculated adroitly in Church lands and made himself a modest fortune; on the other he busied himself with a gigantic educational scheme which, because it threw him into contact with foreigners, brought him into disfavor and resulted in his being put in protective custody. He escaped and then, in a gesture both romantic and truly noble, surrendered himself again when he found that his hotel proprietor had been unjustly accused of collaborating in his escape.

This time he went to jail. But there, in his cell, there came to him the revelation for which he had, in a sense, been waiting all his life. The revelation came, as such visitations do, in a dream; Saint-Simon described it thus:

"During the cruelest period of the Revolution, and during a night of my imprisonment at Luxembourg, Charlemagne appeared to me and said: 'Since the beginning of the world no family has enjoyed the honor of producing both a hero and philosopher of first rank. This honor was reserved for my house. My son, your successes as a philosopher will equal those which I achieved as a warrior and politician.' "

Saint-Simon asked for no more. He obtained a release from prison and the money he had accumulated now poured forth in a fantastic search for knowledge. This man actually set out to know everything there was to know—scientists, economists, philosophers, politicians, all the savants of France were invited to his house, financed in their work, and endlessly queried that Saint-Simon might encompass the world's intellectual scope. It was a bizarre endeavor. At one time, having come to the conclusion that he still lacked a firsthand acquaintance with family life for the pursuance of his social studies, he married—on a three-year contract. One year was enough: his wife talked too much and his guests drank too much, and Saint-Simon decided that marriage as an educational institution had its limitations. Instead he sought the hand of the most brilliant woman in Europe, Mme. de Staël; she was the only woman, he declared, who could understand his plans. They met, but it was an anticlimax; she found him full of *esprit,* but hardly the greatest philosopher in the world. In the circumstances, his enthusiasm also waned.

But the search for encyclopedic knowledge, while stimulating, was financially disastrous. His expenditures had been lavish to the point of recklessness; his marriage unexpectedly expensive. He found himself reduced first to modest circumstances and then to real poverty; he was forced to find a clerical job and then to depend on the kindness of an old servant for board and lodging. Meanwhile he was writing, furiously writing an endless stream of tracts, observations, exhortations, and examinations of society. He sent his works to the leading patrons of the day with a pathetic note:

> Monsieur:
>
> Be my saviour, I am dying of hunger. . . . For 15 days I have lived on bread and water . . . sold everything but my clothes, to pay for the expense of copies of my work. It is the passion for knowledge and the public welfare, the desire to find a peaceful means of ending the frightful crisis which engages all European society which has brought me to this state of distress. . . .

No one subscribed. In 1823, although his family now accorded him a small pension, he shot himself in despair. But he could never quite do anything as he wished. He only succeeded in losing an eye. He lived two more years, ill, impoverished, dedicated, and proud. When the end came, he gathered his few disciples around him and said, "Remember that in order to do great things one must be impassioned!"

But what had he done to justify such an operatic end?

A strange thing: he had founded an industrial religion. He had not done it through his books, which were voluminous enough but unread, nor through lectures, nor through doing "great things." Somehow the man himself had inspired a sect, had gathered a small band of followers, and had given society a new image of what it might be.

It was a strange, semimystical, and disorganized religion, and little wonder, for it was built on an unfinished and lopsided edifice of ideas. It was not even meant to be a religion as such— and yet after his death there was actually a Saint-Simonian Church with six departmental churches in France and with branches in Germany and England. Perhaps it is better compared to an order of brotherhood: his disciples dressed in shades of blue and ranked each other as "fathers and sons." And as a nice symbol of what the founder himself had stood for, they wore a special waistcoat which could be neither put on nor taken off unassisted and which thus emphasized the dependence of every man on his brothers. But the church soon degenerated into little more than a cult, for the latter-day Saint-Simonians devised their own code of morality, which in some instances was little more than a respectably codified immorality.

The gospel which Saint-Simon had preached is hardly shocking to modern eyes. It proclaimed that "man must work" if he is to share in society's fruits. But compared with the conclusions drawn from this premise, Robert Owen's society of parallelograms was clarity itself.

"We suppose," writes Saint-Simon, "that France suddenly loses her fifty leading physicists, her fifty leading chemists, her fifty leading physiologists . . . mathematicians . . . mechanics" and so on until three thousand savants, artists, and artisans have been accounted for (Saint-Simon is not noted for the economy of his style). What would be the result? It would be a catastrophe which would rob France of her very soul.

But now suppose, says Saint-Simon, that instead of losing these few individuals, France were to be deprived at one blow of its social upper crust: suppose it should lose M. the brother to the king, the Duke de Berry, some duchesses, the officers of the Crown, the ministers of state, its judges, and the ten thousand richest proprietors of the land—thirty thousand people in all.

The result? Most regrettable, says Saint-Simon, because these are all good people, but the loss would be purely a sentimental one; the State would hardly suffer. Any number of people could discharge the functions of these lovely ornaments.

So the moral is clear. It is the workers—*les industriels*—of all ranks and hierarchies who merit the highest rewards of society and the idlers who deserve the least. But what do we find? By a strange miscarriage of justice, it is just the opposite: those who do the least get the most.

Saint-Simon proposes that the pyramid be set aright. Society is actually organized as a gigantic factory and it should carry out the factory principle to its logical conclusion. Government should be economic, not political: it should arrange things and not direct men. Rewards should be apportioned to one's social contribution: they should accrue to the active members of the factory and not to the lazy onlookers. It is not a revolution that Saint-Simon preaches nor even socialism as we understand the word. It is a kind of paean of the industrial process and a protest that in a society of toil, idlers should take such a lion's share of the wealth.

Not a word about how this is to be done: the later Saint-Simonians went a step beyond their founder and urged the end of private property, but even this left them with little more than a vague program of social reformation. This was a religion of work but it lacked a proper catechism; it pointed to grave injustices in the distribution of society's wealth, but it gave disappointingly little guidance to those who wanted to set things to rights.

Perhaps it was just this lack of a program which helped to account for the success of a man who was quite the opposite of Saint-Simon. For whereas the ex-nobleman had been inspired by a passion for the grand idea, Charles Fourier was inspired by a passion for trivia. Like Saint-Simon, Fourier believed the world was hopelessly disorganized, but the cure he proposed was explicit down to the tiniest detail.

Saint-Simon had been an adventurer in life; Fourier was an adventurer in imagination. His biography is largely a blank: born in 1772, the son of a tradesman of Besançon, he spent his days as an unsuccessful commercial traveler. In a sense he did nothing, not even marry. His passions were two: flowers and cats. It is only at the end of his life that he is appealing, for he spent his last years punctually sitting at advertised hours in his small room awaiting the visit of some great capitalist who would offer to finance his schemes to do over the world. After all, this little salesman had written, "I alone have confounded twenty centuries of political imbecility; and it is to me alone that present and future generations will look for the origin of their immense happiness." With such a responsibility resting on his shoulders, he could hardly afford not to be at hand when the appointed savior capitalist would arrive with his moneybags in train. But no one ever came.

Fourier, to be polite, was an eccentric; to be accurate, he was probably mildly insane. His world was a fantasy: the earth, he believed, had been given a life of eighty thousand years; forty thousand of ascending vibrations and the same number of descending. In between (never mind the arithmetic) lay eight thousand years of the Apogée du Bonheur. We lived in the fifth of eight stages of advancement, having pushed through Confusion, Savagery, Patriarchism, and Barbarousness. Ahead lay Guaranteeism (not a bad bit of insight), and then the upward slope of Harmony. After we reached utter bliss, however, the seesaw would tip and we would work our way right back down through all the stages to the beginning.

But as we worked our way ever deeper into Harmony, things would really begin to pop: a Northern Crown would encircle the Pole shedding a gentle dew; the sea would become lemonade; six new moons would replace the old solitary satellite; and new species would emerge, better suited to Harmony: an anti-lion, a docile beast and most serviceable; an anti-whale, which could be harnessed to ships; an anti-bear; anti-bugs; and anti-rats. We would live to be one hundred and forty-four years old, of which one hundred and twenty years would be spent in the unrestricted pursuit of sexual love.

All this plus a firsthand description of the inhabitants of other planets gives to Fourier's writings the air of a madman. Perhaps he was. But when he turned his starry vision to this earth he saw in it chaos and unhappiness and he saw, as well, a way to reorganize society.

His prescription was very exact. Society should be organized into phalanxes—the French word is *phalanstères*—which would consist of a kind of Grand Hotel arrangement, not too dissimilar from Owen's Villages of Cooperation. The hotel was carefully described: there would be a large central building (its various rooms and their dimensions were all thought out) and around it would be fields and industrial establishments. You could live in the hotel at the scale best suited to your purse; first, second, or third class, with just as much privacy as you desired (including meals in your rooms) and with just enough mingling to spread a leaven of culture. Efficiency would be achieved through centralization; Fourier, the old bachelor, paints a mouth-watering picture of the triumphs of the central cuisine.

Everyone would have to work, of course, for a few hours each day. But no one would shirk work, for each would do what he best liked. Thus the problem of dirty work was solved by asking who *liked* to do dirty work. The children, of course. So there would be Little Hordes who would go off gaily to the slaughter houses or to mend the roads and have the time of their lives. And for the minority of children who shrank from dirty work, there would be Little Bands who would tend the flowers and correct their parents' bad pronunciation. Between all workers there would be a game of competition to see who did best: contests of pear growers and cultivators of spinach and finally (once the phalanstery principle had encircled the globe and the 2,985,984 necessary *phalanstères* established) great battles of omelette chefs and champagne bottlers.

And the whole affair would be profitable in the extreme; gains would run to thirty per cent. But it would be communal profit: the surplus would be divided five-twelfths to labor, four-twelfths to capital, and three-twelfths to "ability," and everybody would be urged to become a part owner as well as a fellow worker.

Weird and fantastic as it seems, the Fourierist idea took some hold, even in that fortress of practicality and common sense, the United States. At one time there were over forty phalansteries in this country, and if one groups together the Owenite communities and the religious movements of various sorts, there were at least one hundred and seventy-eight actual Utopian groups with from fifteen to nine hundred members each.

Their variety was immense: some were pious, some impious; some chaste, some licentious; some capitalistic, others anarchic. There were Trumbull Phalanx in Ohio and Modern Times on Long Island; there were Oneida and Brook Farm and New Icaria and one rather remarkable phalanx—the North American Phalanx in New Jersey—which endured from 1843 to 1855 and then lingered on, half hotel, half community, until the late 1930's. Of all unlikely people, Alexander Woollcott was born there.

None of the dream communities took solid root. Dream worlds have a difficult time contending with the frictions of reality, and of all the projected Utopian rearrangements of society, none was so far removed from practicality as the *phalanstère*. And yet, none is so beguiling. If we could live in a *phalanstère*, who would not like to? Fourier, gentle dreamer that he was, pointed with devastating truth to the miserable unhappiness of the world in which he lived, but his prescription was too much compounded of heavenly ingredients for the mortal ills he wished to cure.

Do they appear ridiculous, these Utopians? It is true that they were all dreamers—but as Anatole France has said, without dreamers, mankind would still live in caves. There was not one without a touch of madness: even Saint-Simon speculated solemnly on the possibility of the beaver, as the most intelligent animal, someday replacing humankind. But they are not noteworthy because they were eccentrics or because of the richness and appealing quality of their fantasies. They are worth our attention because they were courageous, and to appreciate that courage we must appraise and understand the intellectual climate in which they lived.

They lived in a world which was not only harsh and cruel but which rationalized its cruelty under the guise of economic law. Necker, the French financier and statesman, said at the turn of the century, "Were it possible to discover a kind of food less agreeable than bread but having double its sustenance, people would be reduced to eating only once in two days." And such a sentiment, hard though it might have sounded, did ring with a kind of definitiveness. It was the world which was cruel, not the people in it. For the world was run by economic laws, and economic laws were nothing with which one could or should trifle: they were simply *there* and to rail about whatever injustices might be tossed up as an unfortunate consequence of their working was as foolish as to lament the ebb and flow of the tides.

The laws were few but final. We have seen how Adam Smith, Malthus, and Ricardo elaborated the laws of economic distribution. These laws seemed to explain not only how the produce of society tended to be distributed but how it *should* be distributed. The laws showed that profits were evened out and controlled by competition, that wages were always under pressure from population, and that rent accrued to the landlord as society expanded. And that was that. One might not necessarily *like* the result, but it was apparent that this result was the natural outcome of society's dynamics: there was no *personal* ill-will involved nor any personal manipulation. Economic laws were like the laws of gravitation and it seemed as nonsensical to challenge one as the other. Hence an elementary economics textbook of the times said: "A hundred years ago only savants could fathom them [economic laws]. Today they are commonplaces of the nursery, and the only real difficulty is their too great simplicity."

No wonder the Utopians went to such extremes. The laws did look inviolable—and yet the state of society for which they were held responsible was intolerable. So the Utopians took their courage in both hands and said in effect, the whole system must change. If this is capitalism—with a nod of the head at Robert Blincoe chained to a machine—let us have anything else—Villages of Cooperation, moral codes, or the delightful resort atmosphere of a *phalanstère*. The Utopians—and there were many besides those mentioned in this chapter—were reformers of the heart rather than the head. Their heritage is to be found in the welfare ideals of the New Deal of Britain or Scandinavia rather than in the "scientific" conviction of the Russian Soviets.

Note that they were *Utopian* socialists. The "utopia" was not merely a matter of idealistic ends; it was also a key to the means. For, in contradistinction to the Communists, these were reformers who hoped to persuade the members of the *upper* classes that social change would be for their own ultimate benefit. The Communists talked to the masses and urged violence, if necessary, to encompass their ends; the Socialists appealed to their own kind —to the intelligentsia, the *petit bourgeois,* the freethinking middle-class citizen or the intellectually emancipated aristocrat—for adherents to their schemes. Even Robert Owen hoped to get his brother millowners to see the light.

But secondly, note that these were Utopian *Socialists.* This meant they were *economic* reformers. Utopia-builders had existed since Plato but it was not until the French Revolution that they began to react to economic as well as political injustice. And since it was early capitalism which provided the chamber of horrors against which they revolted, not unnaturally they turned their backs on private property and the struggle for private wealth. Few of them thought of reform *within* the system: remember that this was the age of the very first watered-down factory legislation and that such grudging reforms as were painfully won were largely honored in the breach. The Utopians wanted something better than reform—they wanted a new society in which Love Thy Neighbor could somehow be made to take priority over the mean gouging of each for himself. In the communality of property, in the warmth of common ownership, was to be found the touchstone of human progress.

They were men of very good will. And yet, for all their good intentions and their earnest theories, the Utopians lacked the stamp of respectability; they needed the imprimatur of someone with them in heart but whose head would be somewhat more firmly attached to his shoulders. And they found such a person in the most unlikely place—in the ultimate conversion to Socialism of the greatest—by common consent the greatest—economist of the age: John Stuart Mill.

Everyone in this chapter is a somewhat unbelievable character but perhaps J. S. Mill is the most remarkable of them all. His father was James Mill, historian, philosopher, pamphleteer, friend and intimate of Ricardo and Jeremy Bentham, one of the leading intellects of the early nineteenth century. James Mill had definite ideas about almost everything, and especially about education. His son, John Stuart Mill, was the extraordinary result.

John Stuart Mill was born in 1806. In 1809 (not 1819) he began

to learn Greek. At age seven he had read most of the dialogues of
Plato. The next year he began Latin, having meanwhile digested
Herodotus, Xenophon, Diogenes Laërtius, and part of Lucian.
Between eight and twelve, he finished Virgil, Horace, Livy, Sal-
lust, Ovid, Terence, Lucretius, Aristotle, Socrates, and Aristoph-
anes; had mastered geometry, algebra, and the differential calculus; written a Roman History, an Abridgment of the Ancient
Universal History, a History of Holland, and a few verses. "I
never composed at all in Greek, even in prose, and but little in
Latin," he wrote in his famous *Autobiography*. "Not that my
father could be indifferent to the value of this practice . . . but
because there really was not the time for it."

At the ripe age of twelve, Mill took up logic and the work of
Hobbes. At thirteen he made a complete survey of all there was
to be known in the field of political economy.

It was a strange, and by our standards a dreadful, upbringing.
There were no holidays, "lest the habit of work should be broken,
and a taste for idleness acquired," no boyhood friends, and not
even a real awareness that his education and rearing were significantly different from the normal. The miracle is not that
Mill subsequently produced great works, but that he managed
to avoid a complete destruction of his personality. He did have
a kind of nervous breakdown: in his twenties, the delicate dry
intellectual world of work and effort on which he had been nour-
ished suddenly became sterile and unsatisfying, and while other
youths had to discover that there could be beauty in intellectual
activity, poor Mill had to find that there could be beauty in
beauty. He underwent a siege of melancholy; then he read
Goethe, then Wordsworth, then Saint-Simon—all people who
spoke of the heart as seriously as his father had spoken of the
brain. And then he met Harriet Taylor.

There was, worse luck, a Mr. Taylor. He was ignored; Harriet
Taylor and Mill fell in love and for twenty years wrote each
other, traveled together, and even lived together—all (if we are
to believe their correspondence) in perfect innocence. Then the
barrier of Mr. Taylor was removed by his death and the two
finally married.

It was a superlative match. Harriet Taylor (and her belated
daughter, Helen) completed for Mill the emotional awakening

which had begun so late; together, the two women opened his eyes to women's rights and, even more importantly, to mankind's right. After Harriet's death, when he was reflecting on the story of his life, he reviewed their converging influences on himself, and he wrote: "Who, either now, or hereafter, may think of me and of the work I have done, must never forget that it is the product not of one intellect and conscience, but of three."

Mill, as we have seen, learned all the political economy there was to know at the age of thirteen. It was not until thirty years later that he wrote his great text, the two long, masterfully written volumes of the *Principles of Political Economy*. It was as if he had accumulated thirty years of knowledge just for this purpose.

The book is a total survey of the field: it takes up rent and wages and prices and taxes and retreads the paths that had been first mapped by Smith and Malthus and Ricardo. But it is far more than a mere updating of doctrines that had by now received the stamp of virtual dogma. It goes on to make a discovery of its own, a discovery of monumental importance. For Mill brings to light a principle which forever after rescues economics from the category of a dismal science.

The discovery, like so many great insights, was very simple. It consisted in pointing out that the true province of economic law was production and not distribution.

What he meant was very clear: the economic laws of production concern nature. There is nothing arbitrary about whether labor is more productive in this use or that, nor is there anything capricious or optional about such economic phenomena as the diminishing powers of productivity of the soil. Scarcity and the obduracy of nature are real things and the economic rules of behavior which tell us how to maximize the fruits of our labor are as impersonal and as absolute as the laws of the expansion of gases or the interaction of chemical substances.

But—and this is perhaps the biggest *but* in economics—the laws of economics have nothing to do with distribution. Once we have produced wealth as best we can, we can do with it as we like. "The things once there," says Mill; "mankind, individually or collectively, can do with them as they please. They can place them at the disposal of whomsoever they please, and on whatever terms. . . . Even what a person has produced by his individual toil, unaided by anyone, he cannot keep, unless by the permission of society. Not only can society take it from him, but individuals could and would take it from him, if society . . . did not . . . employ and pay people for the purpose of preventing him from being disturbed in [his] possession. The distribution of wealth, therefore, depends on the laws and customs of society. The rules by which it is determined are what the opinions and feelings of the ruling portion of the community make them, and are very different in different ages and countries, and might be still more different, if mankind so chose. . . ."

It was a body blow to the followers of Ricardo who had rigidified his objective findings into a strait jacket for society. For what Mill said was transparently obvious—once it had been said. Never mind if the "natural" action of society was to depress wages or to equalize profits or to raise rents or whatever. If society did not like the "natural" results of its activities, it had only to change them. Society could tax and subsidize, it could expropriate and redistribute. It could give all its wealth to a king, or it could run a gigantic charity ward; it could give due heed to incentives, or it could—at its own risk—ignore them. But whatever it did, there was no "correct" distribution—at least none that economics had any claim to fathom. There was no appeal to "laws" to justify how society shared its fruits: there were only men sharing their wealth as they saw fit.

It was a discovery of profound consequence. For it lifted the whole economic debate from the stifling realm of impersonal and inevitable law and brought it back into the arena of ethics and morality. After Mill, economists might argue that men *deserved* such and such remuneration for this and that reason, but they could never again pretend that some abstract arithmetical force *decreed* that this was the way it should be done.

The discovery did not make Mill a Socialist in quite the sense of his Utopian brethren. Simply because society *could* reorder its distribution as it saw fit did not mean that it should upset the applecart. Mill believed that the world could advance within its given structural framework and he put little faith in a wholesale reorganization of the state.

"I confess," he wrote, "I am not charmed with an ideal of life held out by those who think that the normal state of human beings is that of struggling to get on; that the trampling, crushing, elbowing, and treading on each other's heels, which form the existing type of social life, are the most desirable lot of human kind, or anything but the disagreeable symptoms of one of the phases of industrial progress."

But a distaste for acquisitiveness did not blind him to its usefulness. "That the energies of mankind should be kept in employment by the struggle for riches as they were formerly by the struggle for war, until the better minds succeed in educating the others into better things, is undoubtedly better than that they should rust and stagnate. While minds are coarse they require coarse stimuli and let them have them."

It was a philosophy of resignation—and hope. Mill was a supreme believer in the ability of men to control their fate through reason. He believed that the working classes would come to see the Malthusian specter and that they would thereupon gladly and voluntarily regulate their numbers. And if this hurdle was passed the rest would be easy. For Mill's recognition that distribution obeyed no laws but human ones allowed him to see the world as capable of progress. Eventually the world would reach a stationary level: profits would have disappeared and there would be no more growth, but within the existing framework of society, improvements could still be made. The state would prevent the landlord from reaping an unearned benefit and it would tax away inheritances; men would turn from the struggle for gain to the pursuit of arts and life itself.

It would not be thoroughgoing socialism. While Mill recognized that property had its abuses, he saw as well that the property system was still in its infancy and capable of refinement; the abuses need not be inseparable from the institution. And then, in the system called communism, he saw a danger. For despite its claimed superiority on economic grounds, Mill sensed in it a noneconomic but supremely important threat, and he set down his misgivings in these farsighted words:

> . . . It is not by comparison with the present bad state of society that the claims of Communism can be estimated.
> . . . The question is, whether there would be any asylum

left for individuality of character; whether public opinion
would not be a tyrannical yoke; whether the absolute dependence of each on all, and the surveillance of each by
all, would not grind all down into a tame uniformity of
thoughts, feelings, and actions. . . . No society in which
eccentricity is a matter of reproach can be in a wholesome
state.

Mill lived until 1873, a venerated, almost worshiped man. His
mildly Socialist leanings were forgiven in exchange for his vista
of hope and his removal of the pall of despair. After all, what he
advocated was not so shocking but that it could be embraced
by almost everybody: taxation of rents, and inheritance taxes,
and the formation of workmen's cooperatives. He was not very
sanguine about the possibilities of trade-unions, and that was
all to the good, as far as respectable opinion went. It was a doctrine English to the core: gradualist, optimistic, realistic, and
devoid of radical overtones.

Principles of Political Economy was an enormous success. It
went into seven editions in the expensive two-volume edition
during his own lifetime and, characteristic of Mill, he had it
printed at his own expense in one cheap volume which would be
within the reach of the working class. Five cheap editions also
sold out before he died. Mill became the Great Economist of his
day; he was talked of as Ricardo's rightful successor and heir,
and compared not unfavorably with Adam Smith himself.

And economics aside, the man himself was so respected. Mill
was the author of *Logic,* of *Liberty,* of *Considerations on Representative Government,* and of *Utilitarianism,* all classics in their
fields. And more than merely brilliant, he verged on being saintly.
When Herbert Spencer, his great rival in the area of philosophy,
found himself so straitened in circumstances that he was unable
to complete his projected series on social evolution, it was Mill
who offered to finance the project. "I beg that you will not consider this proposal in the light of a personal favor," he wrote his
rival, "though even if it were I should still hope to be permitted
to offer it. But it is nothing of the kind—it is a simple proposal
of cooperation for an important public purpose, for which you
give your labor and have given your health."

There was never a more typical gesture. Mill cared only for two things: his wife, for whom he conceived a devotion which his friends thought verged on blindness, and the pursuit of knowledge, from which nothing could deflect him. When he was elected to Parliament his defense of human rights exceeded the temper of the day; he was thereupon defeated, but he cared not a whit either way. As he saw the world, so he wrote and spoke, and the only person who mattered, as far as approval went, was his beloved Harriet.

After she died, there was her daughter, Helen, now equally indispensable. In gratitude, Mill wrote in his *Autobiography:* "Surely no one before was so fortunate as, after such a loss as mine, to draw another prize in the lottery of life." He retired to spend his last days with Helen in Avignon, near Harriet's grave, a wonderfully wise and thoroughly great man.

One last coincidence. His masterwork on economics, with its message of progress and the opportunity for peaceful change and betterment, was published in 1848. Perhaps it was not an epoch-making book, but it was certainly an epoch-marking one. For by a curious quirk of fate another far smaller book—a pamphlet—was published in the same year. It was entitled *The Communist Manifesto* and in its few pages it undid, in bitter words, all the calm and buoyant reasonableness with which J. S. Mill had endowed the world.

VI

The Inexorable System
of Karl Marx

THE *Manifesto* opened with portentous words: "A spectre is haunting Europe—the spectre of Communism. All the powers of old Europe have entered into a holy alliance to exorcise this spectre: Pope and Tsar, Metternich and Guizot, French Radicals and German police-spies."

The specter certainly existed: 1848 was a year of terror for the old order on the Continent. There was a revolutionary fervor in the air and a rumble underfoot. For a moment—for a brief moment—it looked as if the old order might break down. In France the plodding regime of Louis Philippe, the portly middle-class king, wrestled with a crisis and then collapsed; the king abdicated and fled to the security of a Surrey villa, and the workingmen of Paris rose in a wild uncoordinated surge and ran up the Red Flag over the Hôtel de Ville. In Belgium a frightened monarch offered to submit his resignation. In Berlin the barricades went up and bullets whistled; in Italy mobs rioted; and in Prague and Vienna popular uprisings imitated Paris by seizing control of the cities.

"The Communists disdain to conceal their views and aims," cried the *Manifesto*. "They openly declare that their ends can be attained only by the forcible overthrow of all existing social relations. Let the ruling classes tremble at a Communist revolution. The proletarians have nothing to lose but their chains. They have a world to win."

The ruling classes did tremble and they saw the threat of communism everywhere. Nor were their fears groundless. In the French foundries the workmen sang radical songs to the accompaniment of blows from their sledge hammers, and Heinrich Heine, the German romantic poet who was touring the factories, reported that "really people in our gentle walk of life can have no idea of the demonic note which runs through these songs."

But despite the clarion words of the *Manifesto,* the demonic note was not a call for a revolution of communism; it was a cry born only of frustration and despair. For all of Europe was in the grip of reaction compared with which conditions in England were positively idyllic. The French government had been characterized by John Stuart Mill as "wholly without the spirit of improvement and . . . wrought almost exclusively through the meaner and more selfish impulses of mankind" and the French had no monopoly on such a dubious claim to fame. As for Germany, well, here it was, the fourth decade of the nineteenth century, and Prussia still had no parliament, no freedom of speech or right of assembly, no liberty of the press or trial by jury, and no tolerance for any idea which deviated by a hair's breadth from the antiquated notion of the divine right of kings. Italy was a hodgepodge of anachronistic principalities. Russia under Nicholas I (despite the Tsar's onetime visit to Robert Owen's New Lanark) was characterized by the historian de Tocqueville as "the cornerstone of despotism in Europe."

Had the despair been channeled and directed, the demonic note might have changed into a truly revolutionary one. But as it was, the uprisings were spontaneous, undisciplined, and aimless; they won initial victories and then, while they were wondering what next to do, the old order rocked invincibly back into place. The revolutionary fervor abated, and where it did not, it was mercilessly crushed. At the price of ten thousand casualties, the Paris mobs were subdued by the National Guard, and Louis Napoleon took over the nation and soon exchanged the Second Republic for the Second Empire. In Belgium the country decided that it had better ask the king to stay after all; he acknowledged the tribute by abolishing the right of assembly. The Viennese and Hungarian crowds were cannonaded from their strongholds, and in Germany a constitutional assembly which had been bravely debating the question of republicanism broke

down into factional bickering and then ignominiously offered
the country to Frederick William IV of Prussia. Still more ignominiously, that monarch declared that he would accept no
crown proffered by the ignoble hands of commoners.

The revolution was over. It had been fierce, bloody, but inconclusive. There were a few new faces in Europe but the policies were much the same.

But to a little group of working-class leaders who had just
formed the Communist League, there was no cause for deep despair. True, the revolution for which they had entertained high
hopes had petered out and the radical movements pocketed
throughout Europe were being more ruthlessly hounded than
ever before. But all that could be regarded with a certain equanimity. For according to their understanding of history, the
uprisings of 1848 were only the small-scale dress rehearsals of a
gigantic production that was scheduled for the future, and of the
eventual success of that awesome spectacle there could be not the
shadow of a doubt.

The league had just published its statement of objectives and
called it the *Communist Manifesto*. But for all its slogans and
its trenchant phrases, the *Manifesto* had not been written merely
to whip up revolutionary sentiment or to add another voice of
protest to the clamor of voices that filled the air. The *Manifesto*
had something else in mind: a philosophy of history in which a
communist revolution was not only desirable but demonstrably
inevitable. Unlike the Utopians who also wanted to reorganize
society closer to their desires, the Communists did not appeal to
men's sympathies or to their addiction to building castles in the
air. Rather, they offered men a chance to hitch their destinies
to a star and to watch that star move inexorably across the historical zodiac. There was no longer a contest in which one side
or the other ought to win for moral or sentimental reasons or
because it thought the existing order was outrageous. Instead
there was a cold analysis of which side *had* to win, and since
that side was the proletariat, their leaders had only to wait. In
the end, they could not lose.

The *Manifesto* was a program written for the future. But one
thing would have surprised its authors. They were prepared
to wait—but not for *seventy* years. They were already scanning

Europe for the likeliest incubator of revolt. And they never even cast a glance in the direction of Russia.

The *Manifesto,* as everybody knows, was the brain child of that angry genius, Karl Marx. More accurately, it was the result of collaboration between him and his remarkable companion, compatriot, supporter, and colleague, Friedrich Engels.

They are interesting, and, of course, enormously important men. The trouble is, they are no longer just men; Marx the human being is obscured behind Marx the Figure; and Engels behind the shadow of Marx. If we are to judge by a count of worshiping noses, Marx must be considered a religious leader to rank with Christ or Mohammed, and Engels thus becomes a sort of Saint Paul or a John. In the Marx-Engels Institute in Moscow, scholars have pored over their works with all the idolatry they ridicule in the antireligious museums down the street; but while Marx and Engels are canonized in Russia, they are still crucified in much of the world.

They merit neither treatment, for they were neither saints nor devils. Nor is their work either Scripture or anathema. It belongs in the great line of economic viewpoints which have successively clarified, illuminated, and interpreted the world for us, and like the other great works on the shelf, it is neither without flaw nor devoid of merit. The world has been preoccupied with Marx the Revolutionary. But had Marx not lived there would have been other socialists and other prophets of a new society. The real and lasting impact of Marx and Engels is not their revolutionary activity, none of which bore too much fruit during their own lifetimes. It is with Marx the Economist that capitalism must finally come to grips. For the final imprint he made on history was his prediction that capitalism must inevitably and necessarily collapse. On that prediction, on that "scientific" prognostication, communism has built its edifice.

But let us see the men.

They were very much opposites in appearance. Marx *looked* like a revolutionary. His children called him "The Moor," for his skin was dark and his eyes deep-set and flashing. He was stocky and powerfully built and rather glowering in expression with a formidable beard. He was not an orderly man; his home was a dusty mass of papers piled in careless disarray in the midst of which Marx himself, slovenly dressed, padded about in an eye-stinging haze of tobacco smoke. Engels, on the other hand, would pass for a member of his despised *bourgeoisie;* tall and fair and rather elegant, he had the figure of a man who liked to fence and to ride to hounds and who had once swum the Weser River four times without a break.

It was not only in their looks that they differed; their personalities were at opposite poles. Engels was gay and observant and gifted with a quick and facile mind; it was said that he could stutter in twenty languages. He had a taste for the bourgeois pleasures in life, including a good palate for wine, and it is amusing to note that although he turned to the proletariat for his amours, he spent much of his time romantically (and unsuccessfully) trying to prove that his working-class mistress, Mary Burns (and later, after her death, her sister, Lizzie), was actually descended from the Scottish poet.

Marx was much more ponderous. He is the German scholar par excellence, slow, meticulous, and painstakingly, even morbidly, perfectionist. Engels could dash off a treatise in no time at all; Marx was always worrying one to death. Engels was fazed only by Arabic with its four thousand verb roots; Marx, after twenty years of practice, still spoke hideously Teutonic English. When he writes to Engels of the great "chock" which events have caused him, we can almost hear him speak. But for all his heaviness, Marx is the greater mind of the two; where Engels supplied breadth and dash, he provided the depth.

They met, for the second time, in 1844 in Paris and their collaboration begins at this date. Engels had come merely to call on Marx, but they had so much to say to each other that their conversation lasted for ten days. Thereafter there is hardly a product of the one that was not edited or rewritten or at least debated with the other, and their correspondence fills several volumes.

Their paths to that common meeting ground in Paris were widely divergent. Engels was the son of a pietist, Calvinist, narrow-minded father, a manufacturer in the Rhineland. When Friedrich as a young man had shown an incomprehensible taste for poetry, his father had packed him off to Bremen to learn the export business and to live with a cleric: religion and money-making, according to Caspar Engels, were good cures for a romantic soul. Engels had dutifully applied himself to business, but everything he saw was colored by a personality in revolt, a happy-go-lucky personality but one that was incompatible with his father's rigid standards. He went down to the docks in the course of business, but his observant eye took in not only the first-class accommodations "in mahogany ornamented with gold" but the steerage as well, where the people were "packed in like the paving-stones in the streets." He began to read the radical literature of his time and by the age of twenty-two he was converted to the ideals of "communism"—a word which then had no very clear definition except insofar as it rejected the idea of private property as a means for organizing society's economic effort.

Then he went to Manchester to enter his father's textile business there. Manchester, like the ships in Bremen, seemed to Engels a façade. There were pleasant streets lined with shops and suburbs ringing the city with pleasant villas. But there was a second Manchester as well. It was hidden behind the first and laid out so that the millowners never had to see it on their trips to their offices. It harbored a stunted population living in a state of filth and despair, turning to gin and evangelism and doping themselves and their children with laudanum against a life that was hopeless and brutal. Engels had seen similar conditions in the factory towns of his Rhineland home, but now he explored Manchester until he knew every last hovel and each ratlike abode. He was to publish his findings in the most terrible verdict ever passed on the world of industrial slums: *The Condition of the Working Class in England in 1844*. One time he talked of the misery of the place to a gentleman friend and remarked that he had never seen so "ill-built a city." His companion listened to him quietly and then said, "And yet there is a great deal of money made here; good day, sir."

He was writing now—treatises to show that the great English economists were only apologists for the existing order—and one of his contributions made an especial impression on a young man named Karl Marx who was editing a radical philosophical magazine in Paris.

Unlike Engels, Marx came from a liberal, even mildly radical, family background. He was born in 1818 in Trier, Germany, the second son of a prosperous Jewish family which shortly thereafter adopted Christianity so that Heinrich Marx, an advocate, might be less restricted in his practice. Heinrich Marx was a respected man; he was, in fact, even appointed *Justizrat,* an honorary title for eminent lawyers, but in his day he had joined illegal banquet clubs which drank toasts to a republican Germany, and he had reared his young son on a diet of Voltaire, Locke, and Diderot.

Heinrich Marx hoped that his son would study law. But at the universities of Bonn and Berlin, young Marx found himself swept up in the great philosophical debate of the day. The philosopher Hegel had propounded a revolutionary scheme and the conservative German universities found themselves split wide open over it. Change, according to Hegel, was the rule of life. Every idea irrepressibly bred its opposite and the two merged into a synthesis which in turn produced its own contradiction. And history, said Hegel, was nothing but the expression of this flux of conflicting and resolving ideas as they fired now this and then that nation. Change—dialectical change—was immanent in human affairs. With one exception: when it came to the Prussian state, the rules no longer applied; the Prussian government, said Hegel, was like "God walking on earth."

This was a powerful stimulus for a young student. Marx joined a group of intellectuals known as the Young Hegelians which debated such daring questions as atheism and pure theoretical communism in terms of the Hegelian dialectic, and he decided to become a philosopher himself. He might have, had it not been for the action of that godlike state. Marx's favorite professor, Bruno Bauer, who was eager to procure an appointment for him at Bonn, was dismissed for proconstitutional and antireligious ideas (one evidently as bad as the other), and an academic career for young Dr. Marx became an impossibility.

He turned instead to journalism. The *Rheinische Zeitung,* a small middle-class liberal newspaper, to which he had been a frequent contributor, asked him to take on its editorship. He accepted; his career lasted exactly five months. Marx was then a radical, but his radicalism was philosophical rather than political. When Friedrich Engels came respectfully to call on him, Marx rather disapproved of that brash young man brimming with communist ideas, and when Marx himself was accused of being a Communist, his reply was equivocal: "I do not know communism," he said, "but a social philosophy which has as its aim the defense of the oppressed cannot be condemned so lightly." But regardless of his disavowals, his editorials were too much for the authorities. He wrote a bitter denunciation of a law which would have prevented the peasants from exercising their immemorial rights to gather dead wood in the forests; for this he was censured. He wrote editorials deploring the housing situation; for this he was warned. And when he went so far as to say some uncomplimentary things about the Tsar of Russia, the *Rheinische Zeitung* was suppressed.

Marx went to Paris to take over another radical journal which was to be almost as short-lived as the newspaper. But his interests were now turned in the direction of politics and economics. The undisguised self-interest of the Prussian government, the implacable resistance of the German *bourgeoisie* toward anything which might alleviate the condition of the German working classes, the almost caricaturesque attitudes of reaction which characterized the wealthy and ruling classes of Europe—all this had coalesced in his mind to form part of a new philosophy of history. And when Engels came to visit him and the two struck up their strong rapport, that philosophy began to take formal shape.

The philosophy was to take the name of dialectical materialism; *dialectical* because it incorporated Hegel's idea of inherent change, and *materialism* because it grounded itself not in the world of ideas, but on the terrain of social and physical environment.

"The materialist conception of history," wrote Engels many years later in a famous tract entitled "Anti-Dühring" (because it was aimed against a German professor named Eugen Dühring), "starts from the principle that production, and with production the exchange of its products, is the basis of every social order; that in every society which has appeared in history the distribution of the products, and with it the division of society into classes or estates, is determined by what is produced and how it is produced, and how the product is exchanged. According to this conception, the ultimate causes of all social changes and political revolutions are to be sought, not in the minds of men, in their increasing insight into eternal truth and justice, but in changes in the mode of production and exchange; they are to be sought not in the *philosophy* but in the *economics* of the epoch concerned."

The reasoning is not difficult to follow. Every society, says Marx, is built on an economic base, is ultimately grounded in the hard reality of human beings who have organized their activities in order to clothe and feed and house themselves. That organization can differ vastly from society to society and from era to era. It can be pastoral or built around hunting or grouped into handicraft units or structured into a complex industrial whole. But whatever the form in which men organize to solve their basic economic problem, society will require a whole superstructure of noneconomic activity and thought—it will need to be bound together by laws, supervised by a government, inspired by religion and philosophy.

But the superstructure of thought cannot be selected at random. It must mirror the foundation on which it is raised. No hunting community will evolve or could use the legal framework of an industrial society, and similarly an industrial community obviously requires an entirely different conception of law, order, and government than does a primitive village. Note that the doctrine of materialism does not toss away the catalytic function and creativity of ideas. It only maintains that thoughts and ideas are the *product* of environment, even though they aim to change that environment.

Materialism by itself would reduce ideas to mere passive accompaniments of economic activity. That was not Marx's contention. For the new theory was *dialectical* as well as materialist: it envisaged change, constant and inherent change; and in that never-ending flux the ideas emanating from one period would help to shape another. "Men make their own history," wrote Marx, commenting on the *coup d'état* of Louis Napoleon in 1852, "but they do not make it just as they please; they do not make it under circumstances chosen by themselves, but under circumstances directly found, given, and transmitted from the past."

But the dialectical—the changing—aspect of this theory of history did not depend merely on the interplay of ideas and social structures. There was another and far more powerful agent at work. The economic world itself was changing; the ultimate reality on which the structure of ideas was built was itself constantly in flux.

For example, the isolated markets of the Middle Ages began to lock fingers under the impetus of exploration and political unification, and a new commercial world was born. The old hand mill was replaced by the steam mill under the impetus of invention, and a new form of social organization called the factory came into being. In both cases the ultimate reality of economic life itself changed its form, and as it did, it forced a new social adaptation from the community in which it was embedded.

And once such a change had taken place, it carried with it a whole train of consequences. The market and the factory were incompatible with the feudal way of life—even though they were born amidst it. They demanded a new cultural and social context to go with them. And they helped in that difficult birthing process by creating their own new social classes: the market created a professional merchant class and the factory a proletariat.

But the process of social change was not merely a matter of new inventions pressing on old institutions: it was a matter of new classes displacing old ones. For each society is organized into a class structure, into aggregates of men who stand in some common relationship—favorable or otherwise—to the existing form of production. And social change threatens all of that. As the technical conditions of production change—as factories destroy handicraft industry, for example—the old classes find that their accustomed situation is changing too; those on top may find the ground cut from under them, while those who were on the bottom may be carried higher. We have seen just such an upset of the relative position of social classes in Ricardo's day in England, when the capitalists, riding the wave of the Industrial Revolution, were threatening to usurp the time-honored prerogatives of the landed gentry.

Hence conflict develops. The classes whose position is jeopardized fight the classes whose position is enhanced: the feudal lord fights the rising merchant, and the guild master despises the young capitalist.

But the process of history pays no attention to likes and dislikes. Gradually conditions change and gradually, but surely, the classes of society are rearranged. Amid turmoil and anguish the division of wealth is altered. And thus history is a pageant of ceaseless struggle between classes to partition social wealth. For as long as the technics of society change, no existing division of wealth is immune from attack.

What did this theory augur for the present? It pointed to revolution—inevitable revolution. For capitalism, according to this analysis, must also consist of a technical base of economic reality and a superstructure of a social class system. And if its technical base was evolving, then necessarily, its superstructure must be subject to increasing strain.

That is exactly what Marx and Engels saw in 1848. The technical base of capitalism—its anchor in reality—was industrial production. Its superstructure was the system of private property, under which a portion of society's output went to those who owned its great technical apparatus. The conflict lay in the fact that the base and superstructure were incompatible.

Why? Because the base of industrial production—the actual making of goods—was a highly organized, integrated, interdependent process, whereas the superstructure of private property was the most highly individualistic of social systems. Hence the superstructure and the base clashed: factories necessitated social planning, and private property abhorred it; *capitalism* had become so complex that it needed direction but *capitalists* insisted on a ruinous freedom.

The result was twofold. First, capitalism must destroy itself. The planless nature of production must lead to a constant disorganization of economic activity—to crises and slumps and the social chaos of depression. The system was simply too complex; it was constantly getting out of joint, losing step, and overproducing one good while underproducing another.

Secondly, capitalism would unknowingly breed its own successor. Within its great factories it would not only create the technical base for socialism—mass production—but it would create as well a trained and disciplined *class* who would be the agent of socialism—the embittered proletariat. By its own inner dynamic, capitalism would produce its own downfall, and in the process, it would nourish its own enemy.

It was a profoundly revolutionary insight into history, not only for what it betokened for the future, but for the whole new perspective it opened upon the past. We have come to be familiar with the "economic interpretation" of history, and we can accept with equanimity a re-evaluation of the past with respect to the struggle, say, of the nascent seventeenth-century commercial classes and the aristocratic world of land and lineage. But for Marx and Engels, this was no mere exercise in historical rein-terpretation. The dialectic led to the future and that future, as revealed by the *Communist Manifesto,* pointed to an *inevitable* communist revolution which this same dialectic would produce. In somber words the *Manifesto* proclaimed: "The development of modern industry . . . cuts from under its feet the very founda-tion on which the bourgeoisie produces and appropriates prod-ucts. What the bourgeoisie therefore produces, above all, are its own gravediggers. Its fall and the victory of the proletariat are equally inevitable."

The *Manifesto,* with its rumbling, inexorable interpretation of history, was not written in Paris. Marx's career had been brief in that city. He edited a caustic, radical magazine; he again rubbed the sensibilities of the Prussian government, and at its behest, he was expelled from the French capital.

He was married now—in 1843 he had married Jenny von West-phalen, who lived next door to him as a child. Jenny was the daughter of a Prussian aristocrat and Privy Councillor, but Baron von Westphalen was nevertheless a humanist and liberal thinker. He had talked to young Marx about Homer and Shakespeare and even told him about the ideas of Saint-Simon despite their pronouncement by the local bishop as heresy. As for Jenny —she was the belle of the town. Beautiful and with suitors galore, she could easily have made a more "suitable" match than the dark young man next door. But she was in love with him and both families smiled their approval. For the Marxes such a mar-riage would be a not inconsiderable social triumph and for the baron it was, perhaps, a happy vindication of his humanist ideas. One wonders if he would have given his consent could he have foreseen what was to happen to his daughter. For Jenny was to be forced to share the bed of a common prostitute in jail and would have to beg the money from a neighbor to buy a coffin to bury one of her children. In place of the pleasant comforts and the social prestige of Trier, she was to spend the years of her life in two dismal rooms in a London slum, sharing with her husband the calumny of a hostile world.

And yet it was a deeply devoted union. In his dealings with outsiders, Marx was unkind, jealous, suspicious, and wrathful; but he was a devoted husband and father. Later, much later, when Jenny was dying and Marx was ill, this lovely scene was witnessed by her daughter.

> Mother lay in the big front room and The Moor lay in the little room next to it. . . . I shall never forget the morning when he felt strong enough to get up and go into Mother's room. It was as though they were young again together—she a loving girl and he an ardent youth starting out together through life and not an old man shattered by ill-health and a dying lady taking leave of each other forever.

The Marxes had moved to London in 1849. Expulsion from Paris, four years before, had landed them in Brussels, where they stayed (and the *Manifesto* was composed) until the revolutionary outbursts in 1848. Then when the Belgian king had secured a firm enough grip on his shaky throne, he rounded up the radical leaders in his capital and Marx went briefly to Germany.

It was the same pattern all over again. Marx took over the editorship of a newspaper and it was only a matter of time before the government closed it down. He printed the last edition in red —and sought a haven in London.

He was now in desperate financial shape. Engels was in Manchester, leading his strange double life (he was a respected figure on the Manchester Stock Exchange), and he supplied the Marxes with a never-ending stream of checks and loans. But the family faced the bitterest poverty, nonetheless. There were, in all, five of them, plus Lenchen, the Westphalen family maid who stayed with them, unpaid, all their days. Marx had no work—except his never-ending stint in the British Museum from ten o'clock every morning until seven o'clock at night. He tried to make a little money by writing articles on the political situation for the New York *Tribune*, whose editor, Charles A. Dana, was a Fourierist himself and not averse to a few slaps at European politics. It helped for a while, although it was Engels who bailed Marx out by composing many of his pieces for him—Marx meanwhile advising by letter as follows: "Du musst dein war-articles colour a little more." When the articles stopped, he tried to get a clerical job with a railway, but was rejected for his atrocious handwriting. Thereafter he pawned what was left to his name, all the family silver and valuables having been sold long ago. At times his want was so intense that he was forced to sit home because his coat and even his shoes were at pawn; on other occasions he lacked the money to buy postage stamps to send his works to the publisher. And to compound his difficulties, he suffered from the most painful boils. When he arrived home one evening after writing in misery all day long in the Museum he remarked, "I hope the bourgeoisie as long as they live will have cause to remember my carbuncles." He had just composed the terrible chapter of *Das Kapital* which describes the Working Day.

There was only Engels to fall back on. Marx wrote him constantly, touching on economics, politics, mathematics, military tactics, on everything under the sun, but especially on his own situation. A typical excerpt reads:

> My wife is ill. Little Jenny is ill. Lenchen has a sort of nervous fever and I can't call in the doctor because I have no money to pay him. For about eight or ten days we have all been living on bread and potatoes and it is now doubtful whether we shall be able to get even that. . . . I have written nothing for Dana because I have not had the money to buy newspapers. . . . How am I to get out of this devilish mess? During the past week or so I have borrowed a few shillings and even pence from workers. It was terrible but it was absolutely necessary or we should have starved.

Only the last years were a little easier. An old friend left Marx a small bequest and he never again touched the lower depths of poverty. Engels, too, finally came into an inheritance and left his business; in 1869 he went to his office for the last time and came over the fields to meet Marx's daughter, "flourishing his stick and laughing and singing all over his face."

In 1881 Jenny died; she had buried two of her five children including her only son; she was old and tired. Marx was too ill to go to the funeral; when Engels looked at him he said, "The Moor is dead, too." Not quite; he lingered for two more years; disapproved of the husbands whom his two married daughters had chosen; grew weary of the bickering of the working-class movement and delivered himself of a statement that has never ceased to bedevil the faithful ("I am not a Marxist," he said one day); and then on a March afternoon, quietly slipped away.

What had he done, in these long years of privation?

He had produced, for one thing, an international working-class movement. As a young man Marx had written: "The philosophers hitherto have only interpreted the world in various ways; the thing, however, is to change it." Marx and Engels had given the accolade to the proletariat in their interpretation of history; now they set about steering and guiding the proletariat so that it should exert its maximum leverage on history.

It was not an attempt crowned with much success. Coincident with the publication of the *Manifesto*, the Communist League had been formed, but it was never much more than a paper organization; the *Manifesto,* which was its platform, was not then even placed on public sale, and with the demise of the revolution of 1848, the League died too.

It was followed in 1864 with a far more ambitious organization, the International Workingmen's Association. The International boasted seven million members and was real enough to have a hand in a wave of strikes which swept the Continent and to earn for itself a rather fearsome reputation. But it, too, was doomed to have a brief history. The International did not consist of a tough and disciplined army of Communists, but a motley crew of Owenists, Proudhonists, Fourierists, lukewarm Socialists, rabid nationalists, and trade-unionists who were leery of any kind of revolutionary theory whatsoever. With considerable skill Marx kept his crew together for five years and then the International fell apart; some followed Bakunin, a giant of a man with a true revolutionist's background of Siberia and exile (it was said that his oratory was so moving that his listeners would have cut their throats if he had asked them to), while others turned their attention back to national affairs. The last meeting of the International was held in New York in 1874. It was a lugubrious failure.

But far more important than the creation of the First International was the peculiar tone which Marx injected into working-class affairs. This was the most quarrelsome and intolerant of men, and from the beginning he was unable to believe that anyone who did not follow his line of reasoning could possibly be right. As an economist his language was precise, as a philosopher-historian it was eloquent, as a revolutionary it was scurrilous. He called his opponents "louts," "rascals," even "bedbugs." Early in his career, when he was still in Brussels, Marx had been visited by a German tailor named Weitling. Weitling was a tried son of the labor movement; he had scars on his legs from the irons of Prussian prisons and a long history of selfless and valiant efforts on behalf of the German workingman. He came to speak to Marx on such things as justice and brotherhood and solidarity; instead he found himself exposed to a merciless cross-examination on the "scientific principles" of socialism. Poor Weitling was confused, his answers were unsatisfactory. Marx, who had been sitting as the chief examiner, began to stride angrily about the room. "Ignorance has never helped anybody yet," he shouted. The audience was over.

Willich was another to be excommunicated. An ex-Prussian captain, he had fought in the German revolution, and later was to become an outstanding general on the Union side of the American Civil War. But he clung to the "un-Marxist" idea that "pure will" could be the motive power of revolution instead of "actual conditions"; for this notion—which Lenin was one day to prove was not so farfetched after all—he, too, was dropped from the movement.

And the list could be extended endlessly. Perhaps no single incident was more provocative, more prophetic of a movement which was one day to degenerate into an internal witch-hunt for "deviationists" and "counterrevolutionaries" than the feud between Marx and Pierre Proudhon. Proudhon was the son of a French barrelmaker, a self-educated brilliant socialist who had rocked the French intelligentsia with a book entitled *What Is Property?* Proudhon had answered, Property is Theft, and he had called for an end to huge private riches although not to all private property. Marx and he had met and talked and corresponded and then Marx asked him to join forces with himself and Engels. Proudhon's answer is so profoundly moving and so frighteningly indicative of the future that it is worth quoting at some length.

"Let us by all means collaborate," he wrote, "in trying to discover the laws of society, the way in which these laws work out, the best method to go about investigating them; but, for God's sake, after we have demolished all the dogmatisms *a priori*, let us not of all things attempt in our turn to instill another kind of doctrine into the people. . . . I applaud with all my heart your idea of bringing to light all the varieties of opinion; let us have good and sincere polemics; let us show the world the example of a learned and far-sighted tolerance; but simply because we are at the head of a new movement, let us not set ourselves up as the leaders of a new intolerance, let us not pose as the apostles of a new religion—even though this religion be the religion of logic, the religion of reason itself. Let us welcome, let us encourage all the protests; let us condemn all the exclusions, all the mysticisms; let us never regard a question as closed, and even after we have exhausted our last argument, let us begin again, if necessary, with eloquence and irony. On that condition, I shall be delighted to take part in your association—but otherwise, no!"

Marx's answer was this: Proudhon had written a book called *The Philosophy of Poverty;* Marx now annihilated it with a rejoinder entitled *The Poverty of Philosophy.*

The pattern of intolerance was never to disappear. The First International would be followed by the mild and well-meaning Second—which included socialists of such caliber as Bernard Shaw, Ramsay MacDonald, and Pilsudski (as well as Lenin, Mussolini, and Laval!), and then by the infamous Third, organized under the aegis of Moscow. And yet, the impact of these great movements is perhaps less than the persistence of that narrowness, that infuriating and absolute inability to entertain a dissenting opinion, that autocratic air, and that antipathy for democracy which communism has inherited from its single greatest founder.

Had Marx produced nothing more in his long years in exile than a revolutionary labor movement, he would not loom today so important a figure in the world. Marx was only one of a dozen revolutionaries and by no means the most successful; he was only one of at least that many prophets of socialism and as a matter of fact he wrote next to nothing about what that new society might be like. His final contribution lies elsewhere: in his dialectical materialist theory of history, and even more important, in his pessimistic analysis of the outlook for a capitalist economy.

"The history of capitalism," Stalin has written, "has entirely confirmed the theories of Marx and Engels concerning the laws of development of capitalist society . . . that must inevitably lead to the downfall of the whole capitalist system." What were those laws? What was Marx's prognosis for the system that he knew?

The answer lies in that enormous work *Das Kapital*—(Capital). With Marx's agonizing meticulousness, it is remarkable that the work was ever finished—in a sense it never was. It was eighteen years in process; in 1851 it was to be done "in five weeks"; in 1859 "in six weeks"; in 1865 it was "done"—a huge bundle of virtually illegible manuscripts which took two years to edit into Volume I. When Marx died in 1883 two volumes remained: Engels put out Volume II in 1885 and the third in 1894. The final (fourth) volume did not emerge until 1910.

There are twenty-five hundred pages to read for anyone intrepid enough to make the effort. And what pages! Some deal with the tiniest of technical matters and labor them to a point of mathematical exhaustion; others swirl with passion and anger. This is an economist who has read *every* economist, a German pedant with a passion for footnotes, and an emotional critic who can write that "capital is dead labour, that vampire-like, only lives by sucking living labour" and who tells us that capital came into the world "dripping from head to foot, from every pore, with blood and dirt."

And yet one must not jump to the conclusion that this is

merely a biased and irascible text inveighing against the sins of
the wicked money-barons. It is shot through with remarks which
betray the total involvement of the man with his theoretical
adversary, but the great merit of the book, curiously enough, is
its utter detachment from all considerations of morality. The
book describes with fury, but it analyzes with cold logic. For
what Marx has set for his goal is to discover the intrinsic tendencies of the capitalist system, its inner laws of motion, and in so
doing, he has eschewed the easy but less convincing means of
merely expatiating on its manifest shortcomings. Instead he erects
the most rigorous, the purest capitalism imaginable and within
this rarefied abstract system, with an imaginary capitalism in
which all the obvious defects of real life are removed, he seeks his
quarry. For if he can prove that the best of all possible capital-
isms is nonethless headed for certain disaster, it is certainly easy
to demonstrate that real capitalism will follow the same path,
only quicker.

And so he sets the stage. We enter a world of perfect capitalism: no monopolies, no unions, no special advantages for anyone.
It is a world in which every commodity sells at exactly its proper
price. And that proper price is its *value*—a tricky word. For the
value of a commodity, says Marx (and Smith and Ricardo before
him), is the amount of labor it has within itself. If it takes twice
as much labor to make hats as shoes, then hats will sell for twice
the price of shoes. The labor, of course, need not be direct
manual labor; it may be overhead labor which is spread over
many commodities or it may be the labor which once went into
making a machine and which the machine now slowly passes on
to the products it shapes. But no matter what its form, everything
is eventually reducible to labor, and all commodities, in this perfect system, will be priced according to the amount of labor,
direct or indirect, which they contain.

In this world stand the two great protagonists of the capitalist
drama: worker and capitalist—the landlord has by now been
relegated to a minor position in society. They are not quite the
same protagonists we have met earlier in similar economic tab-
leaux. The worker is no longer the slave to his reproductive urge.
He is a free bargaining agent who enters the market to dispose
of the one commodity he commands—labor-power—and if he gets

a rise in wages he will not be so foolish as to squander it in a self-defeating proliferation of his numbers.

The capitalist faces him in the arena. He is not a bad fellow at heart, although his greed and lust for wealth are caustically described in those chapters which leave the abstract world for a look into 1860 England. But it is worth noting that he is not money-hungry from mere motives of rapacity; he is an owner-entrepreneur engaged in an endless race against his fellow owner-entrepreneurs; he *must* strive for accumulation, for in the competitive environment in which he operates, one accumulates or one gets accumulated.

The stage is set and the characters take their places. But now the first difficulty appears. How, asks Marx, can profits exist in such a situation? If everything sells for its exact value, then who gets an unearned increment? No one dares to raise his price above the competitive one, and even if one seller managed to gouge a buyer, that buyer would only have less to spend elsewhere in the economy—one man's profit would thus be another man's loss. How can there be profit in the *whole* system if everything exchanges for its honest worth?

It seems like a paradox. Profits are easy to explain if we assume that there are monopolies in the system which need not obey the leveling influences of competition or if we admit that capitalists may pay labor less than it is worth. But Marx will have none of that—this is to be *pure* capitalism which will dig its own grave.

He finds the answer to the dilemma in one commodity which is different from all others. That commodity is labor-power. For the laborer, like the capitalist, sells his product for exactly what it is worth—for its value. And its value, like the value of everything else that is sold, is the amount of labor that goes into it—in this case, the amount of labor that it takes to "make" labor-power. In other words, a laborer's salable energies are worth the amount of socially necessary labor it takes to keep that laborer alive. Smith and Ricardo would have agreed entirely: the true value of a workman is the wage he needs in order to exist. It is his subsistence wage.

So far, so good. But here comes the key to profit. The laborer who contracts to work can only ask for a wage which is his due.

What that wage will be depends, as we have seen, on the amount of labor-time it takes to keep a man alive. If it takes six hours of society's labor to maintain a workingman, then (if labor is priced at one dollar an hour), he is "worth" six dollars a day. No more.

But the laborer who gets a job does not contract to work only six hours a day. That would be just long enough to support himself. On the contrary, he agrees to work a full eight-hour, or in Marx's time a ten- or eleven-hour, day. Hence he will produce a full ten or eleven hours' worth of value and he will get paid for only six. His wage will cover his subsistence which is his true "value," but in return he will sell the value which he produces in a full working day. And this is how profit enters the system.

Marx called this layer of unpaid work "surplus value." But it is quite devoid of moral indignation. The worker is only entitled to the *value* of his labor-power. He gets it in full. But meanwhile the capitalist gets the full value of his workers' whole working day, and this is longer than the hours for which he paid. Hence when the capitalist sells his products, he can afford to sell them at *their* true value and still realize a profit. For there is more labor-time embodied in his products than the labor-time for which he was forced to pay.

How can this state of affairs come about? It happens because the capitalists monopolize one thing—access to the means of production themselves. If a worker isn't willing to work a full working day, he doesn't get a job. Like everyone else in the system, a worker has no right and no power to ask for more than his own worth as a commodity. The system is perfectly equitable and yet all workers are cheated, for they are forced to work a longer time than their own self-sustenance demands.

Does this sound strange? Remember that Marx is describing a time when the working day was long—sometimes unendurably long—and when wages were, by and large, little more than it took to keep body and soul together. The idea of surplus value may make little sense in a world where the sweatshop is very largely a thing of the past, but it was not merely a theoretical construct at the time that Marx was writing. One example may suffice: at a Manchester factory in 1862 the average work-week for a period of a month and a half was 84 hours! For the previous 18 months it had been 78½ hours.

But all this is still only the setting for the drama. We have the protagonists, we have their motives, we have the clue to the plot in the discovery of "surplus value." And now the play is set in motion.

All capitalists have profits. But they are all in competition. Hence they try to accumulate and so to expand their scales of output, at the expense of their competitors. But expansion is not so easy. It requires more laborers and to get them the capitalists must bid against each other for the working force. Wages tend to rise. Conversely, surplus value tends to fall. It looks as if the Marxian capitalists will soon be up against the dilemma faced by the capitalists of Adam Smith and David Ricardo—their profits will be eaten away by rising wages.

To Smith and Ricardo the solution to the dilemma lay in the propensity of the working force to increase its numbers with every boost in pay. But Marx has ruled out this possibility. He doesn't argue about it; he simply brands the Malthusian doctrine "a libel on the human race"—after all, the proletariat, which is to be the ruling class of the future, cannot be so shortsighted as to dissipate its gains through mere unbridled physical appetite. But he rescues his capitalists just the same. For he says that they will meet the threat of rising wages by introducing laborsaving machinery into their plants. That will throw part of the working force back onto the street and there, as an Industrial Reserve Army, it will serve the same function as Malthus' teeming population: it will compete wages right back down to their former "value"—the subsistence level.

But now comes the crucial twist. It seems as though the capitalist has saved the day, for he has prevented wages from rising by creating unemployment through machinery. But not so fast. By the very process through which he hopes to free himself from one horn of the dilemma, he impales himself on the other.

For as he substitutes machines for men, he is simultaneously substituting nonprofitable means of production for profitable ones. Remember that in this never-never world, no one makes a profit by merely sharp bargaining. Whatever a machine will be worth to a capitalist, you can be sure that he paid full value for it.

If a machine will yield ten thousand dollars' worth of value over its whole life, our capitalist was charged the full ten thousand dollars in the first place. It is only from his living labor that he can realize a profit, only from the unpaid-for hours of surplus working time. Hence when he reduces the number or proportion of workers, he is killing the goose that laid the golden egg.

And yet, unhappy fellow, he has to. There is nothing Mephistophelean about his actions. He is only obeying his impulse to accumulate and trying to stay abreast of his competitors. As his wages rise, he *must* introduce laborsaving machinery to cut his costs and rescue his profits—if he does not, his neighbor will. But since he must substitute machinery for labor, he must also narrow the base out of which he gleans his profits. It is a kind of Greek drama where men go willy-nilly to their fate, and in which they all unwittingly cooperate to bring about their own destruction.

For now the die is cast. As his profits shrink, each capitalist will redouble his efforts to put new laborsaving, cost-cutting machinery in his factory. It is only by getting a step ahead of the parade that he can hope to make a profit. But since everyone is doing precisely the same thing, the ratio of labor (and hence surplus value) to total output shrinks still further. The rate of profit falls and falls. And now doom lies ahead. Profits are cut to the point at which production is no longer profitable at all. Consumption dwindles as machines displace men and the number of employed fails to keep pace with output. Bankruptcies ensue. There is a scramble to dump goods on the market and in the process smaller firms go under. A capitalist crisis is at hand.

Not forever. As workers are thrown out of work, they are forced to accept subvalue wages. As machinery is dumped, the stronger capitalists can acquire machines for less than their true value. After a time, surplus value reappears. The forward march is taken up again. But it leads to the same catastrophic conclusion: competition for workers; higher wages, labor-displacing machinery; a smaller base for surplus value; still more frenzied competition; collapse. And each collapse is worse than the preceding one. In the periods of crisis, the bigger firms absorb the smaller ones, and when the industrial monsters eventually go down, the wreckage is far greater than when the little enterprises buckle.

And then, one day, the drama ends. Marx's picture of it has all the eloquence of a description of Damnation: "Along with the constantly diminishing number of the magnates of capital, who usurp and monopolize all advantages of this process of transformation, grows the mass of misery, oppression, slavery, degradation, exploitation; but with this too grows the revolt of the working-class, a class always increasing in numbers, and disciplined, united, organized by the very mechanism of the process of capitalist production itself . . . Centralization of the means of production and socialization of labour at last reach a point where they become incompatible with their capitalist integument. This integument bursts asunder. The knell of capitalist private property sounds. The expropriators are expropriated."

And so the drama ends in the inevitable overthrow which Marx had envisioned in the dialectic. The system—the *pure* system—breaks down as it works upon itself to squeeze out its own source of energy, surplus value. The breakdown is hastened by the constant instability which arises from the essentially planless nature of the economy, and although there are forces at work which act both to prolong and to hasten its end, its final death struggle is inescapable. And if the pure system is unworkable, what possible hope can there be for the real system, with all its imperfections, monopolies, cutthroat tactics, and heedless profit seeking?

For Adam Smith, the capitalist escalator climbed ever upward, at least as far as the eye could reasonably see. For Ricardo that upward motion was finally stalled by the pressure of mouths on insufficient cropland, which brought a stalemate to progress and a windfall to the fortunate landlord. For Mill the vista was made more reassuring by his discovery that society could distribute its product as it saw fit, regardless of what "economic laws" seemed to dictate. But for Marx even that saving possibility was untenable. For the dialectic told him that the State was only the political ruling organ of the economic rulers, and the thought that it might act as a neutral body, as an impartial third force which might balance the claims of its conflicting members, would have seemed little else but sheer wishful thinking. No, there was no escape from the inner logic, the inexorable development of a system which would not only destroy itself but which, in so doing, would give birth to its successor.

As to what that successor might look like, Marx had little to say. It would be "classless," of course—by which Marx meant that the basis for an economic division of society based on property would be removed once society owned all the means of production of goods. Just how society would "own" its factories; what was meant by "society"; whether there would or could be bitter antagonisms between the managers and the managed, between the political chieftains and the rank and file—none of this did Marx specify. During a transitional period of "socialism" there would be a "dictatorship of the proletariat"; after that, "pure" communism itself.

Marx, it must be kept in mind, was not the architect of communism. That formidable task would fall to Lenin. *Das Kapital* is the Doomsday Book of capitalism, and in all of Marx there is almost nothing which looks beyond the Day of Judgment to see what lineaments paradise may present.

What are we to make of his apocalyptic argument?

There is an easy way of disposing of the whole thing. Remember that the system is built on value—labor value—and that the key to its demise lies in that special phenomenon called surplus value. But the real world consists not of "values" but of real tangible prices. Marx must show that the world of dollars and cents mirrors, in some approximate fashion, the abstract world that he has created. But in making the transition from a value-world to a price-world, he lands in the most terrible tangle of mathematics. In fact he makes a mistake.

It is not an irreparable mistake and by going through an even worse tangle of mathematics one can make the Marxist equations come out "right"—one can, that is, explain a correspondence between the prices that really obtain in life and the underlying values in terms of labor-time. But the critics who pointed out the error were hardly interested in setting the scheme aright and their judgment that Marx was "wrong" was taken as final. When the equations were finally justified, no one paid much attention.

For regardless of its mathematical purity, the Marxian rigmarole
is at best a cumbersome and difficult framework and an unneces-
sarily laborious method of getting at the required understanding
of how capitalism works.

But while we might be tempted to toss the whole analysis to
one side because it is awkward and inflexible, to do so would be
to overlook its worth. Marx, after all, did not strip capitalism
down to its barest essentials merely to indulge his bent for abstract argument. He did so because he believed that in the simplicity of a theoretical world the mechanics of the actual world
would lie clearly exposed; because he hoped that the very stark-
ness of his model world would highlight tendencies hidden in
real life.

And so it did. For all its clumsines, Marx's model of the capitalist world seemed to *work*, to display a kind of life of its own.
Given its basic assumptions—the *mise en scène* of its characters,
their motives and their milieu—the situation it presented *changed*,
and changed in a way that was foreseeable, precise, and inevitable. We have seen what these changes are: how profits fell, how
capitalists sought new machinery, how each boom ended in a
crash, how small businesses were absorbed in each debacle by
the larger firms. But all this was still within the framework of
an abstract world: now Marx applied his findings on paper to
the real world about him—the actual world of capitalism, he
said, must also display these trends.

He called the trends the "laws of motion" of a capitalist system—the path which capitalism would tread over future time.
And the astonishing fact is that almost all these predictions have
come true!

For profits *do* tend to fall in an enterprise economy. The insight was not original with Marx, nor do profits fall for the reason he gave—we can dispense with the idea of exploitation contained in the theory of surplus value. But as Adam Smith or
Ricardo or Mill pointed out—and as any businessman will vouch-
safe—the pressures of competition and rising wages will serve
quite as well. Impregnable monopolies aside (and these are few),
profits are both the hallmark of capitalism and its Achilles' heel,
for no business can *permanently* maintain its prices much above

its costs. There is only one way in which profits can be perpetuated: a business—or an entire economy—must grow.

But growth implies the second prediction of the Marxist model: the ceaseless quest for new techniques. It was no accident that industrial capitalism dates from the Industrial Revolution, for as Marx made clear, technological progress is not merely an accompaniment of capitalism but a vital ingredient. Business *must* innovate, invent, and experiment if it is to survive; the business that rests content on its past achievements is not long for this enterprising world. It is interesting to note that recently one large chemical company announced that sixty per cent of its income came from products that were unknown ten years ago; and although this is an exceptionally inventive industry, the relationship between industrial inventiveness and profitability generally holds.

The model showed still two more tendencies for capitalism which have also come to pass. We hardly need document the existence of business cycles over the past hundred years nor the emergence of giant business enterprise. But we might remark on the daring of Marx's prediction. When *Das Kapital* appeared, bigness was the exception rather than the rule and small enterprise still ruled the roost. To claim that huge firms would come to dominate the business scene was as startling a prediction in 1867 as would be a statement today that fifty years hence America will be a land in which small-scale proprietorships will have displaced giant corporations.

It was, all things considered, an extraordinary bit of foresight. And note this: all these changes, vast and portentous as they were, could not have been unearthed purely by examining the world as it appeared to Marx's eyes. For these are historical changes, slow in their unfolding and stretched out over time; as real, but as unnoticeable, as the growth of a tree. It was only by reducing the economic system to a microcosm and then by observing that microcosm in its speeded-up life span that this drift of the future could be apprehended.

It was not, of course, exact. Marx thought that profits would not only fall *within* the business cycle, which they do, but that they would display a long downward secular trend; this does not appear to have taken place. Marx did not stop to consider that the economic particles with which he played had feelings and volitions and consciences that could also change and that they would not therefore behave with the imperturbable predictability of the particles under a chemist's microscope. But for all its short-comings— and it is far from infallible, as we shall see—the Marxist model of how capitalism worked was extraordinarily prophetic.

But everything that Marx had predicted so far was, after all, innocuous. There remained the final prediction of the model; for as the reader will remember, in the end Marx's "pure capitalism" *collapsed.*

Let it be said at the outset that this prediction as well cannot be lightly brushed aside. In Russia and Eastern Europe capital-ism has disappeared; in Scandinavia and Britain it has been par-tially abandoned; in Germany and Italy it drifted into fascism and emerged from its bath of fire in less than perfect health. And while wars, brute political power, exigencies of fate, and the de-termined efforts of revolutionaries have all contributed their share, the grim truth is that these changes occurred largely for the very reason Marx foresaw: capitalism broke down.

Why did it break down? Partly because it developed the in-stability Marx said it would. A succession of business crises, com-pounded by a plague of wars, destroyed the faith of the lower and middle classes in the system. But that is not the entire an-swer—we too have had our wars and depressions, and capitalism here is very much alive. Something else spelled the difference between survival and destruction: European capitalism failed not so much for economic as for *social* reasons—and Marx predicted this too!

For Marx recognized that the economic difficulties of the sys-tem were not insuperable. Although antimonopoly legislation or antibusiness cycle policies were unknown in Marx's day, such activities were not inconceivable: there was nothing inevitable in the *physical* sense about Marx's vision. The Marxist prediction of decay was founded on a conception of capitalism in which it was *socially* impossible for a government to set wrongs aright; intellectually, ideologically, even emotionally impossible. The cure for capitalism's failings would require that a government would have to rise above the interests of one class alone—and that, as Marx's doctrine of historical materialism revealed, was to assume that men could free themselves from the shackles of their immediate economic self-interest.

And it is just this lack of social flexibility, this bondage to shortsighted interest, that weakened European capitalism. For one who has read the works of Marx it is frightening to look back at the grim determination with which so many nations steadfastly hewed to the very course which he insisted would lead to their undoing. It was as if their governments were unconsciously vindicating Marx's prophecy by obstinately doing exactly what he said they would. When in Russia under the Tsars all democratic trade-unionism was ruthlessly stamped out, when in England and Germany monopolies and cartels were officially encouraged, the Marxist dialectic looked balefully prescient indeed. Until very recently, when one considered that in France or Italy or Greece capitalist governments could not collect taxes they levied on their own business communities, when one inspected the enormous gulf between rich and poor and saw evidence of the total indifference of the former for the latter, one had the uneasy feeling that the psychological stereotypes which Marx cast in his historical drama were all too truly drawn from life.

And it is these very facts which give us the clue as to why capitalism has survived in the United States. We have had our share of reactionaries and revolutionaries. The economic history of the United States contains more than enough exploitation and ugliness. But capitalism here nonetheless evolved in a land untouched by the dead hand of aristocratic lineage and age-old class attitudes. To some degree this resulted in a harsher social climate in America than in Europe, for here we clung to the credo of "rugged individualism" long after the individual had been hopelessly overwhelmed by the environment of massive industrialism, whereas in Europe a traditional "noblesse oblige" existed side by side with its unconcealed class divisions. Yet out of the American milieu came a certain pragmatism in dealing with power, private as well as public; an unstinting encouragement to enterprise, whatever the social origins of its protagonist; and a general subscription to the ideals of democracy that steered the body politic safely past the rocks on which it foundered in so many nations abroad.

It is in these attributes that the answer to Marxian analysis lies.

Marx was not so much "wrong" in his economic vision as he was wrong in assuming that his psychological and sociological preconceptions were fixed and unalterable. The economic laws of motion which his model of capitalism revealed may still be visible in American capitalism—indeed, they are—but they are faced with a set of remedies which spring from political and social attitudes quite beyond his imagination.

Some of these remedies arise from new attitudes and values on the part of business itself. The rigid antilabor stance of nineteenth- and early-twentieth-century big business has given way to a characteristically matter-of-fact acceptance of unions by big corporations today. The near-religious opposition to social-welfare policies found among the old exponents of the philosophy of rugged individualism has imperceptibly changed into the recognition (however grudging) that programs of social assistance are inescapable in the environment of twentieth-century urban life. In short, the attitudes of business have proved to be as capable of enlightenment as the attitudes of any other class, including (as Marx himself maintained in the case of "neo-Malthusianism") the working class.

Equally important, by way of countering the Marxian argument, are changes in the role of government. As we have seen, for Marx a government was inevitably the tool of the ruling class, and as long as that class was openly hostile to the working class, one could hardly expect the government to be otherwise. But in the New World both political and economic attitudes diverged from those of mid-nineteenth-century Europe. On the one hand, while capitalists fought their workers in America, they never quite feared them as did capitalists in Europe. And on the other hand, while government in America was often tinctured with class interest, its democratic roots prevented it from ever becoming so tainted that it was no longer capable of taking any action against the wishes of the business community. Thus, capitalism in America developed in a milieu of social consensus that brought radically different results from those envisaged by Marx.

In retrospect we can see that capitalism was capable of developing in many directions, just as Communism is today. Marx himself never contended that the underlying structure of the economic system enjoined one and only one kind of legal, political, and social superstructure, but rather that the economic under-pinnings enjoined *limits* on the kind of superstructure that might be compatible with them. Thus, capitalism could give rise to societies as different—although "structurally" similar—as the France of Marcel Proust and the Germany of Thomas Mann, not to mention the United States of Sinclair Lewis and of J. P. Marquand. The tragedy is that for much of the world, and especially for so much of the Communist world, the stereotypes of English capitalism of the 1850's, with its grasping, narrow-minded Manchester millowners and its sodden and bitter working classes, is still taken as the true likeness of capitalism everywhere.

But shorn of its overtones of inevitable doom, the Marxist analysis cannot be disregarded. It remains the gravest, most penetrating examination the capitalist system has ever undergone. It is not an examination conducted along moral lines with head-wagging and tongue-clucking over the iniquities of the profit motive—this is the stuff of the Marxist revolutionary but not of the Marxist economist. For all its passion, it is a dispassionate appraisal and it is for this reason that its somber findings must be soberly considered.

To repeat an earlier statement: it is with Karl Marx the Revolutionary that the world has been preoccupied, with Marxism as an expansive force and an intellectually intolerant one. Certainly that is the immediate concern. And yet it is not with Marx the Revolutionary that capitalism must finally contend. When Khrushchev boasted that communism would "bury" capitalism, it was not military prowess but economic theory that gave him his certitude. In the end the figure who must be proven wrong is Marx the Economist, Marx the finicky scholar who laboriously sought to prove, through the welter of surface distraction, that the essence of capitalism is *self*-destruction. The answer to Marx lies not so much in pointing out the injustices of communism as in demonstrating that capitalism can continue to evolve and to adapt its institutions to the never-satisfied demands of social justice.

VII

The Victorian World
and the
Underworld of Economics

KARL MARX pronounced his sentence of doom on capitalism in 1867; the system was diagnosed as the victim of an incurable disease, and although no timetable was given, it was presumed to be close enough to its final death struggle for the next-of-kin—the Communists—to listen avidly for the last gasp that would signal their inheritance of power. Even before the appearance of *Das Kapital,* the deathwatch had begun, and with each bout of speculative fever or each siege of industrial depression, the hopeful drew nearer to the deathbed and told each other that the moment of Final Revolution would now be soon at hand.

But the system did not die. On the contrary, it seemed to emerge from each attack of weakness with renewed strength and to rebound from each crisis with a vigor that dismayed the critics. True, many of the Marxist laws of motion were amply verified by the march of events: big business did grow bigger and recurrent depressions and unemployment did plague society. But along with these confirmations of the prognosis of doom, another highly important and portentously phrased Marxist symptom was remarkable by its absence: the "increasing misery" of the proletariat failed to increase.

For Marx had believed that with the increasingly difficult struggle of the system to maintain itself, the working classes would be relentlessly ground underfoot, and that when the final death throes of capitalism were at hand, their revolutionary tempers would have snapped. With a kind of grim justice, the cruelties of capitalism would have brought into being its own executioner. And that simply failed to happen. On the contrary, a British Committee on Depression which convened to look into the slump of 1886 reported that "there is no feature in the situation which we have been called upon to examine, as satisfactory as the immense improvement which has taken place in the condition of the working class." And this was not just the patronizing cant of class apologists: conditions were better, enormously better. In 1840, according to the calculations of Arnold Toynbee, the wage of an ordinary laborer came to eight shillings a week, while his family necessaries of life cost him fourteen shillings; he made up the difference by begging, stealing, sending his children to the mills, or simply by drawing in his belt. But by 1875, although necessaries had gone to fifteen shillings and a little over, his wages had nearly drawn abreast. *For the first time* he was making enough to keep body and soul together—a sorry commentary on the past, but certainly a hopeful augury for the future.

And not only had wages gone up, but the very source of surplus value had diminished: hours were far shorter. At the Jarrow Shipyards and the New Castle Chemical Works, for example, the workweek had fallen from sixty-one to fifty-four hours, while even in the sweated textile mills, the stint was reduced to only fifty-seven hours. Indeed the millowners complained that their wage costs had risen by better than twenty per cent. But while progress was expensive, it paid intangible dividends. For as conditions ameliorated, the mutterings of 1848 died down. "You cannot get them to talk of politics so long as they are well employed," testified a Staffordshire manufacturer on the attitude of his working force.

Even Marx and Engels had to recognize the trend. "The English proletariat is becoming more and more bourgeois," mourned Engels in a letter to Marx, "so that this most bourgeois of all nations is apparently aiming ultimately at the possession of a bourgeois aristocracy and a bourgeois proletariat *as well as* a *bourgeoisie.*"

Clearly, Marx was premature in his pronouncement of impending doom. For the Faithful, of course, the unexpected turn of events could be swallowed in the comforting knowledge that "inevitable" still meant inevitable, and that a matter of a generation or two came to little in the grand march of history. But for the non-Marxist surveyors of the scene, the great Victorian boom meant something else. The world again appeared full of hope and promise and the forebodings of a dissenter like Karl Marx seemed merely the ravings of a discontented radical. Hence the great intellectual bombshell that Marx had prepared went off in almost total silence; instead of a storm of abuse, Marx met the far more crushing ignominy of indifference.

For economics had ceased to be the proliferation of world views which now in the hands of a philosopher, now a stock-broker, now a revolutionary seemed to illuminate the whole avenue down which society was marching. It became instead the special province of professors whose investigations threw out pin-point beams rather than the wide-searching beacons of the earlier economists.

There was a reason for this: as we have seen, Victorian England had caught the steady trade winds of late-nineteenth-century progress and optimism. Improvement was in the air, and so quite naturally there seemed less cause to ask disturbing questions about the nature of the voyage. Hence the Victorian boom gave rise to a roster of elucidators, men who would examine the workings of the system in greatest detail, but not to men who would express doubt as to its basic merits or make troublesome prognostications as to its eventual fate. In the new professordom, men like Alfred Marshall, Stanley Jevons, John Bates Clark, Léon Walras, Taussig, Menger—a whole faculty of economists—took over the main line of economic thought. Their contributions were often important, yet they were not vital. Perhaps this was because there were no wolves in the world of economic theory any more. There were only obedient, if imaginary, sheep.

The sheep were never more clearly delineated than in a little volume entitled *Mathematical Psychics* which appeared in 1881, just two years before Marx died. It was not written by the greatest of the academicians, but perhaps by the most revealing of them —a strange, shy professor named Francis Ysidro Edgeworth, a nephew of that Maria Edgeworth who had once played charades with Ricardo.

Edgeworth was undoubtedly a brilliant scholar. In his final examinations at Oxford, when he was asked a particularly abstruse question, he inquired of his examiners, "Shall I answer briefly, or at length?" and then proceeded to hold forth for half an hour, punctuating his reply with excursions into Greek and the differential calculus, while his examiners gaped.

But Edgeworth was not fascinated with economics because it justified or explained or condemned the world, or because it opened new vistas, bright or gloomy, into the future. This odd soul was fascinated because economics dealt with *quantities* and because anything which dealt with quantities could be translated into *mathematics!* The process of translation required the abandonment of that tension-fraught world of the earlier economists, but it yielded in return a world of such neat precision and lovely exactness that the loss seemed amply compensated.

To build up such a mathematical mirror of reality, the world obviously had to be simplified. Edgeworth's simplification was this assumption: *every man is a pleasure-machine.* Jeremy Bentham had originated the conception in the early nineteenth century under the beguiling title of the Felicific Calculus, a philosophical view of humanity as so many living profit-and-loss calculators, each busily arranging his life to maximize the pleasure of his psychic adding machine. To this general philosophy Edgeworth now added the precision of mathematics to produce a kind of economic paradise.

Of all men to have adopted such a view of mankind, Edgeworth seems a most unlikely choice. He himself was as ill-constructed a pleasure-machine as can be imagined. Neurotically shy, he tended to flee from the pleasures of human company to the presumably less pleasure-filled confines of his club; unhappy about the burden of material things, he received few of the pleasures which for most people flow from possessions. His rooms were bare, his library was the public one, and his stock of material wealth did not include crockery, or stationery, or even stamps. Perhaps his greatest source of pleasure was in the construction of his lovely imaginary economic Xanadu.

But regardless of his motives, Edgeworth's pleasure-machine assumption bore wonderful intellectual fruit. For if economics was defined to be the study of human pleasure-mechanisms competing for shares of society's stock of pleasure, then it could be shown—with all the irrefutability of the differential calculus—

that in a world of perfect competition each pleasure-machine would achieve the highest amount of pleasure that could be meted out by society.

In other words, this was the best of all possible worlds—or more accurately, it could be. Unfortunately, the world was not organized as a game of perfect competition; men did have the lamentable habit of sticking together in foolish disregard of the beneficent consequences of stubbornly following their self-interest: trade-unions, for example, were in direct controversion to the principles of each for himself, and the undeniable fact of inequalities of wealth and position did make the starting position of the game something less than absolutely neutral.

But never mind, said Edgeworth. Nature has taken care of that, too. While trade-unions might gain in the short run through combination, it could be shown that in the long run they must lose—they were only a regrettable imperfection in the ideal scheme of things. And if high birth and great wealth seemed at first to prejudice the outcome of the economic game, that could be reconciled with mathematical psychics, too. For while all men were pleasure-machines, some men were *better* pleasure-machines than others. Men, for example, were better equipped to run up their psychic bank accounts than women, and the delicate sensibilities of the "aristocracy of skill and talent" were more responsive to the pleasures of good living than the clodlike pleasure-machines of the laboring classes. Hence, the calculus of human mathematics could still function advantageously; indeed it positively justified those divisions of sex and status which one saw about him in the living world.

But mathematical psychics did more than rationalize the tenets of conservatism. Edgeworth actually believed that his algebraic insight into human activity might yield helpful results in the world of flesh and blood. As he wrote his book, a bloody struggle was going on between the landlords and Irish peasants, and Edgeworth looked into the matter in a chapter entitled "The Present Crisis in Ireland." His analysis involved such terms as these:

$$\frac{d^2y}{dx^2} = \frac{\left(\frac{\partial\pi}{\partial x}\right)^2\left(\frac{\partial^2\pi}{\partial y^2}\right) - 2\frac{\partial\pi}{\partial x}\frac{\partial\pi}{\partial y}\left(\frac{\partial^2\pi}{\partial x\partial y}\right) + \left(\frac{\partial\pi}{\partial y}\right)^2\left(\frac{\partial^2\pi}{\partial x^2}\right)}{-\left(\frac{\partial\pi}{\partial y}\right)^3}$$

"Considerations so abstract," wrote Edgeworth, "it would of course be ridiculous to fling upon the floodtide of practical politics. But they are not perhaps out of place when we remount to the little rills of sentiment and secret springs of motive where every course of action must be originated."

"The little rills of sentiment," indeed! What would Adam Smith have thought of this conversion of his pushy merchants, his greedy journeymen, and his multiplying laboring classes into so many categories of effete pleasure-seekers? Indeed, Henry Sidgwick, a contemporary of Edgeworth's and a disciple of J. S. Mill, angrily announced that he did not eat his dinner because he had toted up the satisfactions to be gained therefrom, but because he was hungry. But there was no use protesting: the scheme of mathematical psychics was so neat, so beguiling, so bereft of troublesome human intransigences, and so happily unbesmirched with considerations of human striving and social conflict, that its success was immediate.

Edgeworth's was not the only such attempt to dehumanize political economy. Even during Marx's lifetime a whole mathematical school of economics had grown up. In Germany an economist named von Thünen came up with a formula which yielded, he claimed, the precise just wage of labor:

$$\sqrt{a \cdot p}$$

Von Thünen liked it well enough to have it engraved on his tombstone; we do not know what the workingmen thought of it. In France a distinguished economist named Léon Walras proved that one could deduce by mathematics the exact prices which would just exactly clear the market: of course, in order to do this one had to have the equation for every single economic good on the market and then the ability to solve a problem in which the number of equations would run into the hundreds of thousands. But never mind the difficulties; the problem could theoretically be done. At the University of Manchester, a professor named W. Stanley Jevons wrote a textbook on economics (it is suggestive that political economy was now called economics, and that its expositions were now texts) in which general depressions were dismissed as "evidently absurd and self-contradictory" and the struggle for existence was reduced to "a Calculus of Pleasure and Pain." "My theory of Economics . . . is purely mathematical in character," wrote Jevons, and he turned out of his focus every aspect of economic life which was not reducible to the jigsaw precision of his scheme.

It was not all foolishness, although certainly much of it was. Economics, after all, does concern the actions of aggregates of people, and human aggregates, like aggregates of atoms, do tend to conform to statistical rules and the laws of probability. The mathematical school did unearth points of interest which the earlier economists, with their eyes on the horizon, had hurried over. But the trouble was, the psychic mathematicians too often forgot that the rules of behavior which underlay their equations were convenient assumptions rather than actually observed activity. They built a kind of ideal menagerie, in which, as it were, intelligent monkeys were taught to count, given money, and set up in business for themselves. While the official observers were busy predicting the resultant price for bananas, they forgot to ask whether trained monkeys in the zoo really behaved like their unrestrained cousins in the jungle.

There were exceptions, of course. Léon Walras, the French economist who was fascinated by the mathematical analysis of markets, did not fall into the tempting error of mistaking his arithmetic for the world. While he developed his equations—far too complex to be solved in actuality—he was careful to stress that this was a tool, a method of inquiry, and not a statement of things as they actually were or should be. In point of fact, Walras was an agrarian socialist and a proponent of ideas far more radical than his dignified counterparts in the British Isles. For him—and for the later generations of economists who would profit by his work—mathematics was an avenue for unraveling such recurrent but elusive words as "equilibrium," and not a mere game to be played for the intellectual hurdles it presented.

But Walras was the exception. For the most part, the official world saw humanity as so many accountants constantly engaged in the careful calculation of their behavior into debits of pain and credits of pleasure. Whether such pallid motives were sufficient to describe and account for the turbulent past or even the placid present was a question which did not seem to matter.

And so, as a counterpart to this pale world of equations, an underworld of economics flourished. There had always been such an underworld, a strange limbo of cranks and heretics, whose doctrines had failed to attain the stature of respectability. One such was Bernard Mandeville who had shocked the eighteenth century with a witty demonstration that virtue was vice and vice virtue. Mandeville merely pointed out that the profligate expenditure of the sinful rich gave work to the poor, while the stingy rectitude of the virtuous penny pincher did not; hence, said Mandeville, private immorality may redound to the public welfare, whereas private uprightness may be a social burden. The sophisticated lesson of his *Fable of the Bees* was too much for the eighteenth century to swallow; Mandeville's book was convicted as a public nuisance by a grand jury in Middlesex in 1723, and Mandeville himself was thus consigned to economic limbo.

But whereas the earlier eccentrics and charlatans were largely banished by the opinions of some sturdy thinker like Smith or Ricardo, now the underworld claimed its recruits for a different reason. There was simply no longer any room in the official world of economics for those who wanted to take the whole burly gamut of human behavior for their forum, and there was little tolerance in the stuffy world of Victorian correctness for those whose diagnosis of society left room for moral doubtings or seemed to indicate the need for radical reform.

And so the underworld took on new life. Marx went there because his doctrine was unpleasant and full of the kind of behavior which would never do in a well-mannered zoo. Malthus went there because his idea of "general gluts" was an arithmetical absurdity and because his doubts about the benefits of saving were totally at variance with the Victorian admiration for thrift. The Utopians went there because what they were talking about was arrant nonsense and wasn't "economics" anyway, and finally anyone went there whose doctrine failed to accord with the dry and elegant world which the academicians erected in their classrooms and fondly believed existed outside them.

It was a far more interesting place, this underworld, than the serene realms above. It abounded with wonderful personalities and in it sprouted a weird and luxuriant tangle of ideas. There was, for example, a man who has been almost forgotten in the march of economic ideas. He is Frédéric Bastiat, a delightful Frenchman, who lived from 1801 to 1850, and who in that short space of time and an even shorter space of literary life—six years —brought to bear on economics that most devastating of all weapons, ridicule. Look at this madhouse of a world, says Bastiat. It goes to enormous efforts to tunnel underneath a mountain in order to connect two countries. And then what does it do? Having labored mightily to facilitate the interchanges of goods, it sets up customs guards on both sides of the mountain and makes it as difficult as possible for merchandise to travel through the tunnel!

Bastiat had a gift for pointing out absurdities; his little book *Economic Sophisms* is as close to humor as economics has ever come. When, for example, the Paris-Madrid railroad was being debated in the French Assembly, one M. Simiot argued that it should have a gap at Bordeaux, because a break in the line there would redound greatly to the wealth of the Bordeaux porters, commissionaires, hotelkeepers, bargemen, and the like, and thus, by enriching Bordeaux, would enrich France. Bastiat seized on the idea with avidity. Fine, he said, but let's not stop at Bordeaux alone. "If Bordeaux has a right to profit by a gap . . . then Angoulême, Poitiers, Tours, Orléans . . . should also demand gaps as being for the general interest. . . . In this way we shall succeed in having a railway composed of successive gaps, and which may be denominated a *Negative Railway*."

Bastiat was a wit in the world of economics, but his private life was tragic. Born in Bayonne, he was orphaned at an early age and, worse yet, contracted tuberculosis of the lungs. He studied at a university, and then tried business, but he had no head for commercial details. He turned to agriculture, but he fared equally badly there; like Tolstoi's well-meaning count, the more he interfered in the running of his family estate, the worse it did. He dreamed of heroism, but his military adventures had a Don Quixote twist: when the Bourbons were run out of France in 1830, Bastiat rounded up six hundred young men and led them to storm a royalist citadel, regardless of cost. Poor Bastiat —the fortress meekly hauled down its flag and invited everyone in for a feast instead.

It seemed that he was doomed to disappointment. But his enforced idleness turned his interests to economics and he began to read and discuss the topics of the day. A neighboring country gentleman urged him to put his ideas on paper and Bastiat wrote an article on free trade and sent it in to a Parisian journal. His thoughts were original and his style wonderfully sharp. The article was printed and overnight this mild scholar of the provinces was famous.

He came to Paris. "He had not had time to call in the assistance of a Parisian hatter and tailor," writes M. de Molinari, "and with his long hair, his tiny hat, his ample frock-coat and his family umbrella, you would have been apt to mistake him for an honest peasant who came to town for the first time to see the metropolis."

But the country scholar had a pen that bit. Every day he read the Paris papers in which the deputies and ministers of France argued for and defended their policies of selfishness and blind self-interest; then he would answer with a rejoinder that rocked Paris with laughter. For example, when the Chamber of Deputies in the 1840's legislated higher duties on all foreign goods in order to benefit French industry, Bastiat turned out this masterpiece of economic satire:

PETITION OF THE MANUFACTURERS OF CANDLES, WAXLIGHTS, LAMPS, CANDLESTICKS, STREET LAMPS, SNUFFERS, EXTINGUISHERS, AND OF THE PRODUCERS OF OIL, TALLOW, RESIN, ALCOHOL, AND GENERALLY EVERYTHING CONNECTED WITH LIGHTING

To Messieurs the Members of the Chamber of Deputies

Gentlemen,

. . . We are suffering from the intolerable competition of a foreign rival, placed, it would seem, in a condition so far superior to our own for the production of light, that he absolutely *inundates* our *national market* with it at a price fabulously reduced. . . . This rival . . . is no other than the sun.

What we pray for, is, that it may please you to pass a law ordering the shutting up of all windows, skylights, dormer-windows, outside and inside shutters, curtains, blinds, bull's-eyes; in a word of all openings, holes, chinks, and fissures.

. . . If you shut up as much as possible all access to natural light and create a demand for artificial light, which of our French manufacturers will not benefit by it?

. . . If more tallow is consumed, then there must be more oxen and sheep . . . if more oil is consumed, then we shall have extended cultivation of the poppy, of the olive . . . , our heaths will be covered with resinous trees.

Make your choice, but be logical; for as long as you exclude, as you do, iron, corn, foreign fabrics, *in proportion* as their prices approximate to zero, what inconsistency it would be to admit the light of the sun, the price of which is already at *zero* during the entire day!

A more effective—if fantastic—defense of free trade has never been written. But it was not only against protective tariffs that Bastiat protested: this man laughed at every form of economic double-thinking. In 1848, when the Socialists began to propound their ideas for the salvation of society with more regard for passion than practicability, Bastiat turned against them the same weapons that he had used against the *ancien régime*. "Everyone wants to live at the expense of the state," he wrote. "They forget that the state lives at the expense of everyone."

But his special target, his most hated "sophism," was the rationalization of private greed under the pretentious cover of a protective tariff erected for the "national good." How he loved to demolish the specious thinking that argued for barriers to trade under the guise of liberal economics! When the French ministry proposed to raise the duty on imported cloth to "protect" the French workingman, Bastiat replied with this delicious paradox:

"Pass a law to this effect," wrote Bastiat to the Minister of Commerce. "No one shall henceforth be permitted to employ any beams or rafters but such as are produced and fashioned by blunt hatchets. . . . Whereas at present we give a hundred blows of the axe, we shall then give three hundred. The work which we now do in an hour will then require three hours. What a powerful

encouragement will thus be given to labor! . . . Whoever shall
henceforth desire to have a roof to cover him must comply with
our exactions, just as at present whoever desires clothes to his
back must comply with yours."

His criticisms, for all their penetrating mockery, met with little
practical success. He went to England to meet the leaders of the
free-trade movement there and returned to organize a free-trade
association in Paris. It lasted only eighteen months—Bastiat was
never any good as an organizer.

But 1848 was now at hand and Bastiat was elected to the National Assembly. By then the danger seemed to him the other extreme—that men would pay too much attention to the imperfections of the system and would blindly choose socialism in its
stead. He began a book entitled *Economic Harmonies* in which
he was to show that the apparent disorder of the world was a
disorder of the surface only; that underneath, the impetus of a
thousand different self-seeking agents became transmuted in the
market place into a higher social good. But his health was now
disastrously bad. He could barely breathe and his face was livid
with the ravages of his disease. He moved to Pisa where he read
in the papers of his own death and of the commonplace expres-
sions of regret which accompanied it: regret at the passing of "the
great economist," the "illustrious author." He wrote a friend:
"Thank God I am not dead. I assure you I should breathe my
last without pain and almost wish joy if I were certain of leaving
to the friends who love me, not poignant regrets, but a gentle,
affectionate, somewhat melancholy remembrance of me." He
struggled to finish his book before he himself should be finished.
But it was too late. In 1850 he passed away, whispering at the
end something that the listening priest thought was "Truth,
truth . . ."

He is a very small figure in the economic constellation. He
was not a fanatic, not a crusading reformer, not even a major
system-builder. His function, it seems, was to prick the pom-
posities of his time; but beneath the raillery and the wit lies the
more disturbing question: does the system always make sense?
Are there paradoxes where the public and private weals collide?
Can we trust the automatic mechanism of private interest when

it is perverted at every turn by the far from automatic mechanism of the political structure it erects?

The questions were never squarely faced in the Elysian fields above. The work of J. S. Mill was now the Bible and the official world of economics took little notice of the paradoxes proposed by its jester. Instead it sailed serenely on toward the development of the quantitative niceties of a pleasure-seeking world and the questions raised by Bastiat remained unanswered. Certainly mathematical psychics was hardly the tool with which to unlock the dilemma of the Negative Railway and the Blunt Hatchet; Stanley Jevons, who with Edgeworth was the great proponent of making economics a "science," admitted, "About politics, I confess myself in a fog." Unfortunately, he was not alone.

And so the underworld continued to prosper. In 1879 it gained an American recruit, a bearded, gentle, fiercely self-sure man, who said that "Political Economy . . . as currently taught *is* hopeless and despairing. But this [is] because she has been degraded and shackled; her truths dislocated; her harmonies ignored; the word she would utter gagged in her mouth, and her protest against wrong turned into an indorsement of injustice." And that was not all. For this heretic not only maintained that economics had failed to see the answer to the riddle of poverty although it was clearly laid out before her eyes, but that with his remedy, a whole new world stood ready to unfold: "Words fail the thought! It is the Golden Age of which poets have sung and high-raised seers have told in metaphor! . . . It is the culmination of Christianity—the city of God with its walls of jasper and its gates of pearl!"

The newcomer was Henry George. No wonder he was in the underworld, for his early career must certainly have seemed an uncouth preparation for serious thinking to the cloistered keepers of the true doctrine. Henry George had been everything in life: adventurer, gold prospector, worker, sailor, compositor, journalist, government bureaucrat, and lecturer. He had never even gone to college; at thirteen he had left school to ship out as foremast boy on the 586-ton *Hindoo* bound for Australia and Calcutta. At a time when his contemporaries were learning Latin, he had bought a pet monkey and watched a man fall from the rigging, and become a thin, intense, independent boy with a wanderlust. Back from the East, he tried a job in a printing firm in his home town of Philadelphia, and then at nineteen, shipped out again, this time to California, with the thought of gold in mind.

Before he left, he rated himself on a phrenological chart:

Amativeness	large
Philoprogenitiveness	moderate
Adhesiveness	large
Inhabitiveness	large
Concentrativeness	small

and so on, with a rating of "full" on Alimentativeness, "small" on Acquisitiveness, "large" on Self-esteem, and "small" on Mirthfulness. It was not a bad estimate in some respects—although it is odd to see Caution rated "large," for when George reached San Francisco in 1858 he skipped ashore, although he had signed on for a year, and headed for Victoria and gold. He found gold—but it was fool's gold, and he decided the life at sea was the life for him after all. Instead—his bump of Concentrativeness being small—he became a typesetter in a San Francisco shop, then a weigher in a rice mill, then, in his own words, "a tramp." Another trek to the gold fields was equally unrewarding, and he returned to San Francisco impoverished.

He met Annie Fox, and she appealed to his Amativeness. He eloped with her; she was a seventeen-year-old innocent and he a handsome young lad with a Bill Cody mustache and pointed beard. The trusting young Miss Fox took with her a bulky package on her secret marriage flight; the young adventurer thought it might be jewels, but it turned out to be only the *Household Book of Poetry* and other volumes.

There followed years of the most wretched poverty. Henry George was an odd-job printer and work was hard to come by and ill-paid at best. When Annie had her second child, George wrote: "I walked along the street and made up my mind to get money from the first man whose appearance might indicate he had it to give. I stopped a man—a stranger—and told him I wanted $5. He asked me what I wanted it for. I told him my wife was confined and that I had nothing to give her to eat. He gave me the money. If he had not, I think I was desperate enough to have killed him."

Now—at age twenty-six—he began to write. He landed a job in the composing room of the San Francisco *Times* and sent a piece upstairs to Noah Brooks, the editor. Brooks suspected that the boy had copied it, but when nothing resembling it appeared in any of the other newspapers for several days he printed it, and then went downstairs to look for George. He found him, a slight young man, rather undersized, standing on a board to raise himself to the height of his type case. George became a reporter.

Within a few years he left the *Times* to join the San Francisco *Post*, a crusading journal. George began to write about matters of more than routine interest: about the Chinese coolies and their indenture, and about the land-grabbing of the railroads, and the machinations of the local trusts. He wrote a long letter to J. S. Mill in France on the immigration question and was graced with a long affirmative reply. And in between his newly found political interest he had time for ventures in the best journalistic tradition: when the ship *Sunrise* came to town with a hushed-up story about a captain and mate who had hounded their crew until two men had leaped overboard to their death, George and the *Post* ferreted out the story and brought the officers to justice.

The newspaper was sold, and Henry George wangled himself a political sinecure—Inspector of Gas Meters. It was not that he wanted a life of leisure; rather, he had begun to read the great economists and his central interest was now clearly formed—already he was a kind of local authority. He needed time to study and to write and to deliver lectures to the working classes on the ideas of the great Mill.

When the University of California established a chair of political economy, he was widely considered as a strong candidate for the post. But to qualify he had to deliver a lecture before faculty and students and George was rash enough to voice such sentiments as this: "The name of political economy has been constantly invoked against every effort of the working classes to increase their wages," and then to compound the shock he added: "For the study of political economy, you need no special knowledge, no extensive library, no costly laboratory. You do not even need text-books nor teachers, if you will but think for yourselves."

That was the beginning and the end of his academic career.

A more suitable candidate was found for the post and George went back to pamphleteering and study. And then suddenly, "in daylight and in a city street, there came to me a thought, a vision, a call—give it what name you please. . . . It was that that impelled me to write *Progress and Poverty* and that sustained me when else I should have failed. And when I had finished the last page, in the dead of night, when I was entirely alone, I flung myself on my knees and wept like a child."

As might be expected, it was a book written from the heart, a cry of mingled protest and hope. And as might also be expected, it suffered from too much passion and too little professorial circumspection. But what a contrast to the dull texts of the day—no wonder the guardians of economics could not seriously consider an argument which was couched in such a style as this:

> Take now . . . some hard-headed business man, who has no theories, but knows how to make money. Say to him: "Here is a little village; in ten years it will be a great city—in ten years the railroad will have taken the place of the stage coach, the electric light of the candle; it will abound with all the machinery and improvements that so enormously multiply the effective power of labor. Will, in ten years, interest be any higher?"
>
> He will tell you, "No!"
>
> "Will the wages of common labor be any higher . . . ?"
>
> He will tell you, "No, the wages of common labor will not be any higher. . . ."
>
> "What, then, will be higher?"
>
> "Rent, the value of land. Go, get yourself a piece of ground, and hold possession."
>
> And if, under such circumstances, you take his advice, you need do nothing more. You may sit down and smoke your pipe; you may lie around like the *lazzaroni* of Naples or the *leperos* of Mexico; you may go up in a balloon or down a hole in the ground; and without doing one stroke of work, without adding one iota of wealth to the community, in ten

years you will be rich! In the new city you may have a luxuri-
ous mansion, but among its public buildings will be an
almshouse.

We need not spell out the whole emotionally charged argument: the crux of it lies in this passage. Henry George is outraged at the spectacle of men whose incomes—sometimes fabulous
incomes—derive not from the services they have rendered the
community, but merely from the fact that they have had the good
fortune to hold advantageously situated soil.

Ricardo, of course, saw all this long before him. But at best,
Ricardo had only claimed that the tendency of a growing society
to enrich the holders of its land would redound to the misfortune
of the capitalist. To Henry George, this was only the entering
wedge. The injustice of rents not only robbed the capitalist of
his honest profit but weighed on the shoulders of the workingman as well. More damaging yet, he found it to be the cause of
those industrial "paroxysms," as he called them, which from time
to time shook society to its roots.

The argument was not too clearly delineated. Primarily it
rested on the fact that since rent was assumed from the start to
be a kind of social extortion, naturally it represented an unfair
distribution of produce to landlords at the expense of workers
and industrialists. And as for the paroxysms—well, George was
convinced that rent led inevitably to wild speculation in land
values (as indeed it did on the West Coast) and just as inevitably
to an eventual collapse which would bring the rest of the structure of prices tumbling down beside it.

Having discovered the true causes of poverty and the fundamental check to progress, it was simple for George to propose the
remedy. It would consist of one single massive tax on land, a
tax which would absorb all rents. And then, with the cancer
removed from the body of society, the millennium could be
allowed to come. The single tax would not only dispense with
the need for all other kinds of taxes, but in abolishing rent it
would "raise wages, increase the earnings of capital, extirpate
pauperism, abolish poverty, give remunerative employment to
whoever wishes it, afford free scope to human powers, purify

government, and carry civilization to yet nobler heights." It would be—there is no other word—the ultimate panacea.

It is an elusive thesis when we seek to evaluate it. Of course it is naïve, and the equation of rent with sin could only have occurred to someone as messianic as George himself. Similarly, to put the blame for industrial depressions on land speculation is to blow up one small aspect of an expanding economy quite out of proportion to reality: land speculations can be troublesome, but severe depressions have taken place in countries where land values were anything but inflated.

No, we need not linger here. But when we come to the central body of the thesis, we must pause. For while George's mechanical diagnosis is superficial and faulty, his basic criticism of society is a moral and not a mechanistic one. Why, asks Henry George, should rent exist? Why should a man benefit merely from the brute fact of ownership, when he may render no services to the community in exchange? We may justify the rewards of an industrialist by describing his profits as the prize for his foresight and ingenuity, but where is the foresight of a man whose grandfather owned a pasture on which, two generations later, society saw fit to erect a skyscraper?

The question is provocative, but it is not so easy to condemn the institution of rent out of hand. For landlords are not the only passive beneficiaries of the growth of society. The stockholder in an expanding company, the workman whose productivity is enhanced by technical progress, the consumer whose real income rises as the nation prospers, all these are also beneficiaries of communal advancement. The unearned gains which accrue to a well-situated landlord are enjoyed in different forms by all of us. The problem is not just that of rents, but of all unearned income, and while this may be a serious problem, it cannot be adequately approached through land ownership alone.

And then the problem is not so drastic as it was viewed by Henry George. A vast body of rents goes to small landholders, farmers, homeowners, modest citizens. And even in the monopolistic area of rental incomes—in the real-estate operations of a metropolis—a shifting and fluid market is in operation. Rents are not frozen in archaic feudal patterns, but constantly pass from hand to hand as land is bought and sold, appraised and reappraised. Suffice it to point out that rental income in the United States has shrunk from six per cent of the national income in 1929 to only three per cent in the 1960's.

But no matter whether the thesis held together logically or whether its moral condemnation was fully justified. The book struck a tremendously responsive chord. *Progress and Poverty* became a best seller and overnight Henry George was catapulted into national prominence. "I consider *Progress and Poverty* as *the* book of this half-century," said the reviewer in the San Francisco *Argonaut,* and the New York *Tribune* claimed that it had "no equal since the publication of the *Wealth of Nations* by Adam Smith." Even those publications like the *Examiner* and *Chronicle,* which called it "the most pernicious treatise on political economy that has been published for many a day," only served to enhance its fame.

George went to England; he returned after a lecture tour an international figure. He was drafted to run for mayor of New York and in a three-cornered race he beat Theodore Roosevelt and only narrowly lost to the Tammany candidate.

The single tax was a religion to him now. He organized Land and Labor Clubs and lectured to enthusiastic audiences here and in Great Britain. A friend asked him, "Does this not mean war? Can you, unless dealing with craven conditions among men, hope to take land away from its owners without war?" "I do not see," said George, "that a musket need be fired. But if necessary, war be it, then. There was never a holier cause. No, never a holier cause!"

"Here was the gentlest and kindest of men," comments his friend, James Russell Taylor, "who would shrink from a gun fired in anger, ready for universal war rather than that his gospel should not be accepted. It was the courage . . . which makes one a majority."

Needless to say, the whole doctrine was anathema to the world of respectable opinion. A Catholic priest who had associated himself with George in his mayoralty fight was temporarily excommunicated; the Pope himself addressed an encyclical to the land question and when George sent him an elaborately printed and bound reply, it was ignored. "I will not insult my readers by discussing a project so steeped in infamy," wrote General Francis

A. Walker, a leading professional economist in the United States; but while officialdom looked at his book with shock or with amused contempt, the man himself struck home to his audience. *Progress and Poverty* sold more copies than all the economic texts previously published in the country; in England, his name became a household word. Not only that, but the import of his ideas—albeit usually in watered form—became part of the heritage of men like Woodrow Wilson, John Dewey, Louis Brandeis. Indeed there is a devoted following of Henry George's still active today.

In 1897, old, unwell but still indomitable, he permitted himself to be drafted for a second mayoralty race, knowing full well that the strain of the campaign might be too much for his failing heart. It was; he was called "marauder," "assailant of other people's right," "apostle of anarchy and destruction," and he did die, on the eve of the election. His funeral was attended by thousands. He was a religious man; let us hope that his soul went straight to heaven. As for his reputation—that went straight into the underworld of economics and there he exists today; almost-Messiah, semicrackpot, and disturbing questioner of the morality of our world.

But something else was going on in the underworld, something more important than Henry George's fulminations against rent and his ecstatic vision of a City of God to be built on the foundation of the single tax. A new and vigorous spirit was sweeping England and the Continent and even the United States, a spirit which manifested itself in the proliferation of such slogans as "The Anglo-Saxon race is infallibly destined to be the predominant force in the history and civilization of the world." The spirit was not confined to England: across the Channel, Victor Hugo declared, "France is needed by humanity"; in Russia the spokesman for absolutism, Konstantin Pobyedonostsev, proclaimed that Russia's freedom from the taint of Western decadence had given her the accolade of leadership for the East. In Germany the Kaiser was explaining how *der alte Gott* was on their side, and in the New World Theodore Roosevelt was making himself the American spokesman for a similar philosophy.

The age of imperialism had begun, and the map makers were

busy changing the colors which denoted the ownership of the darker continents. Between 1870 and 1898 Britain added 4 million square miles and 88 million people to its empire; France gained nearly the same area of territory with 40 million souls attached; Germany won a million miles and 16 million colonials; Belgium took 900,000 miles and 30 million people; even Portugal joined the race with 800,000 miles of new lands and 9 million inhabitants.

In truth, three generations had changed the face of the earth. But more than that, they had witnessed an equally remarkable change in the attitude with which the West viewed that process of change. In the days of Adam Smith, it will be remembered, the Scots philosopher regarded with scorn the attempts of merchants to play the role of kings, and he urged the independence of the American colonies. And Smith's contempt for colonies was widely shared: James Mill, the father of John Stuart Mill, called the colonies "a vast system of outdoor relief for the upper classes," and even Disraeli in 1852 had put himself on record as believing that "these wretched colonies are millstones around our necks."

But now all this had changed. Britain had acquired her empire, as it had frequently been remarked, in a fit of absent-mindedness, but absent-mindedness was replaced by single-mindedness as the pace of imperialism accelerated. Lord Rosebery epitomized the sentiment of the day when he called the British Empire "the greatest secular agency for good the world has ever known." "Yes," said Mark Twain, watching a Jubilee procession for Queen Victoria which proudly displayed the pomp of England's possessions, "the English are mentioned in Scripture—'Blessed are the meek, for they shall inherit the earth.' "

By most people, the race for empire was approvingly regarded. In England, Kipling was its poet laureate, and the popular sentiment was that of the music-hall song:

> We don't want to fight, but by jingo if we do,
> We've got the ships, we've got the men, we've got the money too!

Another, rather different nod of approval came from those who agreed with Sir Charles Crossthwaite that the real question between Britain and Siam was "who was to get the trade with them, and how we could make the most of them, so as to find fresh markets for our goods and also employment for those superfluous articles of the present day, our boys."

And then, too, the process of empire building brought with it prosperity for the empire builders. No small part of the gain in working-class conditions which had so pleased the Committee on Depression was the result of sweated labor overseas: the colonies were now the proletariat's proletariat. No wonder imperialism was a popular policy.

Throughout all of this, the officialdom of economics stood to one side, watching the process of imperial growth with equanimity, and confining its remarks to the effect which new possessions might have on the course of trade. So again it was the underworld which fastened on this new phenomenon of history with fascination. For as they looked at the world-wide race for domination, they saw something very different from the mere exciting clash of politics or the inexplicable whims of personalities in power.

They saw a whole new direction to the drift of capitalism; in fact, they saw imperialism as signaling a change in the fundamental character of capitalism itself. More portentous yet, they divined in the new restless process of expansion the most dangerous development which capitalism had yet undergone—a development which led to war.

It was a mild-mannered heretic who made this charge, the product, as he described himself, of "the middle stratum of the middle class of a middle-sized town of the Midlands." John A. Hobson was a frail little man, much worried over his health and plagued by an impediment in his speech which made him nervous about lecturing. Born in 1858, he prepared for an academic career at Oxford; and by all we know of his background and personality (which is not much, for this shy and retiring man even managed successfully to avoid *Who's Who*), he was destined for the cloistered anonymity of English public-school life.

Two factors intervened. He read the works of Ruskin, the British critic and essayist who mocked at the bourgeois Victorian canons of monetary value and who trumpeted, "Wealth is life!" From Ruskin, Hobson acquired an idea of economics as a hu-

manist rather than a scholastic science; and he turned from the
dry refinement of orthodox doctrine to the exciting construction
of a world where cooperative labor guilds would give a higher
value to human personality than the crass world of wages and
profits. Like all Utopians, Hobson insisted that his scheme was
not utopian; on the contrary it was, he claimed, "as certain as a
proposition in Euclid."

As a Utopian he might have been respectable; the English like
eccentrics. It was as a heretic, a trampler on the virtues of tradition, that he became an economic pariah. Chance threw him
into the company of a person called A. F. Mummery, an independent thinker, a successful businessman, and an intrepid mountain climber (he was to meet his death in 1895 on the heights of
Nanga Parbat). "My intercourse with him, I need hardly say,"
writes Hobson, "did not lie on this physical plane. But he was a
mental climber as well. . . ." Mummery had speculated as to the
cause of those periodic slumps in trade which had worried the
business community as far back as the early eighteenth century,
and he had an idea as to their origin, which was, as Hobson put
it, considered by the professordom "as equivalent in rationality
to an attempt to prove the flatness of the earth." For Mummery,
hearkening back to Malthus, thought that the cause of depression lay in the fact of excessive *saving,* in the chronic inability
of the business system to distribute enough purchasing power to
buy its own products back.

Hobson argued at first and then became convinced that Mummery was right. The two wrote *The Physiology of Industry,* setting forth their heretical notion that savings might undermine
prosperity. But this was too much for the official world to swallow. Had not all the great economists, from Adam Smith on-
ward, stressed the fact that saving was only one side of the
golden coin of accumulation? Did not every act of saving automatically add to the fund of capital which was used to put more
people to work? To say that saving might result in unemployment was not only nonsense of the most arrant kind, but it was
positively inimical to one of the legs of social stability—thrift.
The economic world was shocked: the London University Extension Lectures found that they could manage to dispense with
Mr. Hobson's presence; the Charity Organization Society with-

drew an invitation to speak. The scholar had become a heretic and the heretic now became, perforce, an outcast.

All this seems considerably removed from the problem of imperialism. But ideas germinate in devious ways. Hobson's exclusion from the world of respectability led him into the path of social criticism, and the social critic now turned his attention to the great political problem of the day: Africa.

The background of the African problem was complex and emotional. Dutch settlers had set up their independent states in the Transvaal country in 1836, solid communities of "Kaffir-flogging, Bible-reading" farmers. But the land they chose, wide and sunny and exhilarating as it was, hid more wealth than it displayed. In 1869 diamonds were discovered; in 1885 gold. Within a few years the pace of an oxcart settlement was transformed into the frenzied excitement of a community of speculators. Cecil Rhodes appeared on the scene with his projects of railroads and industry; in a moment of madness he sanctioned a raid into the Transvaal and the long-strained tempers of both English and Dutch burst their bonds. The Boer War began.

Hobson had already gone to Africa. This "most timorous of God's creatures," as he called himself, traveled to Capetown and Johannesburg, talked with Kruger and Smuts, and finally dined with Rhodes himself on the eve of the Transvaal raid. Rhodes was a complicated and perplexing personality. Two years before his African adventure, a journalist had quoted him as saying:

"I was in the East End of London yesterday and attended a meeting of the unemployed. I listened to the wild speeches, which were just a cry for 'bread,' 'bread,' 'bread' and on my way home I pondered over the scene. . . . My cherished idea is a solution for the social problems; i.e., in order to save the 40,000,-000 inhabitants of the United Kingdom from a bloody civil war, we colonial statesmen must acquire new lands to settle the surplus population, to provide new markets for the goods produced by them in the factories and mines. The Empire, as I have always said, is a bread and butter question."

We do not know whether he expounded the same sentiments to Hobson; the probabilities are that he did. But it would have made little difference. For what Hobson saw in Africa dovetailed in the most unexpected way with the economic heresy of which he and Mummery had been convicted: the theory of oversaving.

He returned to Britain to write about jingoism and the war in Africa and then in 1902 he presented the world with a book in which his African observations were strangely melded with his heretical views.

The book was called *Imperialism;* it was a devastating volume. For here was the most important and searing criticism which had ever been levied against the profit system. The worst that Marx had claimed was that the system would destroy itself; what Hobson suggested was that it might destroy the world. He saw the process of imperialism as a relentless and restless tendency of capitalism to rescue itself from a self-imposed dilemma, a tendency which necessarily involved foreign commercial conquest and which thereby inescapably involved a constant risk of war. No more profound moral indictment had ever been posed than the charge that the price of the survival of a system was the death of those who lived within it.

What was the substance of Hobson's charge?

It was an argument almost Marxian in its impersonality and inexorable development (although Hobson had no sympathy for the Marxists and their aims). It claimed that capitalism faced an internal and insoluble difficulty and that it was forced to turn to imperialism, not out of a pure lust for conquest, but as a means of ensuring its own economic survival.

That internal capitalist difficulty was an aspect of the system which had received surprisingly little attention in the past—capitalism's unequal distribution of wealth. The fact that the workings of the profit system very often resulted in the rich getting richer and the poor getting children had long been a topic for moral concern, but its *economic* consequences were left for Hobson to point out.

The consequence he saw was most surprising. The inequality of incomes led to the strangest of dilemmas—a paradoxical situation in which neither rich nor poor could consume enough goods. The poor could not consume enough because their incomes were too small, and the rich could not consume enough because their incomes were too big! In other words, said Hobson, in order to clear its own market, an economy must consume everything that it makes: each good must have a buyer. Now if the poor cannot afford to take more than the bare essentials, who is there to take the rest? Obviously, the rich. But while the rich have the money, they lack the physical capacity for *that* much consumption: a man with a million-dollar income would have to consume goods worth a thousand times those bought by a man with only a thousand dollars to spend.

And so, as a consequence of an inequitable division of wealth, the rich—both individuals and corporations—were *forced* to save. They saved not only because most of them wished to, anyway, but because they could not very well help themselves—their incomes were simply too large to be consumed.

And it was this saving that led to trouble. The automatic savings of the rich strata of society had to be put to use, unless the economy was to suffer from the disastrous effects of a steady withdrawal of purchasing power. But the question was *how* to put the savings to work. The classical answer was to invest them in ever more factories and more production and thus to ascend to an even higher level of output and productivity: Smith, Ricardo, Mill, all the great economists agreed on this solution to the problem. But Hobson saw a difficulty in the way. For if the mass of the people were *already* having trouble buying all the goods thrown on the market because their incomes were too small, how, he asked, could a sensible capitalist invest in equipment which would throw still more goods on an overcrowded market? What would be gained from investing savings in another shoe factory, let us say, when the market was already swamped with more shoes than could be readily absorbed? What was to be done?

The answer was devilishly neat. The automatic savings of the rich could be invested in one way which would put them to use without the troublesome accompaniment of more production at home. They could be invested overseas.

And this is the genesis of imperialism. It is, wrote Hobson, "the endeavor of the great controllers of industry to broaden the channel for the flow of their surplus wealth by seeking foreign markets and foreign investments to take off the goods and capital they cannot use at home."

The result is disastrous. It is not one nation only which is sending its surplus wealth abroad. All nations are in the same boat. Hence there ensues a race to partition the world, with each nation trying to fence off for its investors the richest and most lucrative markets it can seize. Thus Africa becomes a huge market (and a source of cheap raw materials) to be split among the capitalists of England and Germany and Italy and Belgium; Asia becomes a rich pie to be carved up among the Japanese and the Russians and the Dutch. India becomes a dumping ground for British industry, and China becomes an India for Japan.

Imperialism thus becomes the road to war—not a royal road nor a road of adventure or misadventure, but a sordid process in which capitalist nations compete for fresh seedbeds for their unemployed wealth. A less inspiring cause for bloodshed could hardly be imagined.

Needless to say, such a theory of violence and struggle found little encouragement in the official world of economists. Hobson, it was said, kept "muddling economics up with other things" and since those "other things" were hardly suggestive of a world organized around the pursuit of pleasure, the official world regarded the theory of imperialism as a display of the sort of bad table manners one would expect of a man whose economics outraged such common-sense doctrines as the social beneficence of thrift.

But while the doctrine was scrupulously avoided by those who might have subjected it to an intelligent, if critical, scrutiny, it was embraced wholeheartedly by another section of the underworld: the Marxists. The idea, after all, was not entirely original with Hobson; it had been worked out by a German economist named Rodbertus, and by Rosa Luxemburg, a fiery German revolutionist. But Hobson's treatment was broader and deeper, and it was embroidered into the royal cloak of Marxist doctrine by none other than their leading theoretician: an exile named Vladimir Ilich Ulyanov—better known as Lenin.

The theory emerged from its baptism somewhat changed. Hobson had puzzled over the question of why capitalist nations so avidly sought colonies after decades of more or less indifference to them. His theory of imperialism was not a dogma, and still less an ironclad prediction of absolutely inescapable war. Indeed, he expressed the hope that rival imperialisms might arrange a kind of final settlement of the world and exist peaceably side by side on a live-and-let-live basis.

But in Marxist garb, the theory took on tones both more menacing and more inexorable. Not only was imperialism placed as the capstone of the Marxist economic arch and given the Marxist consecration of infallibility, but it was broadened and widened beyond Hobson's framework until it accounted for the whole social complexion of latter-day capitalism as well. And what a frightening picture emerged!—

> Being the highest phase of capitalist development, imperialism . . . draws within the orbit of finance-capital exploitation all colonies, all races, and all nations. . . . In squeezing enormous sums of surplus profit out of the millions of colonial workers and peasants and in accumulating colossal incomes from this exploitation, imperialism is creating a type of decaying and parasitically degenerate rentier class, as well as a whole stratum of parasites who live by clipping coupons. In completing the process of creating the material prerequisites of socialism (the concentration of the means of production, the enormous socialization of labour, the growth of labour organization), the epoch of imperialism intensifies the antagonisms among the "Great Powers" and gives rise to wars which cause the break-up of its single world economy. Imperialism is therefore capitalism moribund and decaying. It is the final stage of development of the capitalist system. It is the threshold of social revolution.

The writer: J. V. Stalin. The occasion: The Third Communist International. The date: 1928. But while Stalin is the speaker, the voice is Lenin's. And more disturbing yet, Lenin's conception of a ravaging and ravaged capitalism, internally corrupt and externally predatory, is *still* the formal Soviet explanation of the world in which we live. Its validity was again affirmed by the official program of the Communist party adopted in 1961:

> Imperialism knows no relations between states other than those of domination and subordination, of oppression of the weak by the strong. It bases international relations on

diktat and intimidation, on violence and arbitrary rule. It regards wars of aggression as a natural means of settling international issues.

Of the fact of imperialism there is no doubt. No one who is familiar with the history of the late nineteenth and early twentieth centuries can fail to mark the line of plunder, territorial aggrandizement, and oppressive colonialism which runs like a telltale thread through the endless incidents of international jealousy, friction, and war. If it is no longer fashionable to regard the First World War as "purely" an imperialist conflict, there is no doubt that imperialist jockeying for position did much to bring it into being.

But conquest and colonies are as old as ancient Egypt, and as the recent histories of Russia and China have made clear, they will continue whether capitalism is there to furnish an excuse or not. The question which the *economic* theory of imperialism makes us face is whether the conquest of the last fifty years has been differently motivated from the conquest which came before or which may follow after. It is a simple matter to understand the thirst for power of the dynastic state. Imperialism asks us to consider whether the more impersonal forces of the market economy can lead to the same end result.

The apologists for the colonial system claimed that it could not. In 1876 Bismarck himself wrote: "All the advantages claimed for the mother country are for the most part illusions. England is abandoning its colonial policy; she finds it too costly." And other defenders of the system echoed his remarks: they pointed out that colonies "didn't pay"; that colonization was not undertaken gladly, but that it was forced on the great powers by virtue of their civilizing mission in the world; that colonies gained more than the mother country, and so on.

But they simply missed the point. True, some colonies did not pay—in 1865 a Committee of Commons actually recommended the abandonment of all British holdings save one on the west coast of Africa on the grounds that they were highly unprofitable ventures. But while *all* colonies did not yield a profit, *some* colonies were fabulously rewarding: the tea gardens in Ceylon, for example, would return fifty per cent dividends on invested

capital in a banner year. And while *all* industry did not benefit
from overseas markets, *some* important industries could hardly
have existed without them: the classic case in point is the dependence of the British cotton industry on the Indian market.
When the Japanese eventually undersold the British in India,
the Lancaster cotton mills suffered a blow from which they have
never fully recovered to this day.

To be sure, there were other imperialist motives generously
mixed in with the purely economic, and the economic compen-
satory effect of imperialism was not quite so simple as J. A.
Hobson had described it. But by and large one could hardly
find an explanation for the thrust of European power into Africa
and Asia that did not contain some flavor of economic necessity.
In the case of Holland, for example, the huge plantation economy of Java and Sumatra offered a field for profitable investment
of great importance for Dutch capital; in the case of Malaya,
invaluable and cheap raw materials provided John Bull with a
lucrative international monopoly; in the case of the Middle
East, there were oil and the strategic control over shipping
through the Suez Canal. From country to country the motives
might differ, but the common denominator of economic gain was
to be found in all.

"What our industries lack . . . what they lack more and more, is
markets," said a French minister in 1885; and in 1926 Dr. Schacht,
then president of the German Reichsbank, declared: "The fight
for raw materials plays the most important role in world politics,
an even greater role than before the war. Germany's only solution is her acquisition of colonies." While it was not all quite as
Hobson had foreseen, his somber prognostications seemed confirmed. Capitalism could indeed find itself forced by internal economic pressures to turn to foreign economic exploitation, and
foreign exploitation, as history clearly demonstrated, could lead
easily to war.

Does this mean that imperialism is inseparable from capitalism? The Marxists tell us that it is, and they interpret every
act of sending capital abroad as imperialism in one disguise or
another; thus our efforts to extend assistance to the backward
nations are dubbed "imperialistic" by Communists in exactly
the same way that they label our investments in oil.

The reality seems a good deal more complicated than this Marxian version, however. Imperialism is not just foreign trade nor just foreign investment. It is these *plus* political interference, economic exploitation, military force, and a bland disregard for the interests of the poorer nation by the richer. What is so striking about nineteenth-century British investment in India, for example, is that it was entirely based on England's needs, and not in the slightest degree motivated or shaped by India's requirements.

Some of this old-fashioned imperialism remains. In the Near East vast consortiums of oil continue to maintain in power some of the most corrupt and anachronistic governments in the world. In Africa many capitalist enterprises—British, French, Belgian, Portuguese, South African, and American—have stakes, often immense, in the development of Africa's untapped riches; and in the present turmoil and confusion of African development, the rights of the native Africans to control and develop and enjoy the wealth of their own land may easily be forgotten.

The situation is considerably different when we turn to United States investment in politically more advanced—although economically still very backward—areas such as South America. Here we find large aggregates of American capital that unquestionably exert powerful influences over affairs in their "host" nations. Yet the relationship of American corporations to their foreign hosts is not altogether the same as the typical imperialist relationship of the nineteenth century. Nationals of the host country, far from being excluded from management, are trained for and entrusted with nearly all managerial posts, and they typically sit on (and sometimes control) the board of directors itself. The profits of foreign corporations are usually heavily taxed, and the repatriation of profits are hedged about by exchange restrictions. Most important, the threat of expropriation—always politically popular—is allowed to dangle over the corporation as a reminder of what will happen if it is found to have behaved in some fashion contrary to the national interest of the host nation.

Here, at least, the exercise of traditional economic imperialism is on the wane. And even in the remaining semi-colonial areas, the power of American (or European) capital, while still very great, is contested by changes that have definitively altered the attitude of these areas to their capitalist overlords.

At the crest of imperialism, one sixth of the world was rich and powerful; five sixths were supine, defenseless, needy, and gullible. No more. The rich one sixth is still rich, but it is on the defensive both politically and economically; the poor five sixths are still poor, but angrily aggressive. Asia has turned its back on Europe; the Middle East is bursting with the rage of the beggar who looks at the rich man and who sees—regardless of sober considerations—the gross injustice of differing stations in life. South America resents its subservience to American power; Africa is beginning to dream grandiose dreams of its own.

There is simply less room for the old attitudes of territorial seizure, commercial rape, and cultural disdain. Imperialism is not yet wholly dead, but it is dying, and the cause of its death, by a quirk of justice, lies in its own past excesses. For it was its own injustices and indignities which brought into being the bitter native nationalism to which imperialism is now anathema.

In the whole sordid story, the United States was fortunate enough until recently to play only a peripheral role. We dabbled in imperialism in the Philippines and in our "banana republics"; we had our military adventures in Cuba and Texas. But for all the temptation, we never plunged into a mad race for foreign soil. The reason is not that we were less susceptible to the jingoism of the times or that our economy displayed less of a need for foreign outlets. The saving grace for the United States was that we had an enormous empire, with all its advantages of wider markets, rich materials, and dazzling profits, right in our own back yard: we had the frontier. While Europe had to turn to other continents, we could turn to the West.

Thus, we never became a formidable imperialist power, because we never had to do so: the frontier absorbed all the energy and all the capital we could muster. But if we look at the fury and drive that went into the winning of the West, we may be able better to understand the nature of the dynamism that drove other nations, not so fortunately situated, to send their men and money overseas.

Today we are still not a territorial imperialist in the old-fashioned sense—as we have said, that avenue for the employment of national ambition and capital is largely closed. Yet in recent years we have been driven to a course of action that looks very much like imperialism. Faced with the prospect of radical governments in the underdeveloped world, our instinctive reaction has been to step in before "Communism" could gain a footing. Thus our clandestine overthrow of the radical Guatemala government, our abortive attempt to invade Cuba, our sudden descent upon the Dominican Republic, and our involvement in Vietnam.

Is this imperialism? Certainly not in the classic tradition, for no one could possibly maintain that American policy has been shaped to protect the insignificant investments in those particular areas. To some extent these military activities may have been meant to serve as warnings against the rise, elsewhere, of radical governments which might threaten larger aggregations of American capital. Most probably, however, American "imperialism". (for that is the unflattering word used by much of the world to describe our action) today represents the reaction of a great power placed on the defensive by the thrust of world events and seeking through military force to maintain friendly governments in power and to thwart unfriendly ones. This kind of imperialism is by no means limited to capitalist nations, as the example of Russia in Hungary and that of China in Tibet and India reveal. Here the motive of economics is submerged within the larger motive of the extension and strengthening of political power itself. This does not make modern imperialism—or, if we will, political imperialism—any less dangerous than economic imperialism, but it does make doubtful the claim that capitalism alone must bear the responsibility for aggressive international behavior. If the United States has in fact become an imperialist power—and this is not yet clear—the causes must be sought as much in the Pentagon and in Congress and among the populace at large as in the circles of its corporate leaders.

John Hobson died in 1940; in the London *Times* a properly circumspect obituary duly noted both his prescient ideas and his lack of general recognition.

For unrecognized he was. The most renowned economist of the Victorian world was an economist utterly unlike Hobson:

Alfred Marshall—as considered, middle-of-the-road, and "official"
as Hobson had been intuitive, extreme, and, so to speak, unau-
thorized. Yet it is fitting that we conclude this journey through
the shadowy regions of the underworld by returning again to
Victorian daylight. The economists who worked in that daylight
may not have seen the disturbing sights revealed to more adventurous souls, but they did do one thing which the heretics did
not: they taught their world—and even our world—its "economics."

Merely to look at Alfred Marshall's portrait is already to see
the stereotype of the teacher: white mustache, white wispy hair,
kind bright eyes—an eminently professorial countenance. At the
time of his death in 1924, when the greatest economists in England paid homage to his memory, one of them, Professor C. R.
Fay, produced this indelible portrait of the Victorian professor
chez lui:

> Pigou told me I ought to go and see him about a subject
> for a Fellowship Dissertation. So one afternoon towards twi-
> light I went to Balliol Croft. "Come in, come in," he said,
> running in from a little passage; and I went with him up-
> stairs. "Have you any idea what to do?" he asked me. I said
> "no." "Well, then, listen," he said, producing a small black
> book. He proceeded to read out a list of subjects having pre-
> viously ordered me to hold up my hand when he came to
> one I liked. In my nervousness I tried to close with the first
> subject, but Marshall took no notice and read on. About
> halfway through the second page he arrived at "The Recent
> German Financial Crisis." Having been to Greifswald for a
> summer I signaled acquiescence. "It wouldn't suit you at
> all," he said. I kept quiet for another five minutes, and,
> catching the word "Argentine" made another noise which
> stopped him. My only reason was that two of my uncles had
> been in business there. "Have you been there yourself?" he
> asked. "No," I replied, and he went on. A few moments later
> he stopped and said, "Have you found a subject you like?"
> "I don't know," I began. "No one ever does," he said, "but
> that's my method. Now, what would you like to do?" I
> gasped out "a comparison of German and English labour."

Upon which (for it was now quite dark), he produced a little lantern with an electric button and began prowling around the shelves, handing out books in English and German—von Nostitz, Kuhlman, about 30 in all. "Now," he said, "I'll leave you to smell; when you've finished, blow down the tube and Sarah will bring you some tea."

It was all very remote from the African strife that had disturbed Hobson or the boisterous American speculation that had formed the cradle of environment for Henry George's ideas. Marshall, like his contemporary Edgeworth, was pre-eminently the product of a university. Although he voyaged to America and even across America to San Francisco, his life, his point of view—and inevitably his economics—smacked of the quietude and refinement of the Cambridge setting.

But exactly what did he teach? One word can sum up the basic concern behind Marshall's teaching—the word *equilibrium*. In contrast with Bastiat, who was drawn to the irrationalities of economic sophistry, or with Henry George, who was attracted to the injustices of life cloaked with economic sanction, or with Hobson, who saw the face of Mars behind the impersonal processes of capitalist economics, Marshall was primarily interested in the self-adjusting, self-correcting nature of the economic world. As his most brilliant pupil, J. M. Keynes, would later write, he created "a whole Copernican system, by which all the elements of the economic universe are kept in their places by mutual counterpoise and interaction."

Much of this, of course, had been taught before. Adam Smith, Ricardo, Mill had all expounded the market system as a feedback mechanism of great complexity and efficiency. Yet between the over-all vision and the fine working-out of details there was much unexplored territory and foggy exposition: the theory of market equilibrium which Marshall inherited was a good deal more imposing at a distance than up close. There were sticky bits even about such basic matters as whether prices were really a reflection of the cost of production of a good, or of the final degree of satisfaction yielded by that good—were diamonds high-priced, in other words, because they were hard to find or because people enjoyed wearing them? Perhaps such questions would not make anyone but an economist's heart beat faster, and yet so long as they remained obscure it was hard to think clearly about many problems which economics sought to attack.

It was to these fuzzy questions of economic theory that Marshall applied himself. In his famous *Principles* he combined a mind of mathematical precision with a style that was leisurely, discursive, shot through with homely example, and wonderfully lucid. Even a businessman could understand *this* sort of economics, for all the hard logical proofs were thoughtfully relegated to the footnotes (with the result that Keynes irreverently said that any economist would do better to read the footnotes and forget the text than vice versa). At any rate, the book was a tremendous success: originally published in 1890, it is still prescribed fare for the student who aspires to be an economist.

And what was the great contribution of Marshall to the conceptual tangles of economics? The main contribution—the one to which Marshall himself returned time and again—was the insistence on the importance of *time* as the quintessential element in the working-out of the equilibrium process.

For equilibrium, as Marshall pointed out, changed its basic meaning according to whether the adjustment process of the economy took place in a short-run or a long-run period. In the short run, buyers and sellers met to higgle on the market place, but basically the bargaining process revolved about a fairly fixed quantity of goods—the diamonds which the diamond merchants brought along with them in their suitcases. Over the long run, however, the quantity of diamonds was not fixed. New mines could be opened if the demand warranted it; old mines could be abandoned if supply was superabundant. Hence in the very short run it was the psychic utility of diamonds—that is, the demand for them—which exercised the more immediate influence on their market price, but over the long run, as the recurring flow of supply was adjusted to consumers' wants, cost of production again asserted its upper hand. Neither cost nor utility, of course, could ever be quite divorced from the determination of price: demand and supply, in Marshall's own words, were like "the blades of a pair of scissors," and it was as fruitless to ask whether supply or demand alone regulated price as to ask whether the upper or lower blade of the scissors did all the cutting. But while both blades cut, one of them, so to speak, was the active and one the passive edge—the utility-demand edge active when the cut took place in the quick time span of the given market; the cost-supply edge active when the cutting extended over the longer period in which scales of output and patterns of production were subject to change.

It was, like everything Marshall touched with his analytic mind, an illuminating insight. And yet more than theoretical brilliance radiated from the *Principles*. If Marshall was the finest intelligence of the "official" world of economics, he was also its most compassionate intelligence. A genuine concern for the laboring poor, for the "cringing wretches" he noted on his trips to the London slums, for economics as a tool for social better-ment—all this was inextricably woven into his book. Economics as he conceived it was "an engine for the discovery of truth," but the particular truth toward which he directed the engine was the cause—and cure—of poverty.

Why, then, was he not as significant in the history of economic thought as his brilliance and balance would seem to have war-ranted? The answer, ironically, lies in the very element of Mar-shall's analysis which was his most important gift to economic analysis—the element of time. For time, to Marshall, was abstract time; it was the time in which mathematical curves exfoliate and theoretical experiments may be run and rerun, but it was not the time in which anything ever really *happens*. That is, it was not the irreversible flow of historic time—and, above all, not *the* historic time in which Marshall himself lived. Think for a mo-ment of what he lived to see: a violent anti-capitalist revolution in Russia, a world-encompassing war, the first rumblings of anti-colonialism. Think of what lay just ahead: the decline of capi-talism in much of Europe, a world-wide change in the conception of government, a world-shaking depression in the United States. Yet of the relevance of economics to all these overwhelming changes, neither Alfred Marshall nor still less his official col-leagues had much, if any, understanding. *Natura non facit saltum*—nature makes no sudden leaps—was the motto of the *Principles* in its last edition in 1920 as in its first, in 1890. The fact that history might make sudden leaps, that the world of economics might be inseparably tied to the world of history, that the long and short run of the textbook implied a totally different conception of "time" from that of the relentless ticking of the social clock—all this was far removed from the notions of equilibrium which Marshall made the center of his economic inquiry. For nothing that he said could he be reproached, for he was a man of gentle faith and deeply felt convictions. The trouble was that nothing he said went far enough.

And even this might be condoned in hindsight were it not for one thing. All the while that Marshall and his colleagues were refining their delicate mechanism of equilibrium, a few unorthodox dissenters were insisting that it was not equilibrium but change—violent change—which characterized the real world and which properly formed the subject for economic inquiry. War and revolution and depression and social tension were to their minds the basic problems for economic scrutiny—not equilibrium and the nice processes of adjustment of a stable textbook society. But when the heretics and the amateurs pointed this out to Victorian academic officialdom, their interruptions were resented, their warnings shrugged aside, their prescriptions scorned.

The complacency of the official world was not merely a rueful commentary on the times; it was an intellectual tragedy of the first order. For had the academicians paid attention to the underworld, had Alfred Marshall possessed the disturbing vision of a Hobson, or Edgeworth the sense of social wrong of a Henry George, the great catastrophe of the twentieth century might not have burst upon a world utterly unprepared for radical social change. It teaches us, in retrospect, that ideas, however heretical, cannot safely be ignored—least of all by those whose interests are, in the best sense of that misused word, conservative.

VIII

The Savage Society of
Thorstein Veblen

O NE hundred and twenty-five years had now passed since the
Wealth of Nations appeared in 1776, and in that span of
time it seemed as if the great economists had left no aspect of the
world unexamined: its magnificence or its squalor, its naïveté or
its sometimes sinister overtones, its grandiose achievements in
technology or its often mean shortcomings in human values. But
this many-sided world, with its dozens of differing interpretations,
had nonetheless one common factor. It was European. For all its
changing social complexion, this was still the Old World, and as
such it insisted on a modicum of punctilio.

Thus it was not without significance that when Dick Arkwright, the barber's apprentice, made his fortune in the spinning jenny he metamorphosed into Sir Richard: the threat to
England's traditional reign of gentlemanliness was neatly solved
by inducting such parvenus wholesale into the fraternity of gentle blood and manners. The parvenus, it is true, brought with
them a train of middle-class attitudes and even a strain of anti-
aristocratic sentiment, but they brought with them, as well, the
sneaking knowledge that there was a higher social stratum than
that attainable by wealth alone. As countless comedies of manners testified, there was a difference between the beer baron,
with all his millions and his purchased crest, and the impoverished but hereditary baron next door. The successful European
money-maker might be rich as Croesus, but the savor of his riches
was a trifle dulled by the recognition that this was only one—
and by no means the final—step up the social ladder.

All this was vastly different in America. Not only had this country been founded by men who were deeply opposed to gradations of name and birth, but the spirit of individual independence and individual achievement had sunk deep into the national folklore. In America a man was as good as he proved himself, and his success needed no validation from a genealogist. Hence, while there was not too much to differentiate the dark and sweated mills of New England from the gloomy mills of old England, when one looked into the manners and behavior of their masters, the resemblance lessened. For while the European capitalist was still caught in the shadow of a feudal past, the American money-maker basked in the sun—there were no inhibitions on his drive to power or in the exuberant enjoyment of his wealth. In the bubbling last half of the nineteenth century, money was the stepping stone to social recognition in the United States, and having acquired a passport of suitable wealth, the American millionaire needed no further visa for his entree into the upper classes.

And so the game of money-making in the New World was a rougher and less gentlemanly affair than the competitive struggle abroad. The stakes were higher and the chances for success were greater. The sportsmanship, accordingly, was somewhat less.

In the 1860's, for example, Cornelius Vanderbilt, a fabulous genius of shipping and commerce, found that his own business associates were threatening his interests—a not too uncommon occurrence. He wrote them a letter:

> Gentlemen:
> You have undertaken to ruin me. I will not sue you, for law takes too long. I will ruin you.
>
> Sincerely,
> CORNELIUS VAN DERBILT

And he did. "What do I care about the law? Hain't I got the power?" asked the Commodore. Later J. Pierpont Morgan was to voice much the same sentiment, if in a slightly more polished form. When his associate, Judge Gary, on a rare occasion ventured a legal caveat, Morgan exploded: "Well, I don't know as I want a lawyer to tell me what I cannot do. I hire him to tell me how to do what I want to do."

It was not only in their neglect of the fine processes of the law that the Americans outdid their European contemporaries; when they fought, they abandoned the gentleman's rapier for the roughneck's brass knuckles. An instance in point is the struggle for the control of the Albany-Susquehanna Railroad, a vital link in a system torn between Jim Fisk and the patrician Morgan. Morgan held one end of the line in his own hands, and the other terminal was a Fisk stronghold. The controversy was accordingly resolved by each side mounting a locomotive on its end of the track and running the two engines, like gigantic toys, into one another. And even then the losers did not give up, but retired as best they could, ripping up tracks and tearing down trestles as they went.

In this _mêlée_ for industrial supremacy no quarter was asked and none given. Even dynamite had its uses, being employed to eliminate one particularly sticky competitor of the Standard Oil group, while less violent means, such as kidnaping, were remarkable more for their ingenuity than their immorality. In 1881, when a great blizzard blew down the telegraph lines in New York, Jay Gould, the ruthless master of the money markets, was forced to send his orders to his broker by messenger. His enemies saw their chance and acted on it: they kidnaped the boy, substituted another of the same general physiognomy, and for several weeks Gould was dismayed to find that his moves were all somehow known to his adversaries in advance.

Needless to say, the pirates who thus forced each other to walk the plank could scarcely be expected to treat the public with reverence. Gulling and milking the investor were taken as a matter of course, and the stock market was regarded as a kind of private casino for the rich in which the public laid the bets and the financial titans fixed the croupier's wheel. As to what would happen to the general run of bets under such an arrangement—well, that was the public's lookout, an attitude which might have been more commendable had not these same titans done everything in their power to entice the public to enter their preserves.

The public, be it noted, responded with a will; when the news "got around" that Gould or Rockefeller was buying rails or coppers or steels, the public rushed to get in for a free ride. The fact that it took a fleecing for every killing never affected

its unbounded faith, and on the strength of this faith a virtual
legerdemain of finance was made possible. A head-spinning example was the purchase of the Anaconda Copper Company by
Henry Rogers and William Rockefeller without the expenditure
of a single dollar of their own. This is how they did it:

1. Rogers and Rockefeller gave a check for $39 millions to
   Marcus Daly for the Anaconda properties, on the condition that he would deposit it in the National City Bank
   and leave it untouched for a specified period.
2. They then set up a paper organization known as the
   Amalgamated Copper Company, with their own clerks
   as dummy directors, and caused Amalgamated to buy
   Anaconda—not for cash, but for $75 millions in Amal-
   gamated stock which was conveniently printed for the
   purpose.
3. From the National City Bank, Rogers and Rockefeller
   now borrowed $39 millions to cover the check they had
   given to Marcus Daly, and as collateral for this loan they
   used the $75 millions in Amalgamated stock.
4. They now sold the Amalgamated stock on the market,
   (first having touted it through their brokers) for $75
   millions.
5. With the proceeds, they retired the $39-million loan from
   the National City Bank, and pocketed $36 millions as
   their own profit on the deal.

Of course this free-for-all involved staggering dishonesty. A. B.
Stickney, president of the Chicago, St. Paul, and Kansas Railway, remarked that as gentlemen he would trust his brother railroad presidents anywhere, but that as rail presidents he wouldn't
leave his watch out of sight with them for a moment. There was
reason for his cynicism. At one meeting of railroad heads called
to agree on a schedule of common freight rates which would
rescue the roads from their constant suicidal game of undercut-
ting one another, one railroad president slipped out during an
intermission in the proceedings to wire the agreed schedule back
to his office so that his line might be the first to undercut the
rest. By chance his wire was intercepted and when the meeting

next convened it was faced with the proof positive of the impossibility of honor even among thieves.

It is an age which we are accustomed to look back upon with a blush. Certainly it was grotesque in its trappings (at some parties cigarettes were wrapped in hundred-dollar bills for the thrill of inhaling wealth), and almost medieval in its warrior spirit. But let us not misconstrue the spirit of the times. While the lords of wealth rode roughshod over the public, they trampled equally ruthlessly over each other, and their bold and unprincipled behavior was less a calculated meanness or a conscious flouting of Christian ideals than an unbridled energy which knew no barriers of conscience and nice usage. "I owe the public nothing," Morgan once said, and he meant that remark literally as a credo of his philosophy rather than as a callous *défi* of the world. Business, in this age of barony, was brutal business, and the price of morality was apt to be defeat.

And what did the economists make of all this?

Not very much. The American professionals had followed in the footsteps of their European teachers and they forced the American world into a mold that was never made for it. The fantastic game of monetary cutthroat was described as the process of "thrift and accumulation"; the outright fraud as "enterprise"; the gilded extravagances of the age as colorless "consumption." Indeed, the world was so scrubbed as to be unrecognizable. One might read such leading texts as John Bates Clark's *Distribution of Wealth* and never know that America was a land of millionaires; one might peruse F. H. Taussig's *Economics* and never come across a rigged stock market. If one looked into Professor Laughlin's articles in the *Atlantic Monthly* he would learn that "sacrifice, exertion, and skill" were responsible for the great fortunes, and he would be told that every man had a right "to enjoy the products of his exertion to the exclusion of everybody else"—presumably this included the right to buy legislatures as well as diamonds.

Official economics, in a word, was apologist and unperceptive; it turned its eye away from the excesses and exuberance which were the very essence of the American scene and painted instead a stereotype in formal lines and lusterless color. What it lacked was not honesty or courage or intellectual competence; those qualities it possessed. What it suffered from was what Malthus had once called "the insensible bias of situation and interest." The American economists were too much bound up in the current of these enthusiastic times to back away from their subject and view it coolly and clearly and at a distance.

What was needed was the eye of a stranger—someone like De Tocqueville or Bryce who could view the scene with the added clarity and perspective that comes of being foreign to it. In the person of Thorstein Bunde Veblen—an American by birth but a citizen of nowhere by nature—such an eye was found.

A very strange man, Thorstein Veblen. He was a peasant in looks, a Norwegian farmer. A photograph shows his hair, lank and flat, parted in the middle of a gnomelike head and falling in an inverted V over a low and sloping forehead. Peasant eyes, shrewd and speculative, peer out from behind a blunt nose. An unkempt mustache hides his mouth and a short scraggly beard engulfs his chin. He is dressed in a thick unpressed suit and there is a large safety pin attached to his vest: it moors his watch. The photograph does not show two more safety pins hooked into his pants where they suspend his socks, and it gives us only a suggestion of a thin wiry frame, and a light, highstepping, hunterlike noiseless gait.

A strange appearance, but it hid a yet stranger personality. Those piercing eyes might hint at an equally piercing mental scrutiny and that rustic exterior might prepare one for a certain blunt quality of inquiry. But there was no external sign of the keynote to Veblen's life: his alienation from society.

Alienation is often a phenomenon of the sick, and by our standards Veblen must have been neurotic indeed. For he had a quality of nearly hermetic insulation. He walked through life as if he had descended from another world, and the goings on which appeared so natural to the eyes of his contemporaries appeared to him as piquant, exotic, and curious as the rituals of a savage community to the eye of an anthropologist. Other economists—and this includes both Adam Smith and Karl Marx —were not only in their society, but they were *of* it; sometimes full of admiration for the world about them and sometimes filled

with despair and rage at what they saw. Not Thorstein Veblen.
In the bustling, boosting, gregarious community in which he
lived, he stood apart: uninvolved, unentangled, remote, aloof,
disinterested, a stranger.

Because he was a stranger, he was a nonconformist, but not a
radical. The world to Veblen was uncomfortable and forbidding; he adapted to it as a missionary might to a land of primitives, refusing to go native, but preserving his integrity at the
cost of frightful solitude. Many admired, even loved him, but he
had no friends: there was no man he called by his first name,
and no woman he could wholly love.

As might be expected, he was a mass of eccentricities. He refused to have a telephone, kept his books stacked along the wall
in their original packing cases, and saw no sense in daily making
up the beds; they were thrown back in the morning and pulled
up again at night. Lazy, he allowed the dishes to accumulate
until the cupboard was bare and then washed the whole messy
heap by turning the hose on them. Taciturn, he would sit for
hours in silence when all his visitors were eager to hear his
pronouncements. A flouter of convention, he gave all his students the same grade, regardless of their work, but when one
student needed a higher mark to qualify for a scholarship, Veblen gladly changed a *C* to an *A*. An *enfant terrible* with an ax
to grind for college administrations, he would (when the authorities so decreed) call the roll with exaggerated care, carefully
placing to one side the cards of the students who were absent,
and then when the sheep were weeded from the goats, he would
seemingly by accident mix the two piles together again. Curiously
sadistic, he was capable of such meaningless practical jokes as
borrowing a sack from a passing farmer and returning it to him
with a hornet's nest inside. Rarely whimsical, he once told a little
girl who inquired what his initials T. B. stood for that they
meant Teddy Bear; she called him that but no one else dared.
Enigmatic, he refused to commit himself on anything; typically,
when someone once asked him his opinion of a certain sociologist's writing in a journal which Veblen edited, he replied: "The
average number of words on a page is 400. Professor ——'s average
375." And perhaps strangest of all, this sardonic and unpre-
possessing man had the indefinable quality of being attractive to

women. He was always engaged in one liaison or another, and
not always of his own doing. "What are you to do if the woman
moves in on you?" he once inquired of a friend.

A bewildering and complex personality, locked within itself
and with only one avenue for expression: he wrote in razorlike
English, in a style much like himself, involuted and laden with
esoteric information and terminology, a kind of surgical style
that left the world raw and exposed but perfectly bloodless, so
fine-edged was his blade. He wrote of philanthropy and called it
"essays in pragmatic romance"; of religion and characterized it
as "the fabrication of vendible imponderables in the nth dimen-
sion." He wrote of the main ecclesiastical organizations as "chain-
stores" and of the individual church as a "retail outlet"—cruel
but telling phrases. He described a walking stick as "an advertisement that the bearer's hands are employed otherwise than
in useful effort" and he noted also that it was a weapon: "The
handling of so tangible and primitive a means of offense is very
comforting to anyone who is gifted with even a moderate share
of ferocity." *Gifted* with ferocity! What a savage and yet curiously dry phrase.

But what had this to do with economics? Nothing, in the conventional sense of the word. Economics for Veblen had no relation to the mannerly and precise game of the Victorians in which
the ways of the world were justified by the differential calculus,
and it bore little kinship with the efforts of earlier economists
to explain how things worked themselves out. Veblen wanted to
know something else: why things were as they were in the first
place. Hence his inquiry began not with the economic play, but
with the players; not with the plot, but with the whole set of
customs and mores which resulted in that particular kind of play
called "the business system." In a word, he delved into the nature
of economic man and his economic rites and rituals, and in this
almost anthropological approach it was as important for him to
notice that gentlemen carried walking sticks and went to church
as that landlords received something which society called rent.
He was seeking to penetrate to the true nature of the society in
which he lived, and in that search through a maze of deceptions
and conventions, he would have to take hints and evidences
wherever they revealed themselves: in dress, manners, speech, or

polite usage. Like the psychoanalyst he often fastened on the smallest trivium when he believed it to be the projecting handle of some important but buried reality, and again like the psycho-analyst he sought for meanings which were often strange and even repugnant to common sense.

His examination of society, as we shall see, is merciless. But its biting quality comes not so much from a wish to disparage as from the peculiar coldness with which our fondest notions are appraised. It is as if nothing were familiar to Veblen, nothing too commonplace to merit his attention, and therefore nothing beyond judgment. Only a singularly detached mind, after all, would see in a walking stick both a disguised advertisement of leisure and a barbaric weapon.

The detachment seems to have been with him always. Veblen was born in 1857, a farm boy on the frontier, the fourth son and sixth child of an immigrant Norwegian family. His father, Thomas Veblen, was an aloof and distant person, slow-thinking and independent; Veblen later described him as the finest mind he ever met. His mother, Kari, was warm, quick, and passion-ate; it was she who taught Thorstein the Icelandic lore and Nor-wegian sagas which were to fascinate him all his life. But from the beginning he was a queer child, lazy, addicted to reading in the attic instead of doing his chores, given to inventing nick-names which stuck, and precociously bright. A younger brother has remarked: "From my earliest recollection I thought he knew everything. I could ask him any question and he would tell me all about it in detail. I have found out since that a good deal he told me was made of whole cloth, but even his lies were good."

To whatever makes an unusual personality was added an up-bringing which served to drive a wedge between himself and the world as a place to be taken at face value. He had a pioneer child-hood: simple, austere, sparse. Clothes were homemade, woolens unknown, overcoats fashioned from calfskin. Coffee and sugar were luxuries; so was such a simple garment as an undershirt. But more important, it was a foreign—a stranger's—boyhood. The Norwegians in America formed their own tight-knit and separate communities where Norwegian was the common tongue and Nor-way the true fatherland. Veblen had to learn English as a foreign tongue, not perfecting it until he went to college, and it is typical of that patriarchal self-enclosed community that the first inkling Veblen had that he was going to college was when he was called in from the fields to find his bags packed and placed waiting in the carriage.

He was then seventeen and the college of his family's choice was Carleton College Academy, a small outpost of East Coast culture and enlightenment near the Minnesota township where the Veblens farmed. Thorstein had been sent with an eye to his entering the Lutheran ministry, and he found Carleton religious to the core. But there was no hope of taming this already active and iconoclastic intellect or fitting it into a pious atmosphere. At the weekly declamation, rather than a conventional discourse on the necessity of converting the heathen, Veblen threw the faculty into an uproar with "A Plea for Cannibalism" and "An Apology for a Toper." When asked if he was defending these instances of depravity, Veblen blandly replied that he was merely engaged in scientific observations. The faculty recognized his genius but was a bit afraid of him. John Bates Clark, his teacher (who was to become one of the outstanding academic economists in the country) liked him, but thought him a "misfit."

This odd and gifted misfit found the unlikeliest of opportunities at Carleton. A romance sprang up between Veblen and the niece of the president of the college, Ellen Rolfe. She was an intellectual and a brilliant personality on her own account, and the two drifted together under a natural gravitation. Veblen read Spencer to Ellen, converted her to agnosticism, and persuaded himself that she was descended from the first Viking hero, Gange Rolfe.

They were married in 1888, but the relationship was to be full of ups and downs. This isolated man who had but little love to bestow seems to have needed the care of a woman and with few exceptions (one beauty pronounced him a "chimpanzee") he found it in abundance. But the particular woman did not seem so much to matter; Veblen was hardly faithful to Ellen and she was to leave him again and again, sometimes for his indiscretions, sometimes for the cruelty with which he treated her, sometimes out of the sheer frustration of trying to read an inscrutable and walled-off mind. For many years, however, Veblen himself would seek a *rapprochement,* coming to her house in the woods unannounced, with a black stocking dangling from his hand and inquiring, "Does this garment belong to you, Madam?"

When Veblen left Carleton he had determined on an academic career. There began instead the long, never-ending cumulation of frustrations that would mark his professional life. He was certainly unaggressive about his interests, and yet a kind of ill luck seemed to dog his footsteps: for example, once he was to ask a former student to investigate for him a position with a civic welfare organization in New York, and the student was to comply—only to take the job for himself. But that was to be many years later. Now Veblen obtained a post at tiny Monona Academy in Wisconsin and then, when Monona closed its doors permanently after a year, he went to Johns Hopkins, hoping for a scholarship to study philosophy. The scholarship, despite flowery recommendations, failed to materialize. Veblen transferred to Yale and in 1884 he graduated with a Ph.D. and a broad *a,* but with no future and no prospects.

He returned home, sick from malaria he had contracted in Baltimore and needing a special diet. But he was anything but a grateful invalid. He pestered his family by taking the horse and buggy when they were most needed, and told them they were all tubercular and that they would never be successful because they were not dishonest enough. And he lay around and loafed. "He was lucky enough," wrote a brother, "to come out of a race and family who made of family loyalty and solidarity a religion. . . . Thorstein was the only loafer in a highly respectable community. . . . He read and loafed, and the next day he loafed and read."

Certainly he read everything: political tracts, economics, sociology, Lutheran hymn books, treatises in anthropology. But his idleness aggravated his isolation from society and made it more bitter and still more ingrown. He did occasional odd jobs, puttered with fruitless inventions, commented wryly on the gaudy events of the day, botanized, talked with his father, wrote a few articles, and looked for a job. None came. He had no divinity degree and hence was unacceptable to religious colleges; he lacked the polish and air which might have commended him to others. When he married Ellen, much to the dismay of her family, it was at least partly to find a livelihood; it was hoped that he would secure a position as economist for the Atchison, Topeka, and Santa Fe Railway of which her uncle was president.

But his capricious bad luck intervened. The railway became involved in financial difficulties and was taken over by a committee of bankers, and the position disappeared. Another opened up with the University of Iowa; with his Ph.D., his letters of recommendation, his wife's connections, the appointment seemed sure. It fell through—his lack of forcefulness and his agnosticism counted heavily against him—and then another at St. Olaf's was refused at the eleventh hour. It was as if the fates were conspiring against him, forcing him to remain in his isolation.

The isolation lasted seven years, and in those seven years Veblen did virtually nothing except read. Finally a family council was held. After all, he was thirty-four now and he had never held a respectable position. It was determined that he should take up his graduate studies again and make another attempt to enter the academic world.

He chose Cornell and in 1891 he walked into the office of J. Laurence Laughlin to announce, "I am Thorstein Veblen." Laughlin, a pillar of conservative economics, must have been taken aback; the speaker wore a coonskin cap and corduroy trousers. But something about him impressed the older man. He went to the president of the university and secured a special grant to take on Veblen as a fellow and the next year, when the University of Chicago opened its doors and took on Laughlin as the head of its economics department, he brought Veblen along at a salary of $520 a year. It might be added that on Laughlin's death, his principal contribution to economics was adjudged to have been the fact that he secured Veblen for Chicago.

The University of Chicago was not only Veblen's first job—at age thirty-five—but it was an institution which peculiarly mirrored the society he was to dissect. Rockefeller had founded the university and a popular student jingle went:

John D. Rockefeller,
Wonderful man is he.

Gives all his spare change
To the U. of C.

The university was not, as might have been expected, tied to a policy of unremitting conservatism. Rather, it was the incarnation, in educational circles, of the empire building which had given it birth in the business world. Its president was William Rainey Harper, an ambitious man of only thirty-six, who was admiringly described by Walter Hines Page as a type of captain of industry. He was an entrepreneur college president, who did not hesitate to rob other colleges of their best men by dangling pay before them, and like the Standard Oil group, which was its father, the U. of C. succeeded, by sheer bulk of financial strength, in cornering a large section of the American intellectual capital. All this was later to be caustically described by Veblen's pen, but at the same time it provided him with an adequate milieu of intellectuals. There was Albert Michelson, who was to determine the speed of light with hitherto unknown precision; Jacques Loeb, the physiologist; Lloyd Morgan in sociology; there was a huge library, and a new journal of economics to edit.

Veblen began to be noticed. His immense learning earned him a reputation. "There goes Dr. Veblen who speaks twenty-six languages," said a student. James Hayden Tufts, a noted scholar, came upon him in an examination room and tells, "When I entered the room, the examination had begun and someone I did not know was asking questions. I thought his speech the slowest I had ever heard—it was difficult for me to keep the beginning of the question in mind until the end was reached. But after a while I began to see that here was a subtle mind penetrating to fundamental issues without disclosing its own views except the one determination to get to the bottom of things."

But his isolated personality was impenetrable. No one knew what he thought about anything. People would ask his wife if he were really a socialist; she had to tell them she herself did not know. He was never without his armor; a polite, controlled objectivity which stripped the world of its emotional content and which kept those who would most have liked to pierce his personal shield at arm's length. "Tell me, Professor Veblen," a student once asked him, "do you take anything seriously?" "Yes," he replied in a conspiratorial whisper, "but don't tell anyone."

In class—this borrows from his later life, but it serves to illumine the man—he would come in gaunt and haggard from a long night over his books and, dropping a bulky German volume on the desk, would begin to turn the pages with nervous fingers yellowed from his sole vanity—a penchant for expensive cigarettes. The Reverend Howard Woolston, a onetime student, has described it thus: "In a low creaking tone, he began a recital of village economy among the early Germans. Presently he came upon some unjust legal fiction imposed by rising nobles and sanctioned by the clergy. A sardonic smile twisted his lips; blue devils leaped to his eyes. With mordant sarcasm, he dissected the torturous assumption that the wish of the aristocrats is the will of God. He showed similar implications in modern institutions. He chuckled quietly. Then returning to history, he continued the exposition."

But not everyone appreciated his teaching methods. His frank feeling about students was the fewer the better and he made no attempt to liven the discussion; indeed, he delighted in driving his students away. He once asked a religious student the value of her church to her in kegs of beer, and to another who sedulously copied his words and who wanted a sentence repeated, he said he thought it not worth repeating. He mumbled, he rambled, he digressed. His classes dwindled; one ended up with but one student, and later at another university a door card which originally read: "Thorstein Veblen, 10 to 11, Mondays, Wednesdays, and Fridays" was changed by slow degrees to read: "Mondays: 10 to 10:05."

But for the few who listened carefully to that bored droning voice, the idiosyncrasies were worth the reward. "Why, it was creepy," writes one former student. "It might have been a dead man's voice slowly speaking on, and if the light had gone out behind those dropped eyelids, would it have made any difference? But we who listened day after day found the unusual manner nicely fitted to convey the detached and slightly sardonic intellect that was moving over the face of things. His detached, free-ranging intellect attracted, and yet it seemed a mutilated personality. The scholarliness of his mind was amazing and delightful. He held in memory detail that would have overwhelmed most minds and become an end in itself, and never lost the magnificent charting of large design. . . . The quiet voice might in one minute make the most adroit use of a bit of current slang or popular doggerel to point out an opinion, and the next might be quoting stanza after stanza of a medieval Latin hymn."

His domestic economy was as tangled as the political economy which he sought to unravel. He was living at Chicago with his wife, Ellen, but that did not prevent him from carrying on notoriously, to the displeasure of President Harper. When he went so far as to go abroad with another woman, his position on the campus became intolerable. He began casting around for another post.

He had spent fourteen years at Chicago, reaching the magnificent salary of one thousand dollars in 1903. But the years were far from wasted, for his insatiably inquisitive, voraciously acquisitive mind had finally begun to bear fruit. In a series of brilliant essays and two remarkable books he established a national reputation—although more perhaps for oddity than for anything else.

His first book was written when Veblen was forty-two. He was still a lowly instructor and that year he had gone to President Harper and asked him for the customary few hundred dollars' raise. Harper replied that he did not sufficiently advertise the university and Veblen replied that he had no intention of doing so. But for the intercession of Laughlin, Veblen would have left; if he had, President Harper would have missed a most signal advertisement. For Veblen was about to publish *The Theory of the Leisure Class*. There is no indication that he expected it to make an especial impression; he had read it to some of his students, dryly remarking that they would find it polysyllabic, and he had had to rewrite it several times before the publishers would accept it. But unexpectedly, it was a sensation. William Dean Howells devoted two long reviews to it and overnight the book became the vade mecum of the intelligentsia of the day:

as an eminent sociologist told Veblen, "It fluttered the dovecotes of the East."

No wonder it excited attention, for never was a book of sober analysis written with such pungency. One picked it up at random to chuckle over its wicked insights, its barbed phrases, and its corrosive view of society in which elements of ridiculousness, cruelty, and barbarousness nestled in close juxtaposition with things taken for granted and worn smooth with custom and careless handling. The effect was electric, grotesque, shocking, and amusing, and the choice of words was nothing less than exquisite. A small sample quote:

> . . . A certain king of France . . . is said to have lost his life through an excess of moral stamina in the observance of good form. In the absence of the functionary whose office it was to shift his master's seat, the king sat uncomplaining before the fire and suffered his royal person to be toasted beyond recovery. But in so doing, he saved his Most Christian Majesty from menial contamination.

For most people the book appeared to be nothing more than just such a satire on the ways of the aristocratic class, and a telling attack on the follies and foibles of the rich. And so, on the surface, it appeared to be. Veblen, in his brocaded prose, embroidered the thesis that the leisure class advertised its superiority through conspicuous expenditure—blatant or subtle—and that its own hallmark—leisure itself—was also enjoyed the more fully by being dangled before the eyes of the public. In a thousand examples it held up to acid examination the attitude that "more expensive" necessarily meant "better." Thus, for example,

> We all feel, sincerely and without misgiving, that we are the more lifted up in spirit for having, even in the privacy of our own household, eaten our daily meal by the help of hand-wrought silver utensils, from hand-painted china (often of dubious artistic value) laid on high-priced table linen. Any retrogression from the standard of living which we are accustomed to regard as worthy in this respect is felt to be a grievous violation of our human dignity.

Much of the book was concerned with such a scrutiny of the economic psychopathology of our daily lives: the canons of monetary propriety were spelled out as completely and in as quaint a light as if they were a recently exhumed archaeological find. That much of the book was savored with relish by everyone; in a land of advertisement and keeping up with the Joneses, it was impossible to do otherwise than shake one's head and ruefully admire the unmistakable self-portrait.

But the descriptions of our penchant for display, however amusing or to the point, were no more than the illustrative material of the book. For as the title made clear, this was an inquiry into the *theory* of the leisure class. Although Veblen might stop along the route to comment on the more striking local scenery, his interest lay at the terminus of his journey, in such questions as What is the nature of economic man? How does it happen that he so builds his community that it will have a leisure class? What is the economic meaning of leisure itself?

To the classical economists such questions would have been answerable in terms of common sense. They saw the world in terms of individuals who rationally sought to better their own self-interest. Sometimes, as with Malthus' hopelessly multiplying laboring classes, brute human nature got the upper hand, but by and large mankind was depicted as a collection of reasoning beings. In the competitive struggle some rose to the top and some stayed at the bottom, and those who were fortunate or sagacious enough to prosper quite naturally took advantage of their fortune to minimize their labors. It was all very simple and quite reasonable.

But such a view of mankind made little sense to Veblen. He was not at all sure that the force which bound society together was the interplay of rationally calculated "self-interest" and he was not even wholly convinced that leisure was in and of itself preferable to work. His readings had introduced him to the ways of little-noticed peoples: the American Indians and the Ainus of Japan, the Todas of the Nilgiri hills and the bushmen of Australia. And these people, in their own simple economies, seemed to lack a leisure class entirely. Even more striking, in such communities where the price of survival was labor, everyone worked, whatever his task, without feeling demeaned by his toil. It was not considerations of profit and loss which provided the positive drive of these economies, but a natural pride of workmanship and a parental feeling of concern for the future generations. Men strove to outdo each other in the honorable performance of their daily stints, and if abstinence from labor—leisure—was condoned at all, it was certainly not respected.

But another kind of community also opened itself to Veblen's gaze. The Polynesians and the ancient Icelanders and the shogunates of feudal Japan were a different kind of preindustrial society: they had well-defined leisure classes. These classes, be it noted, were not idlers. On the contrary, they were among the busiest members of the community. But their "work" was all predatory; they *seized* their riches by force or cunning and took no part in the actual production of wealth by sweat or skill.

But although the leisure classes took without rendering any productive service in return, they did so with the full approval of the community. For these were societies which were rich enough to be able to afford a nonproductive class and aggressive enough in spirit to admire them: far from being regarded as wasters or spoilers, those who rose to the leisured ranks were looked up to as the strong and the able.

As a consequence, a portentous change in fundamental attitudes toward work took place. The activities of the leisure class —the winning of wealth by force—came to be regarded as honorable and dignified. Hence, by contrast, pure labor became tainted with indignity. The irksomeness of work, which the classical economists thought to be inherent in the nature of man himself, Veblen saw as the degradation of a once-honorable way of life under the impact of a predatory spirit: a community that admires and elevates force and brute prowess cannot beatify human toil.

But what had all this to do with America or Europe? A great deal. For modern man, in Veblen's eyes, was only a shade removed from his barbarian forebears. Poor Professor Edgeworth would have shuddered at the view, for it entailed nothing less than the junking of his pleasure-machines and the substitution in their stead of warriors, chieftains, medicine men, braves, and an underlying population of humble awe-struck common folk. "The discipline of savage life," wrote Veblen in a later essay, "has been by far the most protracted and probably the most exacting of any phase of culture in all the life-history of the race; so that by heredity human nature still is, and must indefinitely continue to be, savage human nature."

And so in modern life Veblen saw the heritage of the past. The leisure class had changed its occupation, it had refined its methods, but its aim was still the same—the predatory seizure of goods without work. It did not, of course, any longer seek for booty or women; *that* barbaric it was no more. But it sought for money, and the accumulation of money and its lavish or subtle display became the modern-day counterpart of scalps hanging on one's tepee. Not only was the leisure class still following the old predatory pattern, but it was upheld by the old attitudes of admiration for personal strength. In the eyes of society, the members of the leisure class were still the more warlike and more fearsome members of society, and accordingly, the underlying common folk sought to ape their betters. Everyone, workman and middle-class citizen as well as capitalist, sought through the conspicuous expenditure of money—indeed through its conspicuous waste—to demonstrate his predatory prowess. "In order to stand well in the eyes of the community," explained Veblen, "it is necessary to come up to a certain, somewhat indefinite conventional standard of wealth; just as in the earlier predatory stage it is necessary for the barbarian man to come up to his tribe's standard of physical endurance, cunning, and skill at arms." And similarly, in modern society not only did everyone vie for fierce excellence in the eyes of his fellow man, but as part of the same process, everyone "instinctively" felt the indignity which attached to nonpredatory means of livelihood, such as work.

Does this sound farfetched? We are not accustomed to thinking of ourselves as barbarians and we writhe under the comparison or scoff at it. But for all its strangeness, there is a strain of truth in Veblen's observations. There *is* a social derogation of physical toil as opposed to the more genteel pursuits of office employment. There *is* the fact that the accumulation of wealth typically proceeds—at least in the case of a successful executive —well beyond the point of rational wants and needs. We need not accept Veblen's anthropological explanation (which is rather weak in the light of contemporary research into primitive communities) to profit by his principal insight—that the motives of economic behavior can be far better understood in terms of deep-buried irrationalities than in terms of the nineteenth-century prettification of behavior into reasonableness and common sense.

Just what these irrationalities are—psychological or anthropological—need not detain us here. Suffice it that when we trace our actions to their source, we find ourselves in a substratum buried far below the nice explanations of sweet reasonability. In their classic study of *Middletown,* for example, Robert and Helen Lynd found that all but the poorest section of the working class retrenched on food and clothing before it would cut certain "necessary" luxuries, while in middle- and upper-class behavior the standard of display for display's sake is amply testified to on the advertising pages of any magazine. No one is exempt from the virus of competitive emulation, and if only in a literary way, the attitudes of Veblen's predatory barbarians help us to understand our own.

And there is still a final conclusion to be drawn. The notion of man as a thinly civilized barbarian does more than explain the presence of a leisure class and the acceptance of display as the norm of expenditure. It gives a clue to the nature of social cohesion itself. For the earlier economists were not too successful in explaining what bound society together in the face of the powerful divergent interests of its component classes. If Marx's view was right, for example, and the proletariat was irreconcilably and diametrically opposed to the capitalist, what prevented the revolution from breaking out at once? Veblen provides an answer. The lower classes are not at swords' points with the upper; they are bound up with them by the intangible but steely bonds of common attitudes. The workers do not seek to displace their managers; they seek to *emulate* them. They themselves acquiesce in the general judgment that the work they do is somehow less "dignified" than the work of their masters, and their goal is not to rid themselves of a superior class but to climb up to it. In the theory of the leisure class lies the kernel of a theory of social stability.

After the *Leisure Class* appeared in 1899, Veblen had a reputation—although more as a satirist than as an economist. The radicals and intellectuals adored him, but he despised their praise. His fellow economists still questioned whether he were a socialist, and wondered whether to take him seriously or not. They were justifiably bewildered: he praised Marx in one sentence and criticized him in the next and his most serious social judgments were often cloaked in a kind of intellectual drollery which might be taken as morbid humor or as a perfectly straightforward sentiment.

But meanwhile Veblen was working on another book—his own definition of the business system. "The book, I am credibly told," he wrote to a friend, Mrs. Gregory, "is still more 'beyond' or as my friends who have seen it say, beside the point. Its name is *The Theory of Business Enterprise*—a topic on which I am free to theorize with all the abandon that comes of immunity to the facts."

The new book came out in 1904. Factual or not, it was even more coruscating and still more curious than his first. For the point of view which it advocated seemed to fly in the face of common sense itself. Every economist from the days of Adam Smith had made of the capitalist the driving figure in the economic tableau; whether for better or worse, he was generally assumed to be the central generator of economic progress. But with Veblen all this was turned topsy-turvy. The businessman was still the central figure, but no longer the motor force. Now he was portrayed as the *saboteur* of the system!

Needless to say, it was a strange perspective on society which could produce so disconcerting a view. Veblen did not begin, as Ricardo or Marx or the Victorians, with the clash of human interests; he began at a stage below, in the nonhuman substratum of technology. What fascinated him was the machine. He saw society as dominated by the machine, caught up in its standardization, timed to its regular cycle of performance, geared to its insistence on accuracy and precision. More than that, he envisaged the economic process itself as being basically mechanical in character. Economics meant production and production meant the machinelike meshing of society as it turned out goods. Such a social machine would need tenders, of course—technicians and engineers to make whatever adjustments were necessary to ensure the most efficient cooperation of the parts. But from an over-all view, society could best be pictured as a gigantic but purely matter-of-fact mechanism, a highly specialized, highly co-ordinated human clock-work.

But where would the businessman fit into such a scheme? For the businessman was interested in making money, whereas the machine and its engineer masters knew no end except making goods. If the machine functioned well and fitted together smoothly, where would there be a place for a man whose only aim was profit?

Ideally, there would be none. The machine was not concerned with values and profits; it ground out goods. Hence the business-man would have no function to perform—unless he turned en-gineer. But as a member of the leisure class he was not interested in engineering; he wanted to accumulate. And this was some-thing the machine was not set up to do at all. So the business-man achieved his end, not by working within the framework of the social machine, but by conspiring against it! His function was not to help make goods, but to cause breakdowns in the regular flow of output so that values would fluctuate and he could capitalize on the confusion to reap a profit. And so, on top of the machinelike dependability of the actual production ap-paratus in the world, the businessman built a superstructure of credit, loans, and make-believe capitalizations. Below, society turned over in its mechanical routine; above, the structure of finance swayed and shifted. And as the financial counterpart to the real world teetered, opportunities for profit constantly ap-peared, disappeared, and reappeared. But the price of this profit seeking was high; it was the constant disturbing, undoing, even conscious misdirecting of the efforts of society to provision itself.

It is at first blush a rather shocking thesis. That businessmen should work *against* the interests of production seems worse than heretical. It sounds foolish.

But before we dismiss the theory as the product of a strangely warped and bitter mind, let us look again at the scene from which Veblen drew his subject. This was, let us remember, the age of American industry which Matthew Josephson has aptly called the time of the robber barons. We have already seen examples of the arrogance, the unaccountable, guiltless power which the business titans wielded like so many barbarian chiefs, and we know the bizarre lengths to which they went in the achievement of their often predatory goals. But while all this is grist for Veblen's mill, it does not quite justify his contention of sabotage. For that we must look at one further shortcoming of the robber barons: *these men were uninterested in producing goods.*

We might illustrate with an incident from 1868. At that time Jay Gould was fighting Vanderbilt for control of the Erie Railroad, in a lusty footnote to industrial history in which Gould and his men were forced to flee across the Hudson River in a rowboat and barricade themselves in a New Jersey hotel. But it is not the primitive nature of their combat which we now stop to remark, but their total unconcern for the actual railroad itself. For while he was fighting Vanderbilt, Gould had a letter from a superintendent telling him:

> The iron rails have broken and laminated and worn out beyond all precedent until there is scarcely a mile of your road, between Jersey City and Salamanca or Buffalo, where it is safe to run a train at the ordinary passenger or train speed, and many portions of the road can only be traversed safely by reducing the speed of all trains to 10 or 15 miles per hour.

When accidents piled up, one vice-president of the line said, "The public can take care of itself. It is as much as I can do to take care of the railroad"—by which he meant frantically shoring up its crumbling financial embankments.

And Gould was no exception. Very few of the heroes of the Golden Age of American finance had much interest in the solid realities of what underlay their structure of stocks and bonds and credits. Later on, a Henry Ford might introduce an era of intensely production-minded captains of industry, but the Harrimans, Morgans, Fricks, and Rockefellers were far more interested in the exciting manipulation of huge masses of intangible wealth than in the humdrum business of turning out goods. Henry Villard, for example, was widely heralded in 1883 as a business hero; in that year he hammered in the Gold Spike that connected his great transcontinental Northern Pacific line. Thousands cheered; Chief Sitting Bull (who was specially let out of jail for the purpose) formally ceded the hunting lands of his Sioux tribe to the railroad; and the economists declared that Villard's financial peccadilloes were as nothing compared with his organizing genius. His admirers might have felt differently had they known of a letter written by James Hill, a rival railroad man. He had surveyed the Villard empire with a less enthusiastic glance and declared: ". . . the lines are located in good country, some of it rich and producing a large tonnage; but the capitalization is far ahead of what it should be for what there is to show and the selection of routes and grades is abominable. *Practically it would have to be built over."*

Or a final example: the founding of the United States Steel Corporation in 1901. Viewed through Veblen's eyes, the steel combine was a vast social machine for producing steel, an assemblage of plants, furnaces, rail lines, and mines under a common management for their more efficient coordination. But this was only a minor consideration in the eyes of the men who "made" U. S. Steel. The eventual monster company had real assets of some $682 millions, but against this had been sold $303 millions of bonds, $510 millions of preferred stock, and $508 millions of common stock. The financial company, in other words, was twice as "big" as the real one and nothing more lay behind its common stock than the intangible essence of "good will." In the process of creating these intangibles, however, J. P. Morgan and Co. had earned a fee of $12,500,000, and subscription profits to underlying promoters had come to $50,000,000. Altogether, it cost $150,000,000 to float the venture. But all this might have been condoned had the new monopoly been used for the purpose Veblen had in mind—as an enormously efficient machine for the provision of steel. It was not. For thirteen years steel rails were quoted at $28 a ton, whereas it cost less than half of that to make them. In other words, the whole gain in technological unification was subverted to the end of maintaining a structure of make-believe finance.

In the light of the times, Veblen's theory does not seem so farfetched. It stung because it described, almost in the terms of a savage ritual, practices which were recognized as the ultimate of sophistication. But his essential thesis was all too well documented by the facts: the function of the great barons of business was indeed very different from the functions of the men who actually ran the productive machine. The bold game of financial chicanery certainly served as much to disturb the flow of goods as to promote it.

Oddly enough, the book created less of a furor than the *Theory of the Leisure Class*. *Business Enterprise* never leaped the bounds of professional readership to take the country's intelligentsia by storm, as its predecessor had done. The economists themselves regarded the book with an uneasy eye: how could one take entirely seriously a book which was so *clever* as this one? A sampling of his mordant humor describes the "watchful waiting" of a businessman.

> Doubtless this form of words, "watchful waiting" will have been employed in the first place to describe the frame of mind of a toad who has reached years of discretion and has found his appointed place along some frequented run where many flies and spiders pass and repass on their way to complete that destiny to which it has pleased an all-seeing and merciful Providence to call them; but by an easy turn of speech it has also been found suitable to describe that mature order of captains of industry who are governed by sound business principles. There is a certain bland sufficiency spread across the face of a toad so circumstanced, while his comely bulk gives assurance of a pyramidal stability of principles.

It was certainly a difficult book to appraise. Perhaps the most unexpected commentary was that one reader wrote to Veblen asking his advice on how to make money.

But the *Theory of Business Enterprise* was more than an acid treatment of the business system. It was, as well, a theory of social change. For Veblen believed that the days of the business leaders were numbered, that despite their power, there was ranged against them a formidable adversary. It was not the proletariat (for the *Leisure Class* had shown how the underlying

population looked up to its leaders), but a still more implacable foe: the machine.

For the machine, thought Veblen, "throws out anthropomor-
phic habits of thought." It forced men to think in terms of
matter-of-fact, in terms precise, measurable, and devoid of superstition and animism. Hence those who came in contact with the
machine process found it increasingly difficult to swallow the
presumptions of "natural law" and social differentiation which
surround the leisure class. And so society divided; not poor
against rich, but technician versus businessman, mechanic against
war lord, scientist opposed to ritualist.

In a later series of books, principally *The Engineers and
the Price System* and *Absentee Ownership and Business Enterprise,* he spelled out the "revolution" in greater detail. Eventually a corps of engineers would be recruited from society to
take over the chaos of the business system. Already they held
the real power of production in their hands, but they were as
yet unaware of the incompatibility of the business system with
a system of true industry. But one day they would take counsel
among themselves, dispense with the "lieutenants of absentee
ownership," and run the economy along the principles of a
huge, well-ordered production machine. And if they did not?
Then business would increase in predatoriness until it eventually degenerated into a system of naked force, undisguised pre-
rogative, and arbitrary command in which the businessman
would give way to a recrudescence of the old war lord. We
would call such a system fascism.

But to Veblen, writing on *The Technicians and Revolution*
in 1921, it was all a long way off. "There is nothing in the situation that should reasonably flutter the sensibilities of the Guardians or of that massive body of well-to-do citizens who make up
the rank-and-file of absentee owners, just yet." It is that "just
yet" which is so typical of the man. Despite the studied impersonality of his style, his animus bristles through his writing. And
yet, it is not a personal animus, not the rancor of one who is
privately affronted, but the amused and ironical detachment of a
man apart, a man who sees that all this is transient, and that the
ritual and make-believe will in time give way to something else.

This is not the time to make an appraisal of what he said;

that will come later. But we might note a curious comparison. Veblen's general approach reminds us of a most un-Veblenesque figure—that strange half-mad Utopian Socialist, Count Henri de Saint-Simon. Remember that Saint-Simon also extolled the producer and mocked the ornamental functionary. Perhaps it will serve to temper our judgment of Veblen's scorn of the business overlord if we reflect that at one time Saint-Simon's jibes at "M. the brother to the King" must have similarly shocked public sentiment.

The year 1906 was Veblen's last at Chicago. He was beginning to be famous abroad; he had attended a banquet at which the King of Norway was present and in an unusual display of sentiment had sent the menu to his mother, who was deeply moved that her son had met a king. But at home things were not so good. His philanderings had gone too far, and despite his books and his newly won rank of assistant professor, his conduct was not such as to advertise the university in the manner advocated by President Harper.

He sought a new position. But his fame was closer to notoriety than repute and he had much difficulty in finding another post. Eventually he went to Stanford. His reputation had preceded him: his fearsome scholarship, his personal untouchability, his extramarital proclivities. All were amply vindicated. He impressed those few of his colleagues who could endure his maddening refusal to commit himself on anything, and he became known as "the last man who knew everything." But his home economics were unchanged: on one occasion, hoping to be tactful, a friend referred to a young lady staying at his house as his niece. "That was not my niece," said Veblen. And that disposed of that.

His wife had divorced him in 1911. He must have been an impossible husband (he would leave the letters from his admirers in his pockets where she would be sure to find them), and yet, rather pathetically, it was she who hoped that the marriage would eventually right itself. It never did, more than temporarily; once when Ellen thought that she was pregnant, Veblen sent her home in a panic. He considered himself totally unfit to be a father and rationalized his fears with anthropological arguments on the unimportance of the male in the household. Finally a divorce became an inescapable necessity. "Mr. Veblen," wrote Ellen at the end of a long letter of self-commiseration, "though his part of the bargain is to furnish me with $25 a month—probably will not do it." She was right.

The year of his divorce he moved on again, this time to the University of Missouri. He stayed in the house of his friend Davenport, a well-known economist—a lonely and idiosyncratic man writing in the cellar. Yet it was a period of great productivity for Veblen. He looked back on the days at Chicago and summed up the perversion of centers of learning into centers of high-powered public relations and football in the most stinging commentary ever penned on the American university: *The Higher Learning in America*. While it was still in composition Veblen said, half seriously, that it would be subtitled "A Study in Total Depravity."

But more important, he turned his eyes to Europe where the threat of war was imminent, and he wrote about Germany, comparing her dynastic and warlike state to a tapeworm, in these vitriolic words: ". . . the tapeworm's relation to his host is not something easy to beautify in words, or even to authenticate in such convincing fashion as will ensure his affectionate retention on grounds of use and wont." The book on *Imperial Germany* suffered an unusual fate; although the propaganda office of the government wanted to use it for war purposes, the Post Office found in it so many remarks uncomplimentary to Britain and the United States that they barred it from the mails.

When war finally came, he offered his services to Washington: this man, to whom patriotism was only another symptom of a barbaric culture, was not devoid of it himself. But in Washington he was juggled about like a hot potato; everybody had heard of him, but no one wanted him. Finally they shelved him in an unimportant post in the Food Administration. There he behaved like himself: he wrote memoranda on how best to get in the crops—but since his suggestions involved a wholesale reorganization of rural social and business ways, they were called "interesting" and ignored. He proposed a steep tax on the employers of domestic servants in order to release manpower; that too was overlooked. It was a typical Veblen proposal: butlers and footmen, he said, "are typically and eminently an able-bodied sort, who will readily qualify as stevedores and freighthandlers as soon as the day's work has somewhat hardened their muscles and reduced their bulk."

In 1918 he came to New York to write for the *Dial,* a liberal magazine. He had recently published *An Inquiry into the Nature of the Peace* in which he baldly stated that the alternatives facing Europe were a perpetuation of the old order with all its barbarous incentives to war or the abandonment of the business system itself. The program was at first talked about and then lost its fashion; Veblen touted it in the *Dial,* but with every issue, the circulation dropped. He was asked to lecture at the newly formed New School for Social Research with a bevy of stars: John Dewey, Charles A. Beard, Dean Roscoe Pound. But even that turned sour; he was still a mumbler in the classroom and his lectures, which were filled to overflowing at first, were reduced to a handful in short order.

It was a strange mixture of fame and failure. H. L. Mencken has written that "Veblenism was shining in full brilliance. There were Veblenists, Veblen Clubs, Veblen remedies for all the sorrows of the world. There were, in Chicago, Veblen Girls—perhaps Gibson Girls grown middle-aged and despairing." But for the man himself there was nothing. A bust of himself in the lobby of the New School caused him such acute embarrassment that it was finally less prominently displayed in the library. Personally, he was nearly helpless, nurse-maided through the everyday problems of living by a few devoted former students, Wesley Mitchell and Isadore Lubin, already important economists in their own right. For a while he watched eagerly for a sign of a new world to come: an age of engineers and technicians, and he hoped that the Russian Revolution might usher in such an era. But he was disappointed in what he saw, and as Horace Kallen of the New School has written, "When the thing failed to come off, he gave signs of a certain relaxation of will and interest, of a kind of turning toward death. . . ."

Belatedly he was offered the presidency of the American Economic Association. He turned it down with the comment, "They didn't offer it to me when I needed it." Finally he went back to California. Joseph Dorfman, in a definitive biography, tells of his arriving at his small cabin in the West and thinking that someone had unjustly seized his plot of land. "He took a hatchet and methodically broke the windows, going at the matter with a dull intensity that was like madness, the intensity of a physically lazy person roused into sudden activity by anger." It was all a misunderstanding, and he settled there, in home-built rustic furniture that must have reminded him of his boyhood, in coarse workmen's clothes purchased by mail from Sears, Roebuck, disturbing nothing of nature, not even a weed, and allowing the rats and skunks to brush by his legs and explore his cabin as he sat immobile, wrapped in unhappy distant thoughts.

It was neither a happy nor a successful life on which to look back. A second wife, whom he had married in 1914, had had delusions of persecution and had been institutionalized; his friends were far away; his work had been captured by the dilettantes and was largely disregarded by the economists and unknown to the engineers.

He was seventy now and he wrote no more. "I have decided not to break the Sabbath," he declared. "It is such a nice Sabbath." His friends came to see him and found him more distant than ever. He was subjected to adulation and received letters from self-appointed disciples. "Can you tell me in what house in Chicago it was that you did your early writings and if possible what room?" inquired one.

In 1929, a few months before the great crash, he died. He left behind a will and this unsigned penciled injunction: "It is also my wish, in case of death, to be cremated, if it can conveniently be done, as expeditiously and inexpensively as may be, without any ritual or ceremony of any kind; that my ashes be thrown loose into the sea, or into some sizable stream running into the sea; that no tombstone, slab, epitaph, effigy, tablet, inscription or monument of any kind or nature, be set up in my memory or name at any place or at any time; that no obituary, memorial, portrait, or biography of me, nor any letters written to or by me be printed or published, or in any way reproduced, copied, or circulated."

As is always the case, his request was ignored: he was cremated and his ashes strewn out over the Pacific, but his memorialization by the written word began immediately.

What are we to think of this strange figure?

It is hardly necessary to point out that he went to extremes. His characterization of the leisure class, for example, was a masterpiece of portraiture on one page, but a caricature on the next. When he picks out the silent component of wealth in our accepted canons of beauty, when he slyly mentions that "the high gloss of a gentleman's hat or of a patent-leather shoe has no more intrinsic beauty than a similarly high gloss on a threadbare sleeve," he is on sound ground and we must meekly accept the judgment of snobbery that has been passed on our taste. But when he writes, "The vulgar suggestion of thrift, which is nearly inseparable from the cow, is a standing objection to the decorative use of the animal," he shades off into the absurd. The irrepressible Mencken picked him up on that one: "Has the genial professor, pondering his great problems, ever taken a walk in the country? And has he, in the course of that walk, ever crossed a pasture inhabited by a cow? And has he, in making that crossing, ever passed astern of the cow herself? And has he, thus passing astern, ever stepped carelessly and—."

Much the same criticism can be brought against Veblen's characterization of the businessman, or for that matter, the leisure class itself. That the financial titan of the halcyon days of American capitalism was a robber baron there is no doubt, and Veblen's portrait of him, chilling though it is, is uncomfortably close to the truth. But, like Marx, Veblen did not see that the *climate* of business was susceptible to change, and that the institution of business, much as the monarchy in England, might adapt itself to a vastly altered world. More to the point—because it is closer to Veblen's own approach—he did not see that the machine, that wholesale rearranger of life, would change the nature of the entrepreneurial function just as much as it would alter the thought processes of the workman, and that the businessman himself would be forced into a much more bureaucratic mold by virtue of his duties as a manager of a vast, ongoing machine.

It is true that Veblen's infatuation with the machine leaves us a little wary; it is a jarring note in a philosopher otherwise so devoid of lyricism. It may be that machines make us think matter-of-factly—but about what? Charlie Chaplin in *Modern*

Times was not a happy or well-adjusted man. A corps of engineers might well run our society more efficiently, but whether they would run it more humanely is another question.

Yet Veblen did put his finger on a central process of change, a process that looms larger than any other in our time and that had been strangely overlooked in all the investigations of his contemporary economists. *That process was the emergence of technology and science as the leading forces of historic change in the twentieth century.* There is no doubt that the watershed of the technological age is as great as any in history, and that the gradual introduction of machinery into the finest interstices and over the largest spans of life is accomplishing a revolution comparable to that in which men learned to domesticate animals or to live in cities. Like every great discoverer of that which is obvious but has been unseen, Veblen was far too impatient; processes that will take generations, even centuries, he expected to mature in decades or even years. Yet it is to his credit that he saw the machine as the primary fact of economic life in his time, and for this single brilliant illumination he must be placed in the front rank of economic philosophers.

And then, too, he gave economics a new pair of eyes with which to see the world. After Veblen's savage description of the mores of daily life, the classical picture of society as a well-mannered tea party became increasingly difficult to maintain. His scorn of the old school was bitingly expressed when he once wrote: "A gang of Aleutian Islanders, slushing about in the wrack and surf with rakes and magical incantations for the capture of shellfish, are held . . . to be engaged on a feat of hedonistic equilibration in rent, wages, and interest," and just as he ridiculed the classical attempt to resolve the primitive human struggle by fitting it into a fleshless and bloodless framework, so he highlighted the emptiness of trying to understand the actions of modern man in terms which derived from an incomplete and outmoded set of preconceptions. Man, said Veblen, is not to be comprehended in terms of sophisticated "economic laws" in which his innate ferocity and creativity are both smothered under a cloak of rationalization. He is better dealt with in the less flattering but more fundamental vocabulary of the anthropologist or the psychologist: a creature of strong and irrational drives, credulous, untutored, ritualistic. Leave aside the preconceptions of another age, he asked of the economists, and find out why man actually behaves as he does.

His pupil, Wesley Clair Mitchell, a great economic investigator in his own right, summed him up this way: "There was the disturbing influence of Thorstein Veblen—that visitor from another world who dissected the current commonplaces which the student had unconsciously acquired, as if the most familiar of his daily thoughts were the curious products wrought in him by outside forces. No other such emancipator of the mind from the subtle tyranny of circumstance has been known in social science, and no other such enlarger of the realm of inquiry."

IX

The Heresies of
John Maynard Keynes

A FEW YEARS before his death, Thorstein Veblen had done something oddly out of character—he had taken a plunge in the stock market. A friend had recommended an oil stock, and Veblen, thinking of the financial problems of old age, had risked a part of his savings. He made a little money on the venture at first, but his inseparable bad luck plagued him—no sooner had the stock gone up than it was cited in the current oil scandals. His investment eventually became worthless.

The incident is unimportant in itself except insofar as it reveals one more tiny chink in Veblen's armor. And yet, in another context, this pathetic misadventure is curiously revealing. For Veblen himself had fallen victim to the same dazzling lure that blinded America: when the most disenchanted of its observers could be tempted to swallow a draught, is there any wonder that the country was drunk with the elixir of prosperity?

Certainly the signs of prosperity were visible at every hand. America in the late 1920's had found jobs for 45 million of its citizens to whom it paid some $77 billions in wages, rents, profits, and interest—a flood of income comparable to nothing the world had ever seen. When Herbert Hoover said with earnest simplicity, "We shall soon with the help of God be within sight of the day when poverty will be banished from the nation," he may have been shortsighted—as who was not?—but he rested his case on the incontrovertible fact that the average American family lived better, ate better, dressed better, and enjoyed more of the amenities of life than had any average family hitherto in the history of the world.

The nation was possessed of a new vision, one a great deal more uplifting than the buccaneering ideals of the robber barons. John J. Raskob, chairman of the Democratic party, gave it precise expression in the title of an article he wrote for the *Ladies' Home Journal:* "Everybody Ought to Be Rich." "If a man saves $15 a week," wrote Raskob, "and invests in good common stocks, at the end of twenty years he will have at least $80,000 and an income from investments of around $400 a month. He will be rich."

That bit of arithmetic merely presupposed that such a man would keep reinvesting his dividends, figured at about six per cent a year. But there was an even more alluring road to riches. Had a devotee of Raskob's formula *spent* his dividends and merely allowed his money to increase with the trend of stock prices, he would have achieved his goal of wealth just as rapidly and a good deal less painfully. Suppose he had bought stock in 1921 with the $780 he would have saved at $15 a week. By 1922 his money would be worth $1,092. If he then added another $780 yearly he would have found himself worth $4,800 in 1925, $6,900 a year later, $8,800 in 1927, and an incredible $16,000 in 1928. Incredible? By May 1929 he would have figured his worldly wealth at over $21,000: in less than nine years his savings of $7,020 would have tripled. And when the Great Bull Market had gone on for nearly half a generation in an almost uninterrupted rise, who could be blamed for thinking this the royal road to riches? Barber or bootblack, banker or businessman, everyone gambled and everyone won, and the only question in most people's minds was why they had never thought of it before.

It is hardly necessary to dwell upon the sequel. In that awful last week of October, 1929, the market collapsed. To the brokers on the floor of the Stock Exchange it must have been as if Niagara had suddenly burst through the windows, for a cataract of unmanageable selling converged on the market place. In sheer exhaustion brokers wept and tore their collars; they watched stupefied as immense fortunes melted like spun sugar; they shouted themselves hoarse trying to attract the attention of a buyer. The grim jokes of the period speak for themselves: it was said that with every share of Goldman Sachs you got a complimentary revolver, and that when you booked a hotel room the clerk inquired, "For sleeping or jumping?"

When the debris was swept away the wreckage was fearful to behold. In two insane months the market lost all the ground it had gained in two manic years; $40 billion of values simply disappeared. By the end of three years our investor's inflated paper fortune of $21,000 had diminished by eighty per cent; his original $7,000 of savings was worth barely $4,000. The vision of Every Man a Wealthy Man had been shown up as an hallucination.

In retrospect it was inevitable. The stock market had been built on a honeycomb of loans that could bear just so much strain and no more. And more than that, there were shaky timbers and rotten wood in the foundation which propped up the magnificent show of prosperity. Chairman Raskob's formula for retirement was arithmetically accurate enough, all right, but it left unanswered the important question of how a man was to save $15 out of an average pay envelope which came to only $30.

The national flood of income was indubitably imposing in its bulk, but when one followed its course into its millions of terminal rivulets, it was apparent that the nation as a whole benefited very unevenly from its flow. Some twenty-four thousand families at the apex of the social pyramid received a stream of income three times as large as six million families squashed at the bottom—the average income of the fortunate families at the peak was *six hundred and thirty times* the average income of the families at the base. Nor was this the only shortcoming. Disregarded in the hullabaloo of limitless prosperity were two million citizens out of work, and ignored behind their façade of classical marble, banks were failing at the rate of two a day for *six years* before the crash. And then there was the fact that the average American had used his prosperity in a suicidal way; he had mortgaged himself up to his neck, had extended his resources dangerously under the temptation of installment buying, and then had ensured his fate by eagerly buying fantastic quantities of stock—some 300 million shares, it is estimated—not outright, but on margin.

Inevitable or not, it was far from visible at the time. It was a rare day that did not carry the news of some typical figure assuring the nation of its basic health. Even so eminent an economist as Irving Fisher of Yale was lulled by the superficial evidences of prosperity into announcing that we were marching along a "permanently high plateau"—a figure of speech given a macabre humor by the fact that stocks fell off the brink of that plateau one week to the day after he made his statement.

But dramatic as it was, it was not the wild decline of the stock market which most damaged the faith of a generation firmly wedded to the conviction of never-ending prosperity. It was what happened at home. A few items from those dreary years may serve to illustrate. In Muncie, Indiana—the city made famous by its selection as "Middletown"—every fourth factory worker lost his job by the end of 1930. In Chicago the majority of working girls were earning less than twenty-five cents an hour and a quarter of them made less than ten cents. In New York's Bowery alone, two thousand jobless crowded into breadlines every day. In the nation as a whole, residential construction fell by ninety-five per cent. Nine million savings accounts were lost. Eighty-five thousand businesses failed. The national volume of salaries dwindled forty per cent; dividends fifty-six per cent; wages sixty per cent.

And the worst of it, the most depressing aspect of the Great Depression, was that there seemed to be no end to it, no turning point, no relief. In 1930, the nation manfully whistled "Happy Days Are Here Again," but the national income precipitously fell from $87 billions to $75 billions. In 1931 the country sang "I've Got Five Dollars"; meanwhile its income plummeted to $59 billions. In 1932 the song was grimmer: "Brother Can You Spare a Dime?"—national income had dwindled to a miserable $42 billions.

By 1933 the nation was virtually prostrate. The income of the country was down to $39 billions. Over half the prosperity of only four years back had vanished without a trace; the average standard of living was back where it had been twenty years before. On street corners, in homes, in Hoovervilles, 14 million unemployed sat, haunting the land. It seemed as if the proud spirit of hope had been permanently crushed out of America.

It was the unemployment that was hardest to bear. The jobless millions were like an embolism in the nation's vital circulation; and while their indisputable existence argued more forcibly than any text that something was wrong with the system, the economists wrung their hands and racked their brains and called upon the spirit of Adam Smith, but could offer neither diagnosis nor remedy. Unemployment—this kind of unemployment—was simply not listed among the possible ills of the system: it was absurd, impossible, unreasonable, and paradoxical. But it was there.

It would seem logical that the man who would seek to solve this impossible paradox of not enough production existing side by side with men fruitlessly seeking work would be a Leftwinger, an economist with strong sympathies for the proletariat, an angry man. Nothing could be further from the fact. The man who tackled it was almost a dilettante with nothing like a chip on his shoulder. The simple truth was that his talents inclined in every direction. He had, for example, written a most recondite book on mathematical probability, a book that Bertrand Russell had declared "impossible to praise too highly"; then he had gone on to match his skill in abstruse logic with a flair for making money—he accumulated a fortune of £500,000 by way of the most treacherous of all roads to riches: dealing in international currencies and commodities. More impressive yet, he had written his mathematics treatise on the side, as it were, while engaged in Government service, and he piled up his private wealth by applying himself for only half an hour a day while still abed.

But this is only a sample of his many-sidedness. He was an economist, of course—a Cambridge don with all the dignity and erudition that go with such an appointment; but when it came to choosing a wife he eschewed the ladies of learning and picked the leading ballerina from Diaghilev's famous company. He managed to be simultaneously the darling of the Bloomsbury set, the cluster of Britain's most *avant-garde* intellectual brilliants, and also the chairman of a life insurance company, a niche in life rarely noted for its intellectual abandon. He was a pillar of stability in delicate matters of international diplomacy, but his official correctness did not prevent him from acquiring a knowledge of other European politicians that included their mistresses, neuroses, and financial prejudices. He collected modern art before it was fashionable to do so, but at the same time he was a classicist with the finest private collection of Newton's writings in the world. He ran a theater, and he came to be a Director of the Bank of England. He knew Roosevelt and Churchill and also Bernard Shaw and Pablo Picasso. He played bridge like a speculator, preferring a spectacular play to a sound contract, and solitaire like a statistician, noting how long it took for the game to come out twice running. And he once claimed that he had but one regret in life—he wished he had drunk more champagne.

His name was John Maynard Keynes, an old British name (pronounced to rhyme with "rains") that could be traced back to one William de Cahagnes and 1066. Keynes was a traditionalist; he liked to think that greatness ran in families, and it is true that his own father was John Neville Keynes, an illustrious enough economist in his own right. But it took more than the ordinary gifts of heritage to account for the son; it was as if the talents that would have sufficed half a dozen men were by happy accident crowded into one person.

By a coincidence he was born in 1883, in the very year that Karl Marx passed away. But the two economists who thus touched each other in time, although each was to exert the profoundest influence on the philosophy of the capitalist system, could hardly have differed from one another more. Marx was bitter, at bay, heavy and disappointed; as we know, he was the draftsman of Capitalism Doomed. Keynes loved life and sailed through it buoyant, at ease, and consummately successful to become the architect of Capitalism Viable. Perhaps we can trace Marx's passionate prophecy of collapse to the thread of neurotic failure which marked his practical life; if so we can surely credit Keynes's persuasive salesmanship of reconstruction to the exhilaration and achievement which marked his.

His boyhood was Victorian, Old School, and premonitory of brilliance. At age four and a half he was already puzzling out for himself the economic meaning of interest; at six he was wondering about how his brain worked; at seven his father found him a "thoroughly delightful companion." He went to a Mr. Goodchild's preparatory school where he gave evidence of his flair for handling his fellow men: he had a "slave" who obediently trailed him with his schoolbooks, a service rendered in exchange for assistance with the knottier problems of homework, and a "commercial treaty" with another boy whom he disliked: Keynes agreed to get the boy one book a week out of the library in exchange for which the party of the second part agreed never to approach within fifteen yards of the party of the first.

At fourteen he applied for and won a scholarship to Eton. Horror stories on English public schools to the contrary, he was neither sadistically abused nor intellectually quashed. He bloomed; his marks were superlative; he won prizes by the score; bought himself a lavender waistcoat; acquired a taste for champagne; grew tall and rather stooped and cultivated a mustache; rowed; became a formidable debater; and without turning into a snob became an Eton enthusiast. Yet a letter to his father when he was only seventeen shows a discernment unusual for that age. The Boer War had come to a climax and the headmaster made a speech; Keynes described it perfectly in five phrases: "It was the usual stuff. Ought to show our thankfulness; remember dignity of school; if anything done must be of best; as always before."

Eton was a vast success; King's College at Cambridge was to be a triumph. Alfred Marshall begged him to become a full-time economist; Professor Pigou—Marshall's heir-to-be—had him to breakfast once a week. He was elected Secretary of the Union, a post automatically carrying an eventual presidency of one of the most famous nongovernmental debating societies in the world; he was sought out by Leonard Woolf and Lytton Strachey and the nucleus of what was to be known as the Bloomsbury group came into being; he climbed mountains (Strachey complained at the "multitudes of imbecile mountains"); bought books; stayed up in the small hours arguing; shone. He was a phenomenon.

But even phenomena must eat and there came the question of what to do. He had very little money and the prospect of an academic career offered less. And he had larger visions: "I want to manage a railway or organize a Trust," he wrote to Strachey;

"it is so easy and fascinating to master the principles of these things."

No one offered him a railway or a trust and he chose instead to try the public route to success. He took the civil service examinations with an apparent indifference that made Strachey's sister ask if his insouciance was a pose. No, he had it all figured out and so what was the use of fretting; he was sure to land in the top ten. Of course he did; he was second, and his lowest mark was in the economics section of the examination. "The examiners presumably knew less than I did," he explained later, a remark which would be unforgivably presumptuous if it were not, in this case, entirely true.

Hence, in 1907 to the India Office. Keynes hated it. He was spending his freshest energies at home on an early draft of his mathematical treatise, and he found the post of a minor official in public office a far cry from running a railway. After two years he had had enough. His efforts, he declared, consisted in having one pedigreed bull shipped to Bombay, and all that he had found in government work was that an ill-considered remark might result in your being "snubbed." He resigned and went back to Cambridge. But his years could not have been so utterly useless. From what he learned of Indian affairs he wrote a book in 1913 on *Indian Currency and Finance* which everyone admitted to be a small masterpiece, and when a Royal Commission was formed that same year to look into the Indian currency problem Keynes at twenty-nine was asked to be a member —a remarkable honor.

Cambridge was more to his liking. He was an immediate success and as a mark of the esteem in which he was held, he was given the editorship of the *Economic Journal,* Britain's most influential economic publication—a post he was to hold for thirty-three years.

Even more pleasant than Cambridge was Bloomsbury. Bloomsbury was both a place and a state of mind; the little group of intellectuals to whom Keynes had belonged as an undergraduate had now acquired a home, a philosophy, and a reputation. Perhaps not more than twenty or thirty people ever belonged to that charmed circle, but their opinions set the artistic standards of England—after all, it included Leonard and Virginia Woolf,

E. M. Forster, Clive Bell, Roger Fry, Lytton Strachey. If Bloomsbury smiled, a poet's name was made; if it frowned, a painter
was *déclassé*. It is said that it could use the word "really" in a
dozen different intonations, of which sophisticated boredom was
by no means the least. It was a group at once idealistic and
cynical, courageous and fragile. And slightly mad: there was the
incident known as the Dreadnought Hoax in which Virginia
Woolf (then Stephen) and a few co-conspirators dressed up as
the Emperor of Abyssinia and entourage and were thus escorted
with honors aboard one of His Majesty's most closely guarded
battleships.

In all of this, Keynes was a central figure; adviser, councilor,
referee. He could talk about anything with complete assurance:
William Walton the composer, Frederick Ashton the choreogra-
pher, and many another artist or professional was used to
Keynes's "No, no, you're absolutely wrong about that . . ." His
nickname, it might be added, was Pozzo, a sobriquet pinned on
him after a Corsican diplomat known for his multifarious interests and his scheming mind.

It was a rather dilettantish beginning for one who was to set
the capitalist world by its ears.

The war years somewhat disrupted Bloomsbury. Keynes was
called to the Treasury and assigned to work on Britain's overseas finances. He must have been something of a phenomenon
there, too. An anecdote in point was later recounted by an old
associate: "There was an urgent need for Spanish *pesetas*. With
difficulty a smallish sum was raked up. Keynes duly reported
this to a relieved Secretary to the Treasury who remarked that
at any rate for a short time we had a supply of *pesetas*. 'Oh no!'
said Keynes. 'What!' said his horrified chief. 'I've sold them all;
I'm going to break the market.' And he did."

He was soon a key figure in the Treasury. His biographer and
fellow economist, Roy Harrod, tells us that men of ripe judgment have declared that Keynes contributed more to winning
the war than any other person in civil life. Be that as it may,
he managed to find time for other things. On a financial mission
to France he was seized with the bright idea that it would help
balance the French accounts with the British if they sold some of

their pictures to the National Gallery. He thus casually acquired a hundred thousand dollars' worth of Corot, Delacroix, Forain, Gauguin, Ingres, and Manet for the British, and managed to get a Cézanne for himself: Big Bertha was shelling Paris and prices were pleasantly depressed. Back in London he attended the ballet; Lydia Lopokova was dancing the part of the beauty in "The Good-Humored Ladies" and she was the rage. The Sitwells had her to a party where she and Keynes met. One can imagine Keynes with his classic English and Lydia with her classic struggles with English: "I dislike being in the country in August," she said, "because my legs get so bitten by barristers."

But all this was tangential to the main thing—the settlement of Europe after the war. Keynes was now an important personage—one of those unidentified men one sees standing behind the chair of a head of state ready to whisper a guiding word. He went to Paris as Deputy for the Chancellor of the Exchequer on the Supreme Economic Council with full power to make decisions and as representative of the Treasury at the Peace Conference itself. But he was only second echelon; he had a grandstand seat but no power to interfere directly in the game. It must have been an agony of frustration and impotence, for at close quarters he watched while Wilson was outmaneuvered by Clemenceau and the ideals of a humane peace replaced by the achievement of a vindictive one.

"It must be weeks since I've written anyone," he wrote to his mother in 1919, "but I've been utterly worn out, partly by work, partly by depression at the evil around me. I've never been so miserable as for the last two or three weeks; the Peace is outrageous and impossible and can bring nothing but misfortune behind it."

He dragged himself from the sickbed to protest against what he called the "murder of Vienna," but he could not stop the tide. The peace was to be a Carthaginian one and Germany was to pay a sum of reparations so huge that it would force her into the most vicious practices of international trade in order to earn the pounds and francs and dollars. This was not the popular opinion, of course, but Keynes saw that in the Versailles Treaty lay the unwitting goad for an even more formidable resurgence of German autarchy and militarism.

He resigned in despair; then three days before the treaty was signed he began his polemic against it. He called it *The Economic Consequences of the Peace;* when it appeared that December (he wrote it at top speed and fury), it made his name.

It was brilliantly written and crushing. Keynes had seen the protagonists at work and his descriptions of them combined the skill of a novelist with the cutting insight of a Bloomsbury critic. He wrote of Clemenceau that "He had only one illusion —France; and one disillusion—mankind, including his own colleagues not least"; and of Wilson, ". . . like Odysseus, he looked wiser when seated." But while his portraits sparkled, it was his analysis of the harm that had been done that was unforgettable. For Keynes saw the Conference as a reckless settlement of political grudge in utter disregard of the pressing problem of the moment—the resuscitation of Europe into an integrating and functioning whole.

> The Council of Four paid no attention to these issues, being preoccupied with others,—Clemenceau to crush the economic life of his enemy, Lloyd George to do a deal and bring home something that would pass muster for a week, the President to do nothing that was not just and right. It is an extraordinary fact that the fundamental problems of a Europe starving and disintegrating before their eyes, was the one question in which it was impossible to arouse the interest of the Four. Reparation was their main excursion into the economic field, and they settled it as a problem of theology, of politics, of electoral chicane, from every point of view except that of the economic future of the States whose destiny they were handling.

And he went on to deliver this solemn warning:

> The danger confronting us, therefore, is the rapid depression of the standard of life of the European populations to a point which will mean actual starvation for some (a point already reached in Russia and approximately reached in Austria). Men will not always die quietly. For starvation, which brings to some lethargy and a helpless despair, drives

other temperaments to the nervous instability of hysteria and to a mad despair. And these in their distress may overturn the remnants of organization, and submerge civilization itself in their attempts to satisfy desperately the overwhelming needs of the individual. This is the danger against which all our resources and courage and idealism must now cooperate.

The book was an immense success. The unworkability of the treaty was manifest almost from the moment of its signing, but Keynes was the first to see it, to say it, and to suggest an outright revision. He became known as an economist of extraordinary foresight, and when the Dawes Plan in 1924 began the long process of undoing the impasse of 1919, his gift for prophecy was confirmed.

He was famous now, but there remained the question of what to do. He chose business, the riskiest possible business, and with a capital of a few thousand pounds he began to speculate in the international markets. He nearly lost it all, was helped with a loan from a banker who had never met him but who was impressed by his work during the war, recouped, and went on to roll up a fortune worth then two million dollars. It was all done in the most casual way. Keynes disdained inside information—in fact, he once declared that Wall Street traders could make huge fortunes if only they would disregard their "inside" information—and his own oracles were nothing but his minute scrutiny of balance sheets, his encyclopedic knowledge of finance, his intuition into personalities, and a certain flair for trading. Abed in the morning he would study his items of financial intelligence, make his decisions, phone his orders, and that was that; the day was now free for more important things, like economic theory. He would have gotten along famously with David Ricardo.

He made money, by the way, not only for himself. He became the Bursar of King's College and turned a small fund of £30,000 into one of £380,000. He managed an investment trust and guided the finances of a life insurance company. But he never did—despite his undergraduate wish—run a railway.

Meanwhile—there was always more than one thing going on

at a time with Keynes—he wrote for the *Manchester Guardian,*
gave regular classes in Cambridge, in which he spiced dry theory
with an intimate account of the goings on and personalities of
the international commodity marts, bought more pictures, acquired more books, and married Lydia Lopokova. The ballerina
became the wife of the Cambridge don, a new role which, somewhat to the surprise (and relief) of Keynes's friends, she filled
to perfection. She gave up her professional career, of course, but
a visiting friend later reported hearing alarming thumps and
crashes from above: Lydia was still practicing her art.

She was extremely beautiful; he was altogether the proper
admirer, not handsome but tall and dignified. His large, somewhat gawky frame provided a suitable pedestal for a longish,
triangular inquisitive face: a straight nose, a clipped mustache
held over from Eton days, full, mobile lips, and a rather disap-
pointing chin. The eyes were most revealing; under arching
brows they could be grave, icy, sparkling, or "soft as bees' bot-
toms in blue flowers," as one editor wrote, depending, perhaps,
on whether he was acting as Government emissary, speculator,
Bloomsbury brilliant, or balletomane.

There was one odd mannerism: Keynes liked to sit like an
English variant of a Chinese mandarin, with his hands tucked
out of sight in the opposing sleeves of his coat. It was a gesture
of concealment made all the more curious because of his inor-
dinate interest in other people's hands and his pride in his own.
Indeed, he even went to the extent of having casts made of his
and his wife's hands and talked of making a collection of casts
of his friends'; and when he met a man the first thing he noticed
was the character of his palms and fingers and nails. Later, when
he first talked with Franklin Roosevelt, he noted down this description of the President:

> . . . But at first, of course, I did not look closely at these
> things. For naturally my concentrated attention was on his
> hands. Firm and fairly strong, but not clever or with finesse,
> shortish round nails like those at the end of a business man's
> fingers. I cannot draw them right, yet while not distinguished
> (to my eye) they are not of a common type. All the same, they
> were oddly familiar. Where had I seen them before? I spent

ten minutes at least searching my memory as for a forgotten name, hardly knowing what I was saying about silver and balanced budgets and public works. At last it came to me. Sir Edward Grey. A more solid and Americanized Sir Edward Grey.

It is doubtful whether Roosevelt would have written as he did to Felix Frankfurter: "I had a grand talk with K. and liked him immensely," had he known that he was being summed up in the eyes of the other as a businessman's version of an English Foreign Secretary.

By 1935 it was already a brilliantly established career. The book on *Indian Currency and Finance* had been a tour de force, albeit a small one, *The Economic Consequences of the Peace* had made an éclat, and the *Treatise on Probability* was an equal triumph, although far more specialized. An amusing incident in regard to this last book: Keynes was having dinner with Professor Max Planck, the mathematical genius who was responsible for the development of quantum mechanics, one of the more bewildering achievements of the human mind. Planck turned to Keynes and told him that he had once considered going into economics himself. But he had decided against it—it was too hard. Keynes repeated the story with relish to a friend back at Cambridge. "Why, that's odd," said the friend. "Bertrand Russell was telling me just the other day that he'd also thought about going into economics. But he decided it was too easy."

But mathematics was only a side line, as we know; in 1923 a *Tract on Monetary Reform* again raised the eyebrows of the world. Now Keynes was inveighing against the fetishism of gold, against the peculiar passivity evidenced by men's abdication of conscious control of their own currencies and their transfer of this responsibility to the impersonal mechanism of an international gold standard. It was a technical book of course, but like all of Keynes's works, lit up with telling phrases. One thrust will surely be added to the stock of English aphorisms: talking of the "long run" consequences of some venerable economic axiom, Keynes dryly wrote: "In the long run we are all dead."

Then to top it off, in 1930 he had published a *Treatise on*

Money—a long, difficult, uneven, sometimes brilliant and sometimes baffling attempt to account for the behavior of the whole
economy. The *Treatise* was a fascinating book, for it took as its
central problem the question of what made the economy operate
so unevenly—now bustling with prosperity, now sluggish with
depression.

The question, of course, had absorbed the attention of economists for decades. Great speculative crashes aside—like the
1929 bust and its predecessors in history (we have seen one such
in eighteenth-century France when the Mississippi Company collapsed)—the normal course of trade seemed to evidence a wavelike
succession of expansions and contractions, not unlike a kind of
economic breathing. In England, for example, business had been
bad in 1801, good in 1802, bad in 1808, good in 1810, bad in 1815,
and so on for over a hundred years; in America the pattern
was the same although the dates were slightly different.

What lay behind this alternation of prosperity and depression?
At first the cycles of business were thought to be a sort of mass
nervous disorder: "These periodic collapses are really *mental*
in their nature, depending on variations of despondency, hope-
fulness, excitement, disappointment, and panic," wrote an observer in 1867. But although such a statement was undoubtedly
a good description of the state of mind in Wall Street or Lom-
bard Street, Lancaster or New England, it left unanswered the
basic question: What causes such a widespread nervous hysteria?

Some early explanations looked *outside* the economic process
for an answer. W. Stanley Jevons, whose Victorian economics of
Pain and Pleasure we have met before, ventured an explanation which pinned the blame on *sunspots*—not quite so farfetched an idea as it might at first appear. For Jevons was impressed by the fact that business cycles from 1721 to 1878 had
an average duration, from boom to boom, of 10.46 years, and
that sunspots (which had been discovered in 1801 by Sir William Herschel) showed a periodicity of 10.45 years. The corre-
lation, Jevons was convinced, was too close to be purely accidental. Sunspots, he thought, caused weather cycles, which caused
rainfall cycles, which caused crop cycles, which caused business
cycles.

It was not a bad theory—except for one thing. A more careful calculation of the sunspot cycles lengthened their periodicity to eleven years and the neat correspondence between celestial mechanics and the vagaries of business broke down. Sunspots went the way of astronomy and the quest for the motivating factors of business cycles returned to more earthbound considerations.

It returned, as a matter of fact, to an area first bumblingly but intuitively pointed out by Malthus a century before—the area of saving.

Perhaps we will remember the doubtings of Parson Malthus —his rather inarticulate feeling that saving could somehow result in a "general glut." Ricardo had scoffed; Mill had pooh-poohed; and the idea had become part of the paraphernalia of the underworld. To say that saving might be a source of trouble—why, that was impugning thrift itself! It was almost immoral: had not Adam Smith written, "What is prudence in the conduct of every private family can scarce be folly in that of a great nation"?

But when the early economists refused to consider that saving might be a stumbling block for an economy, they were not indulging in moral proselytizing; they were only observing the facts of the real world.

For in the early 1800's, by and large those who saved were the very same people as those who put savings to use. In the hard-pressed world of Ricardo or Mill, virtually the only people who could afford to save were wealthy landlords and capitalists, and any sums they scraped together were profitably employed in buying lands or enlarging factory operations. Hence saving was rightly called "accumulation," for it represented a two-sided coin; on the one hand the amassing of a sum of money, and on the other hand its immediate employment in purchasing the tools or buildings or land to make still more money.

But toward the middle of the nineteenth century, the structure of the economy changed. The distribution of wealth improved and along with it the possibility of saving became open to more and more members of society. And at the same time, business became larger and more depersonalized; increasingly it looked for new capital not just in the pockets of its individual manager-owners but also in the anonymous pocketbooks of savers all over the country. Hence saving and investing became divorced from one another—they became separate operations carried out by separate groups of people.

And this did introduce trouble into the economy—Malthus was right after all, although for reasons he had never seen.

The trouble is so important—so central to the problem of depression—that we must take a moment to make it clear.

We must start out by understanding how we measure the prosperity of a nation. It is not by its gold—poverty-stricken India is rich in gold. Nor is it by its physical assets—buildings, mines, factories, and forests did not evaporate in 1932. Prosperity and depression are not so much matters of past glories but of present accomplishments; therefore they are measured by the *incomes* that we earn. When most of us individually (and therefore most of us collectively) enjoy high incomes, the nation is well off; when our total individual (or national) income drops, we are in depression.

But income—national income—is not a static concept. Indeed the central characteristic of an economy is the *flow* of incomes from hand to hand. With every purchase that we make, we transfer a part of our incomes into someone else's pocket. Similarly every penny of our own incomes, be it wages, salaries, rents, profits, or interest, ultimately derives from money which someone else has spent. Consider any portion of the income which you enjoy and it will be clear that it has originated from someone else's pocket: when he engaged your services, or patronized your store, or helped maintain the corporation in which you own bonds or stock.

It is by this process of handing money around—taking in each other's wash, it has been described—that the economy is constantly revitalized.

Now to a large extent this process of handing income around takes place quite naturally and without hindrance. All of us spend the bulk of our incomes on goods for our own use and enjoyment—on consumption goods, so-called—and since we go on buying consumption goods with fairly consistent regularity, the handing around of a large portion of our national income is assured. The fact that we must eat and clothe ourselves, and that we crave enjoyment, ensures a regular and steady spending on the part of all of us, and thus further ensures a regular and steady receiving on the part of others.

So far everything is quite simple and direct. But there is one portion of our incomes which does *not* go directly out onto the market place to become another's income: that is the money we save.

If we tucked our savings into mattresses or hoarded them in cash, we should obviously break the circular flow of income. For then we should be simply freezing some part of the income stream that was handed to us, and returning to society less than it gave to us. If such a freezing process were widespread and continued, there would soon be a cumulative fall in everybody's money income, as less and less was handed around at each turn. We should be suffering from a depression.

But this dangerous break in the income flow does not in fact take place. For in a civilized community we do not freeze our savings. We put them into stocks or bonds or banks and in this way make it possible for them to be used again. Thus, if we buy new stock we give our savings directly to business; if we put our savings in a bank, they can be used on loan by business-men who seek capital. Whether we bank our savings or use them to buy insurance or securities, the channels exist for those savings to go back into circulation via the activities of business. For when our savings are taken up and spent by business, they again turn up as someone's wages, someone's salary, or someone's profit.

But—and notice this vital fact—there is nothing *automatic* about this savings-investment channel. Business does not ordi-narily need savings to carry on its operations; it works within its regular budget and pays its expenses from the proceeds of its sales. Business only needs savings if it is *expanding* its operation —for its regular receipts will not usually provide it with enough capital to build a new factory or to add substantially to its equipment.

And here is where the trouble enters. A thrifty community will always attempt to save some part of its income. But busi-ness is not always in a position to expand its operations. To take an obvious case, it is apparent that the days of great expan-sion for the radio industry—as contrasted with the television industry—are pretty much a thing of the past. Now if—for reasons we must look into later—all industry is in the position of the radio industry, then obviously investment will be very small.

And therein lies the possibility of depression. *If our savings do not become invested by expanding business firms, our incomes must decline.* We should be in the same spiral of contraction as if we had frozen our savings by hoarding them.

Can such an eventuality come to pass? We shall see. But note meanwhile that this is a strange and passionless tug of war. Here are no greedy landlords, no avaricious capitalists. There are only perfectly virtuous citizens prudently attempting to save some of their incomes, and perfectly virtuous businessmen who are just as prudently making up their minds whether the business situation warrants taking the risk of buying a new machine or building a new plant. And yet, on the outcome of those two sensible decisions the fate of the economy hangs. For if the decisions are out of joint—if businessmen invest less than the community tries to save, for example—then the whole economy will have to readjust to the crimp of depression. The enormous question of boom or slump depends—more than on anything else—on this.

The vulnerability of our fate to the seesaw of savings and investment is, in a sense, the price we pay for economic freedom. There is no such problem in Soviet Russia nor was there such in the Egypt of the Pharaohs. For in economies of edict both savings and investment are determined from above, and a total control over the nation's entire economic life ensures that the nation's savings will be just the right amount to finance its pyramids or power plants. But not so in a capitalist world. For there both the decision to save and the impetus to invest are left to the free decisions of the economic actors themselves. And because those decisions are free, they can be out of joint. There can be far too little investment to absorb our savings or far too little saving to support our investment. Economic freedom is a highly desirable state—but in bust and boom we must be prepared to face its possible consequences.

We have almost lost sight of John Maynard Keynes and the *Treatise on Money.* But not quite. For the *Treatise* was a sparkling exposition of this seesaw of savings and investment. The idea was not original with Keynes—a long list of important economists had already pointed to the critical roles of these two factors in the business cycle. But, as with everything that Keynes touched, the bare abstractions of economics took on a new luster in his prose. Thus:

> It has been usual to think of the accumulated wealth of the world as having been painfully built up out of that voluntary abstinence of individuals from the immediate enjoyment of consumption, which we call Thrift. But it should be obvious that mere abstinence is not enough by itself to build cities or drain fens.
> . . . It is Enterprise which builds and improves the world's possessions. . . . If Enterprise is afoot, wealth accumulates whatever may be happening to Thrift; and if Enterprise is asleep, wealth decays whatever Thrift may be doing.

But for all its masterful analysis, no sooner had Keynes written the *Treatise* than, figuratively, he tore it up. For the seesaw theory of savings and investment failed at one central point: it did not explain how an economy could *remain* in a state of prolonged depression. Indeed, as the very analogy of the seesaw indicates, it seemed as if an economy which was weighted down by surplus savings must, in fairly short order, right itself and swing the other way.

For savings and investment—Thrift and Enterprise—were not utterly unconnected economic activities. On the contrary, they were tied together in the market where businessmen "bought" savings—or at least borrowed them: the money market. Savings, like any other commodity, had its price: the rate of interest. Therefore (so it seemed), at the bottom of a slump when there was a flood of savings, its price should decline—exactly as when there was a glut of shoes, the price of shoes declined. And as the price of savings cheapened—as the rate of interest went down —the *incentive* to invest appeared very likely to increase: if a new factory was too expensive to build when the money for it would cost six per cent, might it not look much more profitable when the money could be had for a payment of only three per cent?

Hence the seesaw theory seemed to promise that there would be an automatic safety switch built right into the business cycle itself; that when savings became too abundant, they would become cheaper to borrow, and that thereby business would be encouraged to invest. The economy might contract, said the theory, but it seemed certain to rebound.

But that was exactly what failed to happen in the Great Depression. The rate of interest declined, but nothing happened. The old nostrums were trotted out—a pinch of local relief and a large dose of hopeful waiting—and still the patient failed to improve. For all its intellectual elegance, something was patently missing from the neat formulation of the swing of savings and investment with the rate of interest always hovering over the seesaw to see that it was kept in motion. Something else must be holding the economy back.

Keynes's master book had been brewing for some time. "To understand *my* state of mind," he had written to George Bernard Shaw in 1935—he had just reread Marx and Engels at Shaw's suggestion and found them little to his liking, ". . . you have to know that I believe myself to be writing a book on economic theory which will largely revolutionize—not, I suppose at once, but in the course of the next ten years—the way the world thinks about economic problems. . . . I can't expect you or anyone else to believe this at the present stage. But for myself I don't merely hope what I say—in my own mind, I'm quite sure."

He was, as usual, quite right. The book was to be a bombshell. Yet it is very doubtful whether Mr. Shaw would have recognized it as such had he attempted to digest it. It had a forbidding title, *The General Theory of Employment, Interest, and Money,* and a still more forbidding interior: one can imagine Shaw goggling on page 25 at "Let Z be the aggregate supply price of the output from employing N men, the relationship between Z and N being written $Z = \phi(N)$, which can be called the Aggregate Supply Function." And if this were not enough to frighten off almost anyone, there was a great dearth of that panorama of social action which the layman had come to expect from a perusal of Smith or Mill or Marx. This was an endless desert of economics, algebra, and abstraction, with track-less wastes of the differential calculus, and only an oasis here and there of delightfully refreshing prose.

And yet the book was revolutionary: no other word will quite do. It stood economics as decisively on its head as had such other revolutionary works as the *Wealth of Nations* or *Das Kapital*.

For the book had a startling and dismaying conclusion. There was no automatic safety mechanism after all! Rather than a see-saw which would always right itself, the economy resembled an elevator: it could be going up or down, but it could also be standing perfectly still. And it was just as capable of standing still on the ground floor as at the top of the shaft. A depression, in other words, might not cure itself at all; the economy could lie prostrate indefinitely, like a ship becalmed.

But how could this be? Would not the flood of savings at the bottom of the slump push down the rate of interest, and would this not in turn interest business in the possibility of using cheap money to expand its plant?

Keynes found the solution to the problem in the simplest and most obvious (once it had been pointed out) fact of economic life: *there would be no flood of savings at the bottom of the trough*. For what happened when an economy went into an eco-nomic tailspin was that its income contracted, and what hap-pened as its income contracted was that its savings were squeezed out. How could a community be expected to save as much when everyone was hard up as when everyone was prosperous, asked Keynes. Quite obviously, it could not. The result of a depres-sion would not be a glut of savings, but a drying-up of savings; not a flood of saving, but a trickle.

And so it was, in fact. In 1929 the American private citizenry put aside $3.7 billions out of its income; by 1932 and 1933 it was saving *nothing*—in fact it was even drawing down its old savings made in the years before. Corporations, which had tucked away $2.6 billions at the top of the boom *after* paying out taxes and dividends, found themselves losing nearly $6 billions three years later. Quite obviously Keynes was right: saving was a kind of luxury which could not withstand hard times.

But the practical consequence of that decline in saving was more portentous than the individual tragedies which accompanied it. It resulted in a paralyzing situation where the economy was in perfect *economic* balance, even though it was in the throes of social agony. For if there was *no* surplus of savings, there would be *no* pressure on interest rates to encourage businessmen to borrow. And if there was *no* surplus of investment (and the very essence of depression, as we have seen, is that investment is not large enough), then there would be *no* impetus for expansion. The economy would not budge an inch.

Thus the paradox of poverty amidst plenty and the anomaly of idle men and idle machines. To be sure, at the bottom of a slump there is a heartless contradiction between a crying need for goods and an insufficiency of production. But the contradiction is purely a moral one. For the economy does not operate to satisfy human *wants*—wants are always as large as dreams. It turns out goods to satisfy *demand*—and demand is as small as a person's pocketbook. Hence the unemployed are little more than economic zeros; they might as well be on the moon for all the economic influence they exert on the market place.

Once investment has declined and the economy has shrunk in size, social misery appears. But not—as Keynes points out—*effective* social misery: the nation's conscience will not do as an effective substitute for enough investment. And since savings decline along with investment, the economic flow turns over evenly, quite unperturbed by the fact that it is smaller than it used to be.

A peculiar state of affairs, indeed: a tragedy without a villain. No one can blame society for saving, when saving is so apparently a private virtue; it is equally impossible to chastise businessmen for not investing when no one would be so happy to comply as they—if they saw a reasonable chance for success. No, the difficulty is no longer a moral one; this is no question of justice, exploitation, or even human foolishness. It is a technical difficulty, almost a mechanical fault. But its price is no less high for all of that. For the price of inactivity is unemployment.

But worse follows. Keynes had explained how an economy in the trough of depression could fail to generate its own automatic recovery. That was gloomy enough. But when you turned the Keynesian proposition around, it spelled trouble at the top of the business cycle as well.

For just as savings contracted when the economy contracted, so they would expand when the economy expanded. And that simple fact had a frightening consequence: it meant that *every boom was constantly threatened with collapse.* For if at any time investment spontaneously slowed down, the nation's swollen savings would again exert the upper hand; the chain of handing around of incomes would be broken, and the process of contraction would begin.

Hence in the final analysis, the economy hung on the amount of investment which business carried out. When investment was low, the economy shrank in size; when investment was high, it pulled the nation up with it; if investment failed to *remain* high, it permitted the process of contraction to begin again. Riches and poverty, boom and slump, all depended on the willingness of business to invest.

And here was the most indigestible fact of all. The willingness to invest could not go on indefinitely. Sooner or later, investment was *bound* to contract.

For at any time, an industry is limited by the size of the market to which it caters. Let us take the example of the railroads in the 1860's—a time of vast investment in new railroad lines. The early railway magnates were not building for the markets of 1960; had they proceeded to lay the trackage the economy would need a hundred years hence, they would have been building lines to nonexistent cities in uninhabited territory. So they built what could be used—and then they stopped. Similarly with the auto industry. Even if Henry Ford had been able to find the capital to build the present-day River Rouge plant in 1910, he would have gone bankrupt in a hurry: the roads, the gas stations, the *demand* for that many cars were simply lacking. Or to bring the matter to the present, the country's utility plants are now spending $8 billions a year to add to their capacity; but they cannot spend $80 or even $18 billions—although someday they may have to. Today no one could use *that* much power.

Not only is investment limited in size, but typically it proceeds in spurts. You cannot build a railway line mile by mile to keep pace with demand: you build one entire line at a time. You cannot enlarge an auto plant piecemeal beyond a certain size: then you must build an entirely new plant. And having built that line, having constructed that plant, you have satisfied the market for a time. You cease investing.

> Ancient Egypt [wrote Keynes] was doubly fortunate and doubtless owed to this its fabled wealth, in that it possessed *two* activities, namely pyramid-building and the search for the precious metals, the fruits of which, since they could not serve the needs of man by being consumed, did not stale with abundance. The Middle Ages built cathedrals and sang dirges. Two pyramids, two masses for the dead are twice as good as one; but not so two railways from London to York.

And so investment typically has its pattern: at first eagerness to take advantage of a new opportunity; then caution lest enthusiasm lead to overbuilding; then inactivity when the market has been satisfied for the time being.

If, as each separate investment project came to a halt, another immediately appeared, there need never be a slump. But such is not likely to be the case. The mere fact that human wants are vast does not mean that *any* investment will pay for itself: the economy is littered with businesses which have died of rash and foolhardy overexpansion. Most investment needs more than the stimulus of sanguine expectations; it needs something more concrete: some new invention, some better way of doing things, some intriguing product to catch the public eye. And such opportunities, as any businessman will tell you, are not always there.

Hence when one investment project dies, there may not be another ready to step into the breach. If there is—if investment maintains its size, although it changes its composition—the economy will sail smoothly along. But if there is no ready substitute for each investment casualty, the pressure of savings will make itself felt and contraction will begin. And needless to say, investment does not thrive in such a dwindling market.

All this was the gloomy diagnosis of *The General Theory*.

First, that an economy in depression might well stay there; there was nothing inherent in the situation to pull it out.

Second, that prosperity depended on investment; for if savings were not put to use, the dread spiral of contraction began.

And third, that investment was an undependable drive wheel for the economy; through no fault of the businessman it was constantly threatened with satiety, and satiety spelled economic shrinkage.

In a word, the economy lived in the shadow of collapse.

Certainly it was a morbid outlook. But it would have been utterly unlike Keynes to content himself with making a diagnosis of gloom and letting it go at that. With all its prophecy of danger, *The General Theory* was never meant to be a book of doom. On the contrary, it held out a promise and it proposed a cure.

As a matter of fact, the cure had begun before its actual prescription was written; the medicine was being applied before the doctors were precisely sure what it was supposed to do. The Hundred Days of the New Deal had enacted a flood of social legislation that had been backing up for twenty years behind a dam of governmental apathy. These laws were meant to improve the social tone, the morale, of a discontented nation. But it was not social legislation which was designed to revitalize the patient. That tonic was something else: the deliberate undertaking of *government* investment.

It began not so much as investment as makeshift work-relief. Unemployment had reached the point at which some sort of action was dictated by pure political necessity—after all, this was a time when there had recently been riots in Dearborn and a ragged march on Washington, when families huddled for warmth in municipal incinerator buildings and even scrabbled for food in garbage trucks. Relief was essential and began under Hoover; then under Roosevelt relief turned into leaf-raking, and leaf-raking turned into constructive enterprise. The government was suddenly a major economic investor itself: roads, dams, auditoriums, airfields, harbors, and housing projects blossomed forth.

Keynes came to Washington in 1934—this was when he made his notes on the impression of President Roosevelt's hands—and urged that the program be extended further. The statistics showed that the bottom had fallen out of private investment activity: business expansion, which had pumped out $15 billions in wages and salaries and profits in 1929, had fallen to the appalling figure of $886 *millions* in 1932—a drop of ninety-four per cent. Something had to start up the investment motor which pulled the economic car up the shaft, and he hoped that government spending would act as such a stimulus by bolstering the nation's general buying power—"priming the pump" it was called in those days.

Hence when *The General Theory* came out in 1936, what it offered was not so much a new and radical program as a defense of a course of action which was already being applied. A defense and an explanation. For *The General Theory* clearly pointed out that the catastrophe facing America and, indeed, the whole Western World, was only the consequence of a lack of sufficient investment on the part of business. And so the remedy was perfectly logical: if business was not able to expand, the government must take up the slack.

With his tongue only partly in his cheek Keynes had written:

> If the Treasury were to fill old bottles with bank notes, bury them at suitable depths in disused coal mines which are then filled up to the surface with town rubbish, and leave it to private enterprise on well tried principles of *laissez-faire* to dig the notes up again . . . there need be no more unemployment and with the help of the repercussions, the real income of the community would probably become a good deal larger than it is. It would, indeed, be more sensible to build houses and the like; but if there are practical difficulties in the way of doing this, the above would be better than nothing.

To some it no doubt appeared that many of the more unorthodox WPA projects were no more sane than Keynes's whimsical proposal. But now, at least, they had a rationale behind them: if private enterprise found itself unable to carry forward with a big enough program of investment, then the government must fill in as best it could—the need for stimulation of some sort was so imperative that almost anything was better than nothing.

And if investment could not be directly stimulated, why then, at least consumption could. For while investment was the capricious element in the system, consumption provided the great floor of economic activity; hence the WPA projects were thought to attack the problem with a two-edged sword: by directly helping to sustain the buying power of the otherwise unemployed, and by leading the way for a resumption of private business expansion.

Keynes himself in a letter to *The New York Times* in 1934 wrote, "I see the problem of recovery in the following light: How soon will normal business enterprise come to the rescue? On what scale, by which expedients, and for how long is abnormal government expenditure advisable in the meantime?"

Note "abnormal." Keynes did not see the government program as a permanent interference with the course of business or as anything but a helping hand to a system that had slipped and was struggling to regain its balance.

It seemed the essence of common sense; in fact it was the essence of common sense. And yet the pump-priming program never brought the results that the planners had hoped for. Total government spending, which had hovered at the $10-billion level from 1929 until 1933, rose to $12 billions, to $13 billions, then to $15 billions in 1936. Private investment picked itself up from the floor and recovered two-thirds of its loss: private firms invested $10 billions by 1936. The national income and national consumption rose by fifty per cent after three years of government injections. And yet unemployment lingered on; it was manageable now, but there were still at least 9 million out of work—hardly a mark of a new economic era.

There were two reasons why the cure did not work better. First, the government program of investment was never carried out to the full extent that would have been necessary to bring the economy up to full employment. Later, in the Second World War, government spending rose to the monumental figure of $103 billions: that brought not only full employment, but inflation. But within the framework of a peacetime economy in the thirties, such all-out spending was quite impossible; indeed, even a modest program of government investment soon brought murmurs that Federal power was overstepping its traditional bounds.

The second reason is closely allied with the first. Neither Keynes nor the government spenders had taken into account that the beneficiaries of the new medicine might consider it worse than the disease. Government investment was *meant* as a helping hand for business. It was *interpreted* by business as a threatening gesture.

Nor is this surprising. The New Deal had swept in on a wave of antibusiness sentiment; values and standards that had become virtually sacrosanct were suddenly held up to skeptical scrutiny and criticism. The whole conception of "business rights," "property rights," and the "role of government" was rudely shaken; within a few years business was asked to forget its traditions of unquestioned pre-eminence and to adopt a new philosophy of cooperation with labor unions, acceptance of new rules and regulations, reform of many of its practices. Little wonder that it regarded the government in Washington as inimical, biased, and downright radical. And no wonder, in such an atmosphere, that its eagerness to undertake large-scale investment was dampened by the uneasiness it felt in this unfamiliar climate.

Hence every effort of the government to undertake a program of sufficient magnitude to mop up all the unemployed—perhaps a program twice as large as it did in fact undertake—was assailed as further evidence of socialist design. And at the same time, the halfway measures which the government did employ were just enough to frighten business away from the undertaking of a full-scale effort by itself. It was a situation not unlike that found in medicine; the medicine cured the patient of one illness, only to weaken him with its side effects. Government spending never truly cured the economy—not because it was economically unsound, but because it was ideologically upsetting.

It was not meant to be upsetting; it was a policy born of desperation rather than design. Had the government not begun to open the valve of public investment, eventually private business would surely once again have led the way: it always had in the past, and despite the severity of the Great Depression, it would in time unquestionably have found new avenues of adventure. But it was impossible to wait. The American people had waited for four long years, and they were in no mood to wait much longer. Not only were there disturbances in the land, but there were troubling voices in the air. The voice of Marx rang louder than it ever had in the past; many pointed to the unemployed as prima-facie evidence that Marx was right. The mumble of Veblen was discernible in the faddish vogue of the technocrats who wanted to call out not the proletariat but the engineers. And there was the still more chilling voice that never wearied of pointing out that Hitler and Mussolini knew what to do with *their* unemployed. In this welter of remedies and advocacy of desperate action, the voice of *The General Theory,* the gentlemanly tones of Keynes, were certainly moderate and reassuring.

For while Keynes espoused a policy of managing capitalism, he was no opponent of private enterprise. "It is better that a man should tyrannize over his bank-balance than over his fellow citizens," he had written in *The General Theory,* and he went on to state that if the government would only concern itself with providing enough investment, the working of the vast bulk of the economy could and should be left to private initiative. In review, *The General Theory* was not a radical solution; it was, rather, an explanation of why an inescapable remedy should work. If an economy in the doldrums could drift indefinitely, the price of government inaction might be graver by far than the consequences of bold unorthodoxy.

The real question was a moral, not an economic one. During the Second World War, Professor Hayek wrote a book, *The Road to Serfdom,* which, for all its exaggerations, contained a deeply felt and sincere indictment of the overplanned economy. Keynes sympathized with and liked the book. But while praising it, he wrote to Hayek:

I should . . . conclude rather differently. I should say that what we want is not no planning, or even less planning, indeed I should say we almost certainly want more. But the planning should take place in a community in which as many people as possible, both leaders and followers, wholly share your own moral position. Moderate planning will be safe enough if those carrying it out are rightly oriented in their own minds and hearts to the moral issue. This is in fact already true of some of them. But the curse is that there is also an important section who could be said to want planning not in order to enjoy its fruits, but because morally they hold ideas exactly the opposite of yours, and wish to serve not God but the devil.

Is this, perhaps a naïve hope? Can capitalism be managed— in the sense that government planners will turn the faucet of investment on and *off* in such a way as to supplement, but never to displace, private investment? Certainly this is one of the central issues of today. But let us postpone discussion of it to the coming chapter.

For here we are dealing with the man Keynes and his beliefs, however misguided, idealistic, impractical, or salutary we may value them. And it would be a grave error in judgment to place this man, whose aim was to rescue capitalism, in the camp of those who want to submerge it. True, he urged the socialization of investment; but if he sacrificed the part, it was to save the whole.

For at heart he was a conservative and not much inclined to mask the fact. "How can I accept the [communistic] doctrine," he had written in 1931—when the point was by no means so clear to many others, "which sets up as its bible, above and beyond criticism, an obsolete textbook which I know not only to be scientifically erroneous but without interest or application to the modern world? How can I adopt a creed which, preferring the mud to the fish, exalts the boorish proletariat above the bourgeoisie and the intelligentsia, who with all their faults, are the quality of life and surely carry the seeds of all human achievement?"

No, one might quibble with his theories, with his diagnosis, and with his cure—although, in justice, it must be said that no more thoughtful theory, no profounder diagnosis, and no more convincing cure has yet been propounded by those who insist that Keynes was only a mischievous meddler with a system that worked well enough. But no one could gainsay his aim: the creation of a capitalist economy in which unemployment—the single greatest and gravest threat to its continuance—would be forever eliminated.

He was a man incapable of doing only one thing at a time. While he was constructing *The General Theory* in his mind, he was building a theater in Cambridge with his pocketbook. It was a typically Keynesian venture. Starting at a loss, the theater was in the black in two years, and its artistic success was immense. Keynes was everywhere at the same time: financial backer, ticket taker (on one occasion when the clerk failed to materialize), husband of the leading lady (Lydia acted in Shakespeare, with extremely good notices), even concessionaire. He attached a restaurant to the theater and jealously watched its receipts, graphing them against different types of entertainment to ascertain how food consumption varied with the state of one's humor. There was a bar, too, where champagne was sold at a specially low discount to promote its wider consumption. It was probably the most pleasant interlude in his pleasant life.

But it did not go on for long. In 1937 his success story was cut short; he suffered a heart attack and was forced into idleness. Well—comparative idleness. He continued to do an active trading business and to edit the *Economic Journal* and to write a few brilliant articles in defense of *The General Theory*. One academician had said, upon its appearance, "Einstein has actually done for Physics what Mr. Keynes believes himself to have done for Economics," and Keynes was not a man to let someone get away with *that*. When he wanted to, he could wield an acid pen, and he now set to work systematically to demolish his critics, singly and en masse; sometimes with sarcasm, occasionally with brilliance, and not infrequently with petulance: "Mr. X *refuses* to understand me," seemed to rise like a sigh of despair from many of his brief communications.

But the war was approaching; Munich was followed by worse. Keynes watched in indignation the pusillanimous letters of some Left-wingers to the *New Statesman and Nation,* on whose board he managed to find time to serve. He wrote to its columns: "Surely it is impossible to believe that there can really be such a person as 'A Socialist'! I disbelieve in his existence," and then, "When it comes to a showdown, scarce four weeks have passed before they remember that they are pacifists and write defeatist letters to your columns, leaving the defence of freedom and civilization to Colonel Blimp and the Old School Tie, for whom Three Cheers."

When the war came, Keynes was too ill to be a permanent member of the Government. They gave him a room in the Treasury and picked his brains. He had already written another book, *How to Pay for the War,* a daring plan that urged deferred savings as the principal means of financing the war. The plan was simple—a portion of every wage earner's pay would automatically be invested in government bonds which would not be available for redemption until after the war. Then, just when consumer buying would again be needed, the savings certificates could be cashed.

Compulsory saving—what a change from his earlier efforts to achieve a kind of compulsory investment! But the change was in the times and not in Keynes's thinking. The old problem had been too little investment and its symptom had been unemployment. The new problem was too much investment—an all-out armament effort—and its symptom was inflation. But the framework of *The General Theory* was as useful in understanding inflation as it had been in understanding inflation's opposite—unemployment. Only it was upside down. Now more and more incomes were being handed out with each turn of the wheel, instead of less and less. Now savings were far short of what was needed to balance out the flow of income, instead of being embarrassingly large.

Accordingly, the cure was the opposite of the depression tonic. Then Keynes had urged that investment be bolstered by every possible means; now he urged that savings must be increased.

The point is important because many have mistakenly judged Keynes as an economist who favored inflation. He did favor "reflation" a pumping-up of incomes and not prices) from the depths of the depression. But to think that he favored inflation for inflation's sake was to disregard such a passage as this from *The Economic Consequences of the Peace:*

> Lenin is said to have declared that the best way to destroy the Capitalist System was to debauch the currency. By a

continuing process of inflation, governments can confiscate, secretly and unobserved, an important part of the wealth of their citizens. By this method they not only confiscate, but they confiscate *arbitrarily*. . . . Lenin was certainly right. There is no subtler, no surer means of overturning the existing basis of society than to debauch the currency. The process engages all the hidden forces of economic law on the side of destruction, and does it in a manner which not one man in a million is able to diagnose.

But despite its logic and its appeal—Keynes made much of the fact that his deferred savings plan would serve to widen the distribution of wealth by making everyone an owner of government bonds—the plan failed to arouse much support. It was too new; the old methods of taxation and rationing and voluntary-savings drives were tried and trusty weapons of war finance. A deferred-credit scheme was tacked on as an ornamental flourish but it was never given the central place Keynes had envisaged for it.

But he had no time to lament its cool reception; he was now fully embroiled in the British war effort. In 1941 he flew via Lisbon to the United States. It was to be the first of six such trips; Lydia went with him as his nurse and guardian. Ever since his first heart attack she had assumed the role of time-keeper for her indefatigable husband and many a dignitary had been politely but firmly ushered out at the expiration of his allotted stay. "Time, gentlemen," said Lydia, and business stopped.

His trips to the United States involved the precarious problems of Britain's war finance and the overhanging question of what was to happen in the terrible postwar interim. Britain was not the only one concerned; the United States, as well, wanted to lay the foundation for a flow of international trade which would avoid the desperate financial warfare which had already led to physical warfare. An International Bank and an Internation Monetary Fund were to be established which would act as guardians of the international flow of money; in place of the old dog-eat-dog world where each nation sought to undercut everyone else, there would be a new cooperative effort to help out a nation which found itself in monetary difficulties.

The final conference was held at Bretton Woods. Keynes, despite his illness and fatigue, clearly dominated the conference; not when it came to winning all his points, for the final plan was far closer to the American proposals than to the British, but by virtue of his personality. One of the delegates gives us an insight into the man in this entry in his journal:

This evening, I participated in a particularly *recherché* celebration. Today is the 500th anniversary of the Concordat between King's College, Cambridge, and New College, Oxford, and to commemorate the occasion, Keynes gave a small banquet in his room. . . . Keynes, who had been looking forward to the event for weeks as excitedly as a schoolboy, was at his most charming. He delivered an exquisite allocution. . . . It was an interesting example of the curiously complex nature of this extraordinary man. So radical in outlook in matters purely intellectual, in matters of culture he is a true Burkean conservative. It was all very pianissimo, as befitting the occasion, but his emotion when he spoke of our debt to the past was truly moving.

When Keynes made his final speech at the conclusion of the conference—"If we can continue in a larger task, as we have begun in this limited task, there is hope for the world"—the delegates rose and cheered him.

As always, his major efforts did not preclude a few minor ones. He was made a Director of the Bank of England ("Which will make an honest woman of the other is anyone's guess," he had declared) and chairman of a new committee on the music and arts which had been established, like the English universities, under the aegis of the government. Thus, while he was carrying the weight of presenting Britain's point of view to an international economic council, he was also keeping up a stream of correspondence on music travelers, the Vic-Wells Ballet, poetry reading, and library exhibits. And of course he kept on collecting; he scooped the Folger Library on a rare volume of Spenser and explained a little guiltily to the librarian that he had used the Foreign Office bag to have the catalogue sent over to him.

And the honors started to pour in. He was elevated to the peerage: he was now Lord Keynes, Baron of Tilton, an estate which he had bought in middle life only to discover to his delight that one of the branches of the Keynes line had once owned these lands. There were honorary degrees to be accepted at Edinburgh, at the Sorbonne, and from his own university. There was an appointment to the Board of Trustees of the National Gallery. And still there was work: the first loan to Britain had to be negotiated and Keynes, of course, was given the task of presenting Britain's viewpoint. When he returned from that trip and a reporter asked him if it were true that England was now to be the forty-ninth State, Keynes's reply was succinct: "No such luck."

In 1946 the ordeal was over. He went back to Sussex to read and relax and prepare for a resumption of teaching at Cambridge. One morning there was a fit of coughing; Lydia flew to his side; he was dead.

The services were held in Westminster Abbey. His father, John Neville Keynes, aged ninety-three, and his mother, Florence, walked up the aisle. For all their sorrow, few parents could have wished for more in a son. The country mourned the loss of a great leader, gone just at a time when his acumen and wisdom were most needed; as the *Times* said in a lengthy obituary on April twenty-second, "By his death the country has lost a great Englishman."

He was not an angel by any means. This most sparkling of the great economists was only a human being, albeit a remarkable one, with all the faults and foibles of any person. He could win twenty-two pounds from two countesses and a duke at bridge and crow delightedly; he could also undertip a bootblack in Algiers and refuse to rectify his error saying, of all things, "I will not be a party to debasing the currency." He could be extraordinarily kind to a slow-thinking student (economists, he said, should be humble, like dentists) and obnoxiously cutting to a businessman or high official to whom he happened to take an intuitive dislike. Sir Harry Goshen, the chairman of the National Provincial Bank, once rubbed Keynes wrong by urging that "we let matters take their natural course." Keynes replied, "Is it more appropriate to smile or rage at these artless sentiments? Best of all, perhaps, to let Sir Harry take *his* natural course."

Keynes himself gave the clue to his own genius—although he was not at the time writing about himself. Discussing his old teacher Alfred Marshall (whom he both loved and rather lovingly derided as "an absurd old man"), Keynes spelled out the qualifications for an economist:

> The study of economics does not seem to require any specialized gifts of an unusually high order. Is it not, intellectually regarded, a very easy subject compared with the higher branches of philosophy or pure science? An easy subject, at which very few excel! The paradox finds its explanation, perhaps, in that the master-economist must possess a rare *combination* of gifts. He must be mathematician, historian, statesman, philosopher—in some degree. He must understand symbols and speak in words. He must contemplate the particular in terms of the general, and touch abstract and concrete in the same flight of thought. He must study the present in the light of the past for the purposes of the future. No part of man's nature or his institutions must lie entirely outside his regard. He must be purposeful and disinterested in a simultaneous mood; as aloof and incorruptible as an artist, yet sometimes as near the earth as a politician.

Marshall—as Keynes says—only approximated that ideal, for Victorian that he was, his economics lacked the necessary iconoclasm to give it deep social penetration. Keynes came closer: the Bloomsbury attitude of "nothing sacred" spilled over into the sacred precincts of economic orthodoxy; once again the world was put into focus by a man not so blind as to fail to see its sickness, and not so emotionally and intellectually dispossessed as to wish not to cure it. If he was an economic sophisticate, he was politically devout, and it is in this curious combination of an engineering mind and a hopeful heart that his greatness lies.

X

The Modern World

In 1930, while most people were darkly occupied with the deepening depression, Keynes was toying with an idea of a very different hue. In disregard of his own dictum that in the long run we are all dead, he had just taken a glimpse into the future—the long-term future—and he had come up with a prophecy quite in contrast with the Cassandra-like rumblings of the day. For what Keynes saw ahead—barring such catastrophes as an uncontrollable flood of population or a totally destructive war—was not a continuation of the current state of misery and doubt, but a prospect so fair as to be almost unbelievable—nothing less than Adam Smith's heralded land of universal plenty.

Keynes called his little excursion into the future *Economic Possibilities for Our Grandchildren* (of whom, it might be added, he himself had none). And what were these possibilities? Well, not to wax too lyrical, they hinted at something like a modest millennium: by the year 2030 Keynes thought the economic problem might be solved—not just the immediate crimp of depression, but *the* economic problem itself, the age-old fact of Not Enough to Go Around. For the first time in history, mankind—British mankind, at any rate—would have emerged from a struggle against want into a new milieu in which everybody could with ease be given a generous helping at the communal table.

It was a typically Keynesian thrust in an unexpected direction. After the First World War, when the world was basking in a glow of self-congratulation, it was Keynes who had rattled the

262

skeleton in the closet; now in the thirties when the world turned
to self-commiseration, it was the same Keynes who bravely talked
of an impending end to its travail. But he was not merely whis-
tling in the dark. On the contrary, he was only taking up a
strand of economics which had absorbed all the master planners
of the past—the tendency of capitalism to *grow*.

In times of depression that tendency was apt to be overlooked.
And yet, looking backward over two hundred years of capitalism, it was not merely a meaningless succession of exhilarating
booms and frustrating busts which had characterized the system,
but a steady, albeit highly irregular, *upward* climb. The forty
million Englishmen of Keynes's day most certainly did not consider themselves the benefactors of a bountiful providence, but
for all the hardship of the times, they unquestionably enjoyed
a far better seat at Nature's table than the ten million Englishmen of Malthus' time.

It was not that Nature herself had become more generous. On
the contrary, as the famous Law of Diminishing Returns made
clear, Nature yielded up her wealth more grudgingly as she
was more intensively cultivated. The secret to economic growth
lay in the fact that each generation attacked Nature not only
with its own energies and resources, but with the heritage of
equipment accumulated by its forebears. And as that heritage
grew—as each generation added its quota of new knowledge,
factories, tools, and techniques to the wealth of the past—human
productivity increased with astonishing rapidity. A factory worker
in the 1960s in the United States turned out between *four and
five times* as much goods in an hour's toil as a worker at the time
of the Civil War—not because he worked harder or more skillfully, but because he worked with mechanical helpers which made
him a superman compared with his Civil War predecessor.

And if only this process of steadily enhancing productivity
would continue for another century—a mere three generations
—then capitalism would have done the trick. For another hundred years of amassing wealth, Keynes calculated, at the same
pace as the last hundred years, would multiply England's real
productive wealth by *seven and one-half* times. By the year 2030,
every worker would have at his elbow machinery which would

make *him* a superman in terms of his grandfather who lived in 1930.

And such a vast increase in productiveness could make all the difference. It could relegate economics as a science of scarcity to the history books. The new problem of society would be not how to find leisure, but how to cope with unprecedented quantities of it. With a grin Keynes quoted the traditional epitaph of the old charwoman

> Don't mourn for me, friends, don't weep for me never,
> For I'm going to do nothing for ever and ever.
> With psalms and sweet music the heavens'll be ringing,
> But I shall have nothing to do with the singing.

It was, of course, only a theoretical jaunt into the future and no one took it very seriously. The machinery was clanking too alarmingly in 1930 for anyone to regard such a prospectus as much more than a pleasant fantasy, and Keynes himself soon lost sight of it in the immediate problem of analyzing the nature of the unemployment which was paralyzing the world.

But wishful or sober, Keynes's vista is important for us. For with *Economic Possibilities for Our Grandchildren* we are for the first time confronted with the question of our own futures. Everything we have considered heretofore is, after all, only history. The evolution of the regulated and codified world of the seventeenth century into the atomistic market capitalism described by Adam Smith; the near escape of that capitalism from the landlord-dominated economy anticipated by Ricardo or the overpopulated subsistence society feared by Malthus; its presumptive self-destruction forecast by Marx; its chronic depressive tendency dissected by Keynes—all these adventures and misadventures of capitalism, however interesting, nevertheless lacked a certain element of suspense. For we knew at each juncture of history what the outcome would finally be. Now we are placed in a more uncomfortable position. As we turn to the modern economists, we are no longer discussing the ideas which helped shape our past: it is our own society, our own fate, our children's inheritance which lie in the balance.

And so we must turn from a study of our past to an appraisal

of our future. Where does capitalism stand today; where is it
going; what signposts point to the years ahead? These are the
great questions of contemporary economics and it is to them
that we must now bend our attention.

Perhaps we should begin by taking stock. We will be better
able to judge the chances and dangers which may lie in store for
us if we have a clear idea of where the present finds us. So let
us put this crucial question: *How well do Americans fare under
their present economic system?*

Some fare very badly.

In the mid-1960s—years in which *average* living standards were
never higher—a sizable fraction of Americans still lived in conditions of economic misery and want. In the crowded Negro and
Puerto Rican slums of New York, the dreary agricultural back-
wash communities of Mississippi and Tennessee, large numbers
of American families still experienced levels of economic "well-
being" which failed by any standard to provide lives of decency.
Some eight million families—one out of every six—scrimped
along on annual incomes of less than $3,000; and four and a half
million single persons—more than one out of every *three*—subsisted on incomes of $1,500 or less. This was not Asiatic poverty
by a long shot, as witness the forests of television masts even
in the poorest urban neighborhoods, but it was a level of economic meanness in which television was bought at the expense
of decent medical care and was enjoyed in the crowded and
smelly "comfort" of an all-too-often rat-infested living-bedroom.
If we take a family income of $4,000 a year as the beginning of
economic independence—a figure which allots only $19 of ex-
penditure per week for each member of a family of four—then
we find that almost one out of every five non-farm American
families had failed to reach this first rung on the ladder of true
economic adequacy by the middle 1960s. And this does not yet
include the "unattached individuals"—young people just getting
started, older people ending their productive lifetimes—thirty per
cent of whom were under the $2,000 mark.

In a society which boasts of its stupendous economic success
this is hardly cause for unrestrained jubilation. Indeed it means
that for the lowest quarter of the nation, capitalism as a system

of high living standards, personal dignity, or individual "affluence" is still little more than a myth, or, worse, a bitter mockery.

But it is possible to become indignant over such facts without viewing them in perspective. And the perspective is this: nowhere in the world has humanity succeeded in scraping together enough from nature or in sharing out that which it has scraped together in such a way as to provide a measure of decency for all. In the teeming continents of the East, the Malthusian dilemma at its realest and most awful has actually *lowered* human living standards in many nations over the past fifty years. Asiatics stand at the actual threshold of survival itself. In Africa, the Near East, South America, and Eastern Europe, grinding poverty is the rule rather than the exception. In Europe the highest standards that have been achieved—in Switzerland, for example—are only slightly over *half* the average American standard; and Switzerland is twice as well off per capita as the Netherlands.

Nor have the socialist nations done much better. Although some of them have shared out their wealth more equitably than we, they have failed to produce as much wealth, and the resulting slices of cake, although more uniform, are thinner. And Russia, for all her original egalitarian ideals and her hard-driving attempts to catch up with the Western World, is far down the scale of universal plenty. It is difficult to compare Russian standards of living with American, since many services for which we pay—such as medical care, higher education, or rent—are provided free or very inexpensively by the Soviet government, but certainly the enjoyment of material well-being in Russia is still *far* below that of our economy.

Against this somber backdrop, American capitalism has performed exceedingly well. Despite our submerged fourth of a nation, we are closer than any community in history to attaining that bright goal seen by Keynes—an economy without poverty. Indeed, we are almost there! For if the trend of the past continues into the future for another *twenty years,* we may within our own lifetimes usher into being the first economy of universal sufficiency the world has ever seen.

The possibility is clearly there. In 1929 our average income for all families and unattached individuals was $2,340. Translate this into the dollar values of the mid-1960s and you boost the mid-mark of American living standards in the zenith year of pre-Depression capitalism to the equivalent of about $4,500 of 1965 purchasing power.

Today the comparable figure for the average after-tax income of all families and unattached individuals is approaching $7,500. In other words, with all price increases washed out, the average household is some two-thirds better off than it was in the so-called heyday of American capitalism. Now project this rate of improvement forward another thirty-odd years to the year 2000, and a genuinely impressive and certainly unprecedented vista opens. By 2000 our average-household income—at today's values —would be nearly $15,000. And if we should avoid the wasted years of a major depression, the figure would be considerably higher.

Better yet. In that potential world of plenty, the gulf between rich and poor will likely have narrowed still further. For over the past thirty years, the income of less-well-off households has risen half again as fast as the income of upper-income households. Partly this has been due to a great leap in the productivity of the working class; partly it has been due to a deliberate attempt to limit wealth at the top by policies of progressive taxation. As a result, according to the calculations of Dr. Simon Kuznets, the share of the nation's income going to the very apex of the economic pyramid—the upper one per cent of income receivers—has been nearly sliced in half since 1929. And while the concealing of top incomes via expense accounts, tax-exempt interest, and capital gains has undoubtedly made the real decline a good deal less in fact than these figures indicate, there can be no doubt that capitalism is handing out its rewards on a more egalitarian basis than ever before.

So if the trend of the past continues, then in the hopeful vistas of the future we can expect the lowest quarter of the nation to have done better than merely ride with the current. It is not likely that the rich will be much further squeezed, for already tax avoidance has become a dangerous competitor of old-fashioned money-making. But the redistribution may yet be brought about by shunting more of the gains from growth toward the lower income brackets instead of sharing them with rich and poor alike.

To be sure, there is a caveat. The redistribution of the past has been brought about, as we have seen, because the average working person has been carried along on the flood tide of economic growth even faster and farther than the capitalist. Significantly, the factory worker—Karl Marx's proletarian hero and the proverbial underdog of capitalism—is no longer to be found among the ranks of the poor. The worker in an average manufacturing establishment makes $5,000 a year, and one in five makes more than $6,500.

But there is a danger that in our system there will develop a new lower class that will not be lifted up on the general advance. The tenant farmers on submarginal farms, the inhabitants of bypassed areas like the Cumberlands, the discouraged slum families caught in the "culture of poverty," and above all the Negro, victim of decades of oppression that is not yet ended —all these fail to respond to the rise of the economy because they are not *in* the economy. Their poverty is social rather than economic—a fact that reflects well enough on the sheerly functional characteristics of capitalism, but that makes their poverty neither less ugly nor any easier to remedy.

For the majority, however, the outlook is surely hopeful. Does this mean, then, that capitalism has solved its economic problems, whatever its lingering social ones? Is the future now the bright path indicated by Keynes?

Not necessarily. For if capitalism is growing richer, it is also growing in other directions and displaying other trends—not all of them healthy ones. Capitalism has fulfilled its most pressing requirement—the provisioning of its constituents. It holds out a prospect of an even better life. Now we must inquire whether there are other forces at work which may project a very different vision of the future.

We must go back a few years to study what these forces may be. And so we listen first to a warning voice that came in 1932.

Significantly, it had nothing to do with Keynes's vista of the future, and it was certainly not couched in his entertaining mixture of whimsey and hopeful economics. The warning lay in the dry statistics of a book—*The Modern Corporation and Private Property*—and its authors, Adolph Berle and Gardiner Means, wasted no time on the year 2030. They were concerned about a trend which would materialize a great deal sooner.

It was this: If the dominant trend of American business continued for another fifty years, the traditional fabric of capitalism would be destroyed.

For looking at the American market place, Berle and Means found an appalling statistic: in 1932, *one half* of all corporate wealth was in the hands of just two hundred companies. Worse yet, at the rate at which the two hundred behemoths seemed to be growing, compared with the three million pigmies which made up the rest of American enterprise, by 1950 it appeared likely they would control *three quarters* of the nation's incorporated wealth. And by 1975 or thereabouts—to carry Berle and Means's figures to their logical, if unstated, conclusion, the two hundred giants would virtually rule the economic life of the nation, not unlike the feudal principalities which once ran the economic life of Europe.

But it was not just the statistics of size that impressed the two observers—although the biggest of these companies was already wealthier than twenty-one of the States of the Union. The shattering impact of their statistics was in the implication they held for the market system itself. For when the heads of the companies that turned out nearly half the goods America bought could be comfortably seated around the banquet table of a modest hotel, the whole traditional concept of competition suddenly appeared woefully unrealistic.

Were U. S. Steel and Bethlehem Steel, each respectfully and warily eyeing the other, to conduct themselves as if they were just two vegetable hawkers in a crowded market? Were the three firms in automobiles who did two-thirds of the business to act as if they didn't *know* they controlled their industry? Or the three who occupied the same position in cigarettes, or farm machinery, or tires, or office machinery, or tin containers?

Obviously not. It was no longer each man for himself and devil take the hindmost. The new situation dictated a new philosophy of live and let live. And although such a code of behavior might be a great deal easier on the businessman, what did it do to the consumer? The whole moral justification for capitalism lay in the fact that in a competitive market the consumer was king. When

te was carried out under the aegis of enormous enter-
no longer *had* to compete, it looked very much as if
hantle had been shifted to the shoulders of the producers.

And to compound the danger, these producers were no longer
even responsive to the economic interests of their "owners."

Traditionally, of course, it was just the conflict of interests
of owners which made up the mechanism of the market in the
first place. But the men who ran American Telephone and Telegraph or Pennsylvania Railroad were not the owners of those
companies. All they had to show, by way of ownership, was a
tiny fraction of millions of outstanding shares. The average holdings of management among the nation's biggest corporations were
less than three per cent of their shares. In a third of the biggest
companies they were less than one per cent.

The actual owners, in the eyes of the law, were thousands of
stockholders, scattered about the country, who held one, ten,
or even a thousand shares each. But these innumerable owners
displayed none of the time-honored prerogatives of ownership:
they neither operated their businesses nor had a voice, save at
the most distant remove, in their operation. Many didn't even
know what "their" companies made. "Ownership" seemed to
have drifted into a kind of passive speculation, a ticket to income, a piece of paper which might be advantageously traded
on the market.

And this left the managers singularly free to pursue whatever
ends they desired. The element of compulsion, which still drove
the owner-manager of a corner drugstore to behave in the market
as Adam Smith had said he *had* to behave, was lacking for the
great corporation executives. Freed from the immediate pressure
of competition, only remotely responsible to the thousands of
legal "owners" who dutifully voted their proxies as management urged them to, the rulers of giant business were in a state
of economic limbo.

They might, of course, behave as the textbooks preached. Or
they might simply milk their corporations for their own gain:
one tobacco company president, over stockholder protests, paid
himself a million dollars a year. Or they might embark on the
most praiseworthy labor or community relations. But the point

was, it was no longer possible to predict their actions by pointing to the simple motive of "self-interest" in a simple environment of competition.

Such a system of independent managership might be good or bad—but it was certainly not traditional capitalism. For the essence of capitalism was that no producer could set himself up as an independent force, to do exactly as he wished. All were locked together in a chain-step march, and the result—as Adam Smith had never wearied of explaining—was the triumph of the consumer.

Now that seemed like a vanished ideal of the past. The new independent managers shrugged their shoulders at the market, smiled at the fictional character of ownership, and simply ran their businesses—reconciling the claims of labor, stockholder, government, community, and themselves—as best they could and as they saw fit.

One observer—Professor James Burnham in a book called *The Managerial Revolution*—suspected we were drifting into a society in which a self-perpetuating body of professionals would order the economic world, much as Veblen had once hoped his engineers would do. Burnham even had the chilling notion that the professional managers of neocapitalism resembled no one quite so much in the tasks they performed as the professional managers of the Russian commissariats and the Nazi combines.

That was one avenue into the future along which the economy seemed to be moving thirty years ago. We shall return to it later, for the question of whether private property is crystallizing into a kind of latter-day feudalism is obviously of prime importance for any appraisal of the future.

But it was not the only warning voice. From a different quarter of the economic world came a second caution, equally concerned with the decline of traditional capitalism. This time, however, the threat was not huge business: it was huge government.

We have already briefly met its protagonist: Dr. Friedrich Hayek. The reader will perhaps remember that during the Second World War Dr. Hayek attacked government planning in *The Road to Serfdom*, about which Keynes seemed to be of two minds—both liking the book and disagreeing with it.

But while Keynes disagreed with Hayek about the *need* for planning, his defense of the *dangers* of planning did seem rather weak. Hayek had watched the progressive enslavement of his native Central Europe under the iron rule of fascism and he believed he saw in that relentless process something like an internal law. He believed, in fact, that once a government had interfered enough with the market mechanism it had no alternative but to embrace the economy in a top-to-bottom rigid grip.

It was not *every* government action which thus carried the seeds of proliferation. Of some interference—for some welfare purposes, or to redress an obviously inequitable balance of power, or to offset a bad depression—Hayek approved. It was another kind of government activity whose consequences he feared: the direct control over economic activity itself.

For what seemed to mark off this kind of planning from the milder and more beneficent sorts of government interference was that planning was characterized by a peculiar inability to call a halt to itself. Once set in motion, an *inner* necessity forced it to expand.

That necessity did not rise from the personal motives of the planners—one might almost say it arose despite them. For the planners did not set out in every case to control the nation's entire economy. All they wanted to do was to plan a few *sections* of that economy—say, its steel output or its export industry.

But there was a difficulty. It was not so simple to plan just one part of an otherwise planless society—indeed, the task was like trying to walk a straight line through a crowd. However carefully calculated the plan, however thoughtfully hedged against contingencies, something invariably turned up which threw it out of kilter. Perhaps it was a business which failed to meet a deadline with some essential subassembly; perhaps a union which went out on strike; perhaps merely the changing tastes of consumers which upset prices in the rest of the economy.

Such miscarriages of expectations are the despair of every private businessman. But what is only a private misfortune for him is a national calamity for the planner. For if a large and integrated plan for a vital section of the economy collapses, it may endanger the entire productive effort of the community itself. So what is a planner to do when he meets his unavoidable trouble-spots? The answer—the easy and obvious and sensible answer—is to plan *still more,* to widen the original plan so as to embrace the unruly elements of the economy within the smooth mechanism of directed activity.

Thus in England, for example, in order to achieve the planned production of the nationalized coal mines in the late 1940's, it was necessary to introduce a plan for the recruitment of labor, and in order to achieve the planned recruitment of labor, a planned schedule of wages had to be set up, and in order to keep coal-mining wages at a suitable differential over other wages, the whole national pattern of industrial pay became a matter of concern. What had started as a simple output plan became necessarily a far wider one. Just as the easiest way to walk through a crowd is to order it to line up in straight rows, so the easiest way to have a plan work is to *make* it work.

And in the end? Hayek feared that planning led inexorably to what Lenin called Who Whom: who plans whom, who directs, chooses, allocates what to whom? It spelled the end not only of capitalism but of personal liberty as well.

That was a second fate which seemed to lie hidden in the trend of capitalist development. And as if two such prospects for the future were not enough, still a third appeared. This one asked the most depressing question of all: Can capitalism *continue* to grow?

The question was put in the late 1930's by a man who could be seen almost any day hurrying across the Harvard Yard to lecture to his class. Professor Alvin Hansen was one of the most respected of the American economists; behind his back he was called "the American Keynes." When he went down to Washington to testify in the monopoly investigations (he appeared complete with green eye-shade and classroom pointer), he turned the committee into a hushed private seminar. "The discussion is getting so interesting, Doctor," said the chairman, "that we are violating our rules on all sides."

No wonder it was interesting. Hansen felt that the whole environment of capitalism was changing, and changing in a most unfortunate way. A great current which had carried the capitalist ship along in the past was petering out, and henceforth progress would have to be made without the aid of a constant, favoring, urgent stimulus.

What was the stimulus? No one would have been more surprised than Malthus—it was population growth.

Malthus had believed that the great barrier to economic progress was the flood of mouths which gobbled up any slight surplus society might wring from Nature. But Hansen saw population growth in a different light. While a runaway population might swamp society, a reasonable rate of increase should have the opposite effect. It should spur society on by giving it a constantly growing demand for new homes, more clothes, larger quantities of goods of every kind. A regular increase in the nation's census—provided it was held within bounds—was the safest and surest guarantee that an adventurous program of expansion would turn out to have been a sensible undertaking.

In the past that regular increase in population had certainly taken place. Each decade had brought with it a vast new market: between 1800 and 1810 we had added a million Americans to the nation; between 1810 and 1820, 2 million; in the next decade twice that, and in the decade of the Civil War twice that again. The ten years at the turn of the century saw 12 million added to the nation, and in *each* of the decades that ended in 1910, 1920, and 1930 *fifteen* million citizens had been added to our population.

But looking at the census figures of the 1930's, Hansen found an alarming trend. The rate of population growth was slowing down. In England and France it had virtually come to a stop; in America it was rapidly tapering off. We were still a growing nation—but a much more slowly growing one.

In the depression thirties only 8 million new customers enlarged the market—*half* the usual increase. No wonder, said Hansen, that this depression proved so difficult to cure. And in the ten years which loomed ahead from 1940 to 1950 only 6 million were estimated to appear—only *one-third* of the normally expected extra market. Then by the last quarter of the century, if the trend continued, the great era of growth would come to a complete stop. America would face a static population.

Malthus would have been delighted; Hansen was not. For this meant that the single greatest stimulus to investment could not henceforth be counted on. And if investment were to be deprived of its surest ally, if there were to be a slackening in the process of investment growth on which everyone from Adam Smith to Keynes had pinned his hopes, what would happen to the American prospects for the future?

The possibility could not be summarily written off. To be sure, the fabulous enrichment of the American people had not depended entirely on population growth. There had been the West to conquer, and there had been a protean flow of revolutionary want-creating inventions. But just as population growth could no longer be relied upon to exert its powerful impetus (think of the housing alone needed to satisfy a fifteenfold increase in American population in the nineteenth century!), so the old frontier was a thing of the past. The West was no longer unexplored territory where any man might make his fortune; it was a stalwart competitor of the East.

And what did all this imply? It meant that in the future the stimulus for capitalism's investment would rest on the shoulders of technological progress *alone*. And this carried with it a difficulty of a special kind. The great inventive contributions of mankind had always come in sudden bursts: an era of industrial revolution; an era of railroadization; an era of electrification; another of automotive building. Each cluster of inventions had resulted in a spurt of investment, but when each had run its course, the hectic activity of building was succeeded by a period of quiescence.

The future might be equally as inventive as the past—perhaps even more so. But the *pace* of invention was likewise apt to be as sporadic and irregular. Unless the economy were bolstered *between* its periods of technological advance, it would surely develop a succession of depressions—deep depressions made all the more intractable by the lack of an undercurrent of steady population growth or the easy availability of new geographical markets.

And the upshot was this: it looked as though the government motor which had been hastily rigged during the worst of the depression doldrums would have to be converted into a fixed auxiliary engine. The old free-enterprise system would have to settle for a partner—an unwanted but necessary partner—in the shape of a *permanent* stream of government spending to keep the economy moving steadily on ahead. The era of self-directed, self-powered capitalism had come to an end; a new era of state-controlled "mature" capitalism was beginning.

It was hardly an outlook calculated to instill a bland confidence in the future. And these were only the major issues which perturbed the diagnosticians of capitalism in the late 1930's and early 1940's. There was a host of subsidiary questions too, recurring flurries of concern about gold or labor or agriculture or tariffs and international trade. But the three main questions—the drift toward corporate bigness, the danger of over-planning, and the uncertainty of growth—seemed to penetrate to the heart of the matter. For these tendencies appeared as *trends* of capitalist development and as such seemed to pose a series of deep-rooted, indigenous problems for the future.

Were these worries justified, or were the "trends" only transient difficulties? Over a quarter of a century has passed since the questions were propounded, and capitalism has had ample time to rid itself of any temporary aberrations which might have misled its observers in the 1930's. If the trends were only a passing phase, then the dangers they suggested should be much less evident today. Are they?

Well, consider the fact that in the late 1950's the hundred and thirty-odd largest manufacturing corporations accounted for *half* the manufacturing output in the United States, and that the two hundred and fifty biggest firms turned out a flow of goods equal in value to the output of the *entire* economy prior to the war. These figures hardly indicate that Berle's and Means's fears were groundless.

Nor were those of Dr. Hayek. By the late 1960s total state, local, and federal government expenditure had grown to comprise one out of every four dollars of our Gross National Product. Our Federal budget, despite the attempts of Republicans and Democrats alike to pare it down, seemed to display an intractable expansive impetus; Federal expenditures for all purposes rose from $40 billion in 1949 to more than $130 billion by 1967. Most of this, to be sure, was associated with a growing level of national defense. Yet to many people the trend seemed to indicate that Hayek's premonitions of a self-feeding drift to planning were

indeed justified and that the implications for freedom were anything but auspicious.

Dr. Hansen's misgivings with regard to growth looked somewhat less prescient at first. There had been trembles in the line
of economic advance to be sure, but from the late 1930's, through
and then beyond the war, the pace of advance had been spectacular. Gross National Product, which was less than $100 billions
when Hansen issued his warnings about a "mature" economy,
had grown to seven times that size—and measured in tonnages
and yardages of output, rather than in rising prices, total production had quadrupled since 1935. Yet the fact that growth
had been largely brought about by two wars and a mounting
level of government expenditure continued to raise Hansen's
question: would we grow if government spending stopped?

Thus the warnings posed by the investigators of capitalism in
the late 1930's do not seem to have been without substance.
The central questions of a quarter century ago continue today
to comprise the great economic questions facing capitalism. Let
us follow the main lines of contemporary economic thought to
find out what these problems portend for the future.

Are we headed for an economy in which a few business giants
will have swallowed up all economic activity? Certainly the
statistics of business size are awesome. Before World War II when
a company like General Motors achieved a billion dollars' worth
of sales it rated a headline in the financial pages. Nowadays the
only interest that "a billion dollars," as a unit of measurement,
holds for the financial community is whether General Motors will
make once or twice that sum as *profit*.

Yet the raw facts of bigness dramatize but do not elucidate the
issue. And that issue is not the emergence of individual Brobding-
nagian firms, but the question of whether en masse the giants
are taking over more and more of the economic activity of the
nation.

Here the evidence is surprising. The top 100 industrial corporations owned 25 per cent of all industrial corporate wealth in
1929; in 1960 they owned 31 per cent. This is evidence of continued growth of the business giants, but growth at a much less
alarming rate than that feared by Berle and Means. Perhaps

equally important, the degree of concentration within various industrial markets—that is, the proportion of sales in those markets
made by the biggest companies—seems to have remained virtually
unchanged in most cases since the end of World War II.

What has brought about this slowdown in over-all expansion
and this stability in concentration ratios? Many factors have undoubtedly combined to bring about the result—the anti-trust laws
that have prevented big businesses from mergers that might have
affected concentration ratios, the generally prosperous state of the
economy that has encouraged the formation and growth of
smaller businesses, the decline of the old-fashioned tycoon bound
for acquisition by the newer-fashioned "professional" manager
interested in preserving his corporate empire for the long run.

Does this mean that Berle and Means's worries about business
giantism are to be set aside? Far from it. We have avoided the
danger of galloping concentration but we have by no means
avoided the consequences of an economic system in which big
managed businesses, rather than small "owned" businesses are the
main protagonists of the market process.

We can see the result in the changing character of that all-
important regulating force of competition.

Before a Senate Investigating Committee in 1958, for example,
it was made pretty plain that "competition," in the lexicon of
large enterprise, largely meant tempting customers away from
rivals by product "differentiation" or by fancy service or better
advertising or more enticing corporate images. This new definition of competition gave every advantage to the consumer
except one. It no longer gave him a mechanism which automatically operated to push *prices* down to the lowest level
compatible with costs of production. Indeed, sometimes the new
"competition" seemed to ensure that the customer paid not the
lowest but the highest possible price. In 1957, for example, the
Ford Motor Company announced new car prices up some 2.9
per cent over the previous year. Two weeks later General Motors
published a price list which was up an average of 6.1 per cent.
Whereupon the Ford Company quickly revised its prices *upward,*
in order (as a company spokesman explained) "to meet competition."

Thus even if the big corporations were extending their sway

only very slowly within the total economy, within the industries in which they were predominant, something foreseen by Berle and Means was indeed taking place. It was the slow breaking down of the traditional function of the market as the supreme economic authority of a free-enterprise economy. In the old atomistic world on which the theory of capitalism had been based, it could truly be said that the consumer was king and that the business firm was his servant. In the new world of industrial giants, the consumer was no longer the unequivocal master of the economy. Indeed, as Professor Berle wrote in 1957, "some of these corporations are units which can be thought of only in somewhat the way we have heretofore thought of nations."

Does this mean that the corporation is today free of all the traditional web of competitive controls, which from Adam Smith's time on have been relied upon to bend individual self-interest to the social will? Does it mean that the consumer, the much lauded master of capitalism, is now only a puppet-king—encouraged in his ceremonial office, which is buying, but prevented from performing his real office, which is ruling?

The situation is not quite that black. Whereas *within* the oligopolistic markets (to use the technical term for markets controlled by only a few sellers) competition is giving way to "administered" prices, *among* oligopolies a meaningful economic battle rages. The battle of prices no longer is waged between U.S. Steel and Bethlehem, but it still engages *all* steel against all aluminum, all aluminum against all glass, glass against plastics, plastics against wood, wood against concrete, and concrete—to complete the circle—against steel. In this battle of industries, the consumer still plays his pivotal role and still commands a formidable power.

In addition, one contemporary economist, John Kenneth Galbraith, has called attention to a new safeguard in this world of competing oligopolies. Great masses of power on one side of a market, he points out, are often faced by "countervailing" masses of power on the other. Thus the great corporation is matched against the great union; the great producer of raw materials is faced with an equally powerful processor of its products; the enormous manufacturer must contend with the enormous chain retail outlet or chain department store. Such countervailing power does not arise in every case, and not in all circumstances—including, most importantly, the circumstance of inflation when big business and big labor use their power not against each other but in tandem against the consumer. But in "normal" circumstances there often appears to be a division of power *across* the market, which provides some of the price protection no longer afforded by a competitive atomization of power *on each side* of the market.

And then Galbraith has pointed out another overlooked aspect of the world of oligopolies—it is a good deal pleasanter world than the old dog-eat-dog competitive situation. For the old economic combat of competition was not an unmixed blessing: while it held private economic power at a minimum, it did so at a price—it also made men ruthless. Karl Marx's capitalists did not tread on the faces of the poor because they were cruel at heart; as Marx pointed out, they *had* to exploit labor if they were going to stay in business. Hence a degree of oligopoly, by sheltering the businessman from the pitiless pressures of the market, also allows him to lift his workers' noses from the grindstone.

The result is a contradiction of textbook gospel. It is not the nation's competitive industries that pioneer in research or forward-looking labor policies. "The showpieces," writes Galbraith, "are, with rare exceptions, the industries which are dominated by a handful of large firms. The foreign visitor, brought to the United States . . . , visits the same firms as do the attorneys of the Department of Justice in their search for monopoly."

What are we to make of this whole complex issue of corporate power? As with many economic problems, there are no black-and-white answers. If Berle and Means were unduly pessimistic in anticipating an engulfing growth of the giant corporations, they were eminently foresighted in predicting that huge enterprises, managed by men who were no longer beholden either to the "owners" of the business or to the "market," would constitute a form of power quite unlike that on which capitalism was presumably founded. That this power can be used irresponsibly and to the detriment of the consumer is obvious. At the same time it is also evident that the great oligopolies are not yet an encrusted economic feudalism and that their very size leads not only to economic problems but also to some far-reaching social benefits.

In short, we seem to confront a form of economic power great with possibilities for economic good or evil, which is not yet "rationalized" within an overarching philosophy of political economy nor regulated within a system of institutional controls. In the end, of course, unless we are resigned to a kind of business neo-feudalism, the new corporate powers must find a legitimate place within, and not above, their larger social and political matrix. What that place will be, how their responsibilities will ultimately be defined, and in what way the new balance of economic power will be achieved are questions which today—and surely for a long while to come—will remain among the crucial problems with which modern capitalism must be concerned.

One thing is certain, however. The continuing expansion of individual corporate giants makes the continuing expansion of the total economy doubly important—not only as a means of affording more goods and services to the nation, but to ensure that big business growth will *not* engulf the economy.

And hence our concern with corporate bigness brings us, by an unexpected route, back to Professor Hansen's problem. What are the chances that we will continue to grow? And how much must we rely on government support in order to grow?

At first sight, unlike the frightening statistics of business size, the statistics of economic growth seem to dispel all of Hansen's worries. He was concerned, we will remember, with the slowing down of our rate of population growth and with the added burden which would thus be thrust on technology as the principal carrier of capitalism's growth. In the late 1930's these seemed like grave problems, but distance has lent a new perspective to them. For following World War II a totally unexpected upsurge in the birth rate—from about 17 per 1,000 in 1935 to nearly 25 per 1,000 in the 1950s—radically changed the population outlook. In retrospect, the low birth rates of the thirties appear to have been a Depression and post-Depression phenomenon, and the long secular increase in population bids fair to continue for a very considerable period. Indeed, as we have seen in our chapter on Malthus, if there is any worry stemming from the population outlook, it is that our rate of growth may be too high, not too low.

More important, in hindsight it is clear that in the 1930s we seriously underestimated the power of the technological thrust behind the economy. Only recently have we become aware that the curve of technology is rising almost vertically beneath our feet, that we are only *entering* the age of science. A Harvard professor has computed, for example, that of all the scientists of whom history has ever known, *ninety per cent* are alive today; a General Electric vice-president reports that of all the money spent by all public and private sources for research and development in the United States since 1776—$100 billion in all—half was spent in the last ten years.

Thus, the technological prospect for growth also looks bright. Does this lay the ghosts that Hansen conjured up in the committee rooms in the 1930s? Not quite. If the momentum of our economy seems secure—certainly much more secure than it seemed in the anxious days when Hansen warned about the long-term outlook—it still has its problemsome aspects.

The first of these concerns the relationship between arms spending and growth. A fact that is often overlooked when we reflect pridefully on our economic record since World War II is the degree to which our economic expansion has been aided by military expenditures. First the Second World War itself, as the cure for the doldrums of the post-Depression semirecovery; then the stimulus of Korea; then the continuing alerts of the Cold War; and finally Vietnam: with the exception of the first five postwar years, military expenditures never failed to add at least $20 billion and in most years $30 to $50 billion of purchasing power each year. Today roughly a tenth of our total output is bought by the Defense Department, and the indirect repercussions of those purchases sustain an even larger proportion of output.

Does this mean that we are a "war economy"—that in the event of effective world disarmament we would suffer a collapse? Few, if any, economists believe so. A gradual phasing-out of defense spending should enable many arms contractors to switch to peacetime goods, while the taxation rollback associated with lower defense spending would also swell the demand for these goods.

Yet, if few economists see disarmament as the cause of a major depression, most economists do see it as the signal for a considerable increase in peacetime public spending. Why? In part the answer lies in the backlog of unsatisfied public needs that have a high moral priority on output—the repair of our decaying cities, the solution of our snarled transportation problem, the cleansing of our air and water, and the provision of care for the aged, of recreation for the young, and of education for a college-bound generation.

But also in part the reason is that most economists feel that the private sector, left to itself, might well fail to generate *enough* purchasing power to absorb the enormous output of our present-day economy. Although private investment and private spending will continue to be the mainstreams of economic activity, nearly all economists agree that there is need for an important subsidiary stream of public expenditure if we are to be certain that the volume of demand will be large enough to buy up all our production.

What is the reason for this fear? It is that we have experienced a drag of unemployment, even during the best years of our post-war growth. Until the mid-1960s, our rate of joblessness hovered between 4 and nearly 7 per cent—not so serious as to constitute a major threat to our well-being, but certainly not good enough to enable us to consider ourselves a full-scale economic success. Worse, unemployment was concentrated in certain social groups that could least well fend for themselves; in 1966, for example, the unemployment rate was 7.3 per cent among laborers, and reached up to 30 per cent among Negro young people. Only by applying the extra push of public demand, many economists believe, can this waste of human resources be kept to a minimum.

To this we must now add a second problem. It is that technology has been steadily changing the structure of employment. A look at the table below makes the point clear:

DISTRIBUTION OF EMPLOYED WORKERS (PERCENTAGES)

	Agriculture, forests, fisheries	Manufacturing, mining, transportation, construction, utilities	Trade, professional and personal services, government
1900	38	37	25
1963	8	36	56

Concealed within the table is a dramatic fact. Somewhere during the past sixty years—in fact, during the late 1940s—the number of people engaged in providing services of various kinds—clerks, teachers, policemen, lawyers—exceeded the number engaged in making or handling goods. A society concerned primarily with production has given way to one concerned primarily with administration and distribution.

What has brought about this dramatic shift? The answer is largely technology, which has steadily replaced the work done by people in the goods-producing parts of the economy with work done by machines. As a result, labor has left those areas in which machines were more economical than humans and has entered the fields of services in which humans are far superior to machines.

What has this to do with the future? The answer is that we now stand at what may be the threshold of a new era of technological advance—an era in which machines can be made to perform more and more work in the service sector. Anyone who has visited a modern bank or insurance company or corporate office and seen the batteries of silent computers and clunking electric printers knows that machines can now do the work of filing clerks and accountants and tellers and office managers and junior executives. In other words, technology may be entering the fields that have hitherto provided the great refuge for the labor that has been displaced from the farm and the factory. The question is, then, where will future displaced labor go?

The question is not difficult to answer. If we want to apply the skills of tomorrow's workers who may be unable to find work in the traditional places, where would we look? We would look to precisely those areas that the economists have already selected for their high moral urgency—to the repair of the cities, the strengthening of the public safety and convenience, the improvement of education and recreation, and so on. In a word, *the new frontier for employment is apt to lie in the same direction as the new priorities for spending—in the growth of public rather than private activity.*

Thus, curiously enough, Hansen seems to have been right in his final prognosis, even if not in his immediate outlook. The expected slowdown in population growth or in technology did not materialize—indeed, just the contrary—but the expected reliance on government spending did.

Thus, the pursuit of Dr. Hansen's problem brings us back to consider Dr. Hayek's. For if our future expansion is to take place in an environment of government participation, then *planning* will play a far more important role in our economy. Does that portend the road to serfdom? Must planning end in Lenin's Who Whom?

It can. When a country in misfortune plans—say, an underdeveloped country in a desperate hurry for industrialization— then planning almost inevitably encroaches on the prime areas of economic freedom. You cannot plan for survival without allocating men to jobs and materials to producers, and it is doubtful whether you can make such allocations and still retain a free-market system.

But all planning is not planning for survival. In a country such as the United States, planning would not be to ration scarcity but to assure the advent of abundance. And in such a setting there is much less reason to expect an explosion of planning to set in. It is not a matter of indifference to an underdeveloped country if its economic plans fail to live up to expectations; it is a matter of emptier bellies in the whole nation. But not so in a wealthy economy. The main purpose of planning in a rich community is to ensure that *enough* economic activity is carried on to prevent a slump or unemployment, or to assure that the quality of life keeps pace with the sheer quantity of production. Short of defense considerations, it is rare that such planning activities carry a life-and-death urgency. Suppose, for example, that the government should undertake a highway investment program. If such a plan does not mature according to schedule, there is no need to take over the nation's cement plants: the highways—unlike the expenditures of an underdeveloped nation—can wait. It is this lack of urgency which makes the difference. Planning in a wealthy nation can have a flexibility it can never have when every project is a matter of the highest national importance.

Nonetheless, there is a final caveat. Planning in the form of government expenditure need not be a self-feeding process in a society of wealth, but we cannot so easily dismiss the possibility of a cumulative growth of planning in the form of a network of controls over our oligopolistic markets. Indeed, unless we find a way to prevent huge accumulations of market powe from imposing their wills on society, either as producers of commodities or as suppliers of labor, the government will have to provide a planning mechanism which may indeed grow large and tight. No economist has yet provided a compelling prescription for restoring the old market interplay to its traditional role of command. And at least one eminently respectable economist, Ben Lewis, commenting on the decline of the self-regulating market, has written unequivocally on what will take its place: "The years ahead will see a great increase in conscious, collective government controls and of government enterprise. . . . The conviction that great power over the economy must reside only in a government of the people will be acted on relentlessly, bluntly, and with force."

Whether or not such planning may be in fact the road to "serfdom" is hard to say. Much depends on one's political sympathies, on what Malthus called "the insensible bias of situation and interest." Perhaps in the end the crucial factor will be—as Keynes suggested—the moral reservations of the planners themselves (he rather hoped, it will be remembered, that the planners would vaguely disapprove of planning). It may well be that in an economy of want and impatience such moral hopes would be frail and foolish. Whether they will be reasonable hopes in an economy of growing affluence we do not know. Almost surely the future will see a rise in the importance of planning, in part to sustain and guide our growth, in part to control the huge and increasingly independent productive units of the economy. Whether, fifty years from now, the forebodings of Hayek or the more sanguine possibilities envisaged by Keynes will more accurately describe the texture of our economy is perhaps the most important question facing the economic society in which we live. It is not without significance that its outcome may depend as much on moral factors as on the impersonal process of economic evolution alone.

And so the issues remain—only half resolved. The weakening of the traditional competitive mechanism before the power of the great business oligopolies, the seemingly permanent use of government expenditure as a means of assuring growth, the new problems of planning—all remain in mid-development. If the worst fears of the economists and social observers who first spied these trends have not been realized, the trends themselves are very much in evidence. To put it differently, the economic structure of capitalism has developed much as was predicted, but the social consequences of these structural changes are not yet fully clear.

Does this mean that capitalism itself is, so to speak, on trial? That is a question we must postpone to our final chapter. For there is yet one more voice to be heard from. It is by all odds more sympathetically inclined toward capitalism than any we have listened to in this chapter. Strange, then, that it will give us more cause to ponder the future than any of the critics.

XI

Beyond the Economic
Revolution

THE voice belonged to Joseph Schumpeter.
No one ever knew quite what to make of this small, dark,
aristocratic man with a taste for dramatic prose and theatrical
gestures. Typically he said of himself later in life that he had
always had three wishes: to be a great lover, a great horseman, a
great economist. Two of these three wishes, he maintained, had
been granted to him.

Everyone agreed that he was brilliant—and perplexing. His
students at Harvard complained that he was never predictable,
and they were entirely right. At the tender age of twenty-seven—
his teacher said of him that he was never a beginner—Schumpeter
had set the economic world on its ear with a truly path-breaking
exposition of the process of economic growth and at thirty he
had added another feather to his cap with a superb history of
economic doctrines. But the students who attended his classes
in the late 1930's were regularly shocked to hear this expositor
of capitalist growth declare, with obvious enjoyment, that depressions, far from being unmitigated social evils, were actually
in the nature of "a good cold douche" for the economic system!

His fame increased with the years—and so did his perplex-
ingness. His earlier books were followed by a monumental work
on business cycles and then in 1942—a few years before his death
—by one of the most provocative books ever written on the future
of capitalism: *Capitalism, Socialism, and Democracy.* But his
students still had to reconcile the fact that he was the most "hope-

less" of conservatives and at the same time an admirer of Marxist economics; a sarcastic critic of the critics of capitalism, and yet its severest critic himself; a scoffer at those who fussed over every sign of trouble in the economy, and himself a diagnostician of its failing health.

What was most vexing of all was this: Schumpeter had written engagingly on what he called "plausible capitalism"—a capitalism which could achieve Keynes's goal of universal sufficiency. He agreed with his economic brethren that there was no purely economic reason why the system should not have another successful run. He neither punctured the arguments for the defense of capitalism nor raised new economic issues overlooked by the critics. He even went so far as to predict that the system would endure for another fifty or a hundred years.

And yet, in his point-blank fashion, he wrote this final appraisal of the future: "Can capitalism survive? No. I do not think it can."

Had sentiment alone moved his pen, it would never have written such a sentence. Schumpeter was the most romantic of economists, and capitalism to his eyes had all the glamor and excitement of a knightly jousting tourney. But that was just the trouble. The jousting tourney required a properly stirring setting, and in the humdrum, matter-of-fact, *businesslike* atmosphere which business itself was fostering, the old pioneering capitalist spirit could never survive.

For capitalism, to Schumpeter's mind, could maintain its forward momentum only as long as capitalists behaved like knights —or at least pioneers. Not all of them, of course: for every daring entrepreneur, there was bound to be a whole flock of timid followers. But the driving impetus for the system came from men of courage, men who risked their fortunes to implement new ideas, who dared to innovate, to experiment, to expand.

And that type was on the wane. Worse, it was being destroyed by its own civilization. Daring as the capitalist was, his civilization was pre-eminently built on a rational, inquiring, skeptical attitude. Originally that rationalism had destroyed the pretensions of kings and lords. But now it turned its cold and disconcerting gaze on itself. "Money isn't everything," said the intellectuals, and in so doing they sowed a seed of doubt about the values of money-making as an end in itself. "Private property is no more sacred than the divine right of kings," said the intellectuals, and in so doing they exposed the basis of privilege in a business society to be no more necessary or inviolable than that of privilege in a feudal society. The romantic ideals, the sacrosanct ideology of business were thus held up to the harsh light of rationality, and the result was that the values of the business way of life lost their attractive glow. You cannot hold a jousting tourney if the audience thinks the whole performance is slightly ridiculous: even the most ardent of knights will lose his zest if no one applauds his success.

But capitalism was not only falling from an attack by its intellectuals; it was decaying from the inside as well. The once daring, independent, perhaps unscrupulous, but always energetic knight of business was being replaced by a very unknightly figure in a lackluster costume. The new lords of business were "managers," depersonalized experts, private bureaucrats. That was the real impact of big business—not its supposed menace to competition. Big business meant *conservative* business—not necessarily in policies or social ideas, but in economic daring. For as the capitalist metamorphosed into the manager, he ceased to care about capitalism as such: he settled for his large steady income and the security of his position in society and forgot about the days of risk and the quest for boundless wealth.

And so, in the end, capitalism would become old-fashioned. It would no longer be a meaningful word, an idea that could move men to action or rally supporters in a time of crisis. In time it would disappear before the oncoming march of socialism and its disappearance would be marked by neither a bang nor a whimper. Capitalism would fade away with a resigned shrug of the shoulders.

What a peculiar thesis this is!

It can neither be proved nor disproved, for note this fact: *it has nothing to do with the laws of economics.* Whether there are laws of social development, of ideological evolution, we do not know, and in any event, if Schumpeter's estimate of the vitality left in the system is correct, it will only be our children or our grandchildren who will be in a position to appraise the accuracy of his diagnosis.

But right or wrong, Schumpeter's ideas are interesting to us for another reason. For here is the first of the great economists who has carried his *economic* analysis of capitalism to its final optimistic conclusion, and then, disregarding the outcome of his economic thinking, has pronounced doom on the system for a noneconomic reason. For the first time, an economist has said that economic development by itself did not ultimately determine the history-making process by which the fate of capitalism would be settled. If Schumpeter was right, a whole chapter of economic history was coming to a close.

As we have followed that chapter down the short but furiously active avenue which began two hundred years ago, we were struck by the diversity of the worlds into which the economists molded the actual world itself. But behind this diversity was a common thread, a thread of continuity which we should now stop to recognize. It was this: *If one could divine the nature of the economic forces in the world, one could foretell the future.*

It was not that politics or ideas were thought to be unimportant or that the economists did not see that at every juncture in history the power of the sword and the pen played a role of crucial importance. It was that the power of the purse was even more important. Kings might fight parliaments and parliaments might fight wars; presidents might do wise things and foolish ones, but all the while, the economic body of society was playing out its incredibly complicated game of self-aggrandizement, and according to how that game went, so went the future.

And in the largest sense, so it did. Before capitalism came into being wealth followed power, and power was an adjunct of military or ecclesiastical or political prestige. In such a world, the future depended upon the decisions—even the whims—of a few men, and history was very nearly equated with adventure.

But after the economic revolution the old order changed. Now power followed wealth, and wealth accrued to the winners of the game of the market place. Hence when the economists sought to predict what would happen when many men, each seeking to enlarge his worldly scope, collided in the market place, they were in fact predicting the broad future of society. Individuals would still rise above the mass to impose their will on others, but for society as a whole, it was the process of money-making which gave it its *élan*, its movement, and its direction. Business cycles were not the decree of any man, but the upshot of the market; riches and poverty depended on no monarch's pleasure, but rose, fluctuated, and disappeared as the market ruled. To a greater extent than ever before, history became an automatic process, and the mold of the future was cast by an anonymous, predictable, gamelike struggle.

The predictions varied, for they placed different stress on different aspects of the game. Adam Smith saw the accumulation of capital as the decisive feature of the market world, whereas Malthus and Ricardo picked out the counterforce of population growth. Marx emphasized the struggle between worker and capitalist, Veblen the struggle between technicians and financier, and Hobson pointed to the need of huge masses of capital for overseas markets.

No single economic thread extended over the whole chapter of capitalist society. But each thread did for a while provide the motif of the future. Society *did* grow, it *was* threatened with an inundation of population, it *did* witness a class struggle, a contest between finance and production, an imperialist thrust. Indeed, if the Victorians and the Utopians failed to make a significant contribution to an understanding of their futures, it was because they failed to see the imperiousness of the economic forces at work.

But all the while that society was engaging in its single-purposed economic game, another conflicting motive was at work. Capitalism, do not forget, is the only society in human history in which neither tradition nor conscious direction supervises the total effort of the community; it is the only society in which the future, the needs for tomorrow, are entirely left to an automatic system. Scant wonder then that no sooner had the boat been set adrift than the passengers began to worry. A ship without a captain might work very well—at least so the designers promised—but suppose it did not? Suppose, for example, that its social results were not so pleasing as its economic ones—or suppose the economic ones were not so pleasing to some as to others? Then what?

At first, nothing. Adam Smith could afford to scoff at those who hoped to improve society by "doing good," since he firmly believed that welfare was best achieved as a by-product of economic action. To Malthus and Ricardo, the notion that motives other than economic should be allowed to intrude into, perhaps to upset, the market mechanism would have been a willful perversion of a demonstrably proper way of life.

The change began with John Stuart Mill and the Utopians. When Mill pointed out that economics had no ultimate solution to the problem of distribution, that society might do with the fruits of its toil as it saw fit, he introduced into the mechanical calculus of the market a conflicting calculus of moral judgment.

It was not moral judgment only in the laudatory sense. It was moral as opposed to mechanical; it was the assertion of independent conscious decision about the ends we *desired* from the economic process, as opposed to a passive acquiescence in the ends which emerged when we did nothing. The ends we desired might well be less sensible than the ends which evolved from the unimpeded action of the market—but that, of course, depended on whether the person who adjudged a change as being "sensible" was a gainer or a loser from its effect.

But once set in motion, the process of interfering with the market process did not stop. The natural outcome of the social struggle was thwarted, channeled, encouraged, and dammed at every turning—one reason, for example, that Marx's inexorable predictions never quite materialized was that we interceded in the game whenever it appeared it might otherwise proceed to a final checkmate. We curbed monopolies, we encouraged labor unions, we regulated competition, we intervened in the business cycle, we did a thousand and one things to make the economic game yield the results we wanted of it—not the result it would naturally bring.

It is not that economic motives are dead: far from it. Despite our oligopolistic trends, if the principle of "buy cheap and sell dear" did not still organize our otherwise undirected economy, we should face chaos on the market place tomorrow. If the drive to amass wealth did not still impel people to shift from job to job, to change the direction of their business efforts, to expand or contract their business operations, we should have a sluggish, inert, changeless economy instead of an active, fluid, and dynamic one. The economic motive is still present and still vitally important.

And therefore society still displays purely economic trends. Indeed, the forecasts of the modern economists are nothing but the projections of the consequences of the purely economic characteristics of our market society. But society no longer obeys its economic impulse *alone*. The very fact that the trends and problems of the last chapter are inconclusive is evidence that there is more at work than impersonal, mechanical forces. The questions which face us in the future are not the purely economic ones of whether corporations will naturally grow larger or whether we will suffer from unemployment, but the moral ones of whether we will *let* corporations grow unchecked and whether we will *allow* unemployment to develop unchecked. Government planning, public investment, antimonopoly policy—these are the tools of the antieconomic, moral impulse.

To the extent that this is true, to the extent that we no longer let the game of economics proceed unhindered to its natural outcome, we are going beyond the economic revolution. After two centuries of sailing almost as the winds directed us, the tiller of society is again in our grasp. More and more we have taken on our own shoulders the responsibility for selecting our destination —with all the inescapable dangers as well as the chances for progress that active navigation must bring. We are leaving behind us a world in which our futures were shaped, at least in the large, by the pressures of economic action; we are proceeding into a world where economic forces will play an important but no longer a predominant role.

What new factors will come to bear on us in that future we do not entirely know. We are by no means a fully controlled economy and so we can count with certainty on many of the old economic problems—booms and busts, the struggle between monopoly and competition, the endless squabble over the division of the economic cake. The problems may be muted in the new environment, but they will be there to contend with. Perhaps we shall face such subtle problems as those raised by Joseph Schumpeter—a slow but penetrating change in the atmosphere of capitalism and in its attitudes toward private property. Such possibilities must be reckoned with, but they are beyond the scope of our foreknowledge.

But two great issues we shall surely face and their importance for our survival as a free economy will be more important than all the old economic pressures or any of the new ideological ones.

First, we must face the political problem of isolation.

For there is a disturbing fact which we must take into account: most of mankind has never had, does not now have, and in all probability will never have any contact with capitalism whatsoever. Capitalism is not the dominant system of organizing man's economic activities; on the contrary—if we judge by nosecounting —it is something of a rarity, and almost an antique rarity at that.

The whole turbulent drama which we have followed in these pages has been confined to a fraction of the earth's surface, and during all these two hundred years, to countless millions of Chinese, Indians, Arabs, Africans, or South American peons the notion of a fluid and dynamic economy in which new products appeared and disappeared, in which a great chain of transactions bound together man and man, has never been anything but a tangential curiosity—strange, rude, disturbing, and often exploitative.

That is still true today. But whereas a century ago one might have guessed that the precapitalist world would develop into capitalism, today for a billion people, at least, that is a vanished hope. Perhaps four human beings out of ten live under regimes which have turned their backs on capitalism, and even if those regimes fail and fall, it is doubtful in the extreme whether their subjects will turn to a system which they have been taught to believe is harsh, cruel, and wicked.

Even in those areas of the world—like part of South America— where the development *into* capitalism is still possible, it is very unlikely that the end product will much resemble the kind of world we know. When we see the strange anachronisms of skyscrapers and peons plowing with a wooden stick, airplanes and oxcarts that give to Latin America its picturesqueness, we are perhaps reminded of seventeenth-century England, with its half-formed market economy. But there is a difference—a vital difference. In the seventeenth century, England led the world; in the twentieth century, the precapitalist countries are furiously struggling to catch up with it.

And this long and arduous process of catching up cannot be thought of solely in economic terms. For *economic* development —the long, steady rise in output and living standards—will not take place without *social and political* change. And it is here that we find the most difficult and dangerous problems of the backward nations.

For it is not easy to remake the social and political fabric of a nation just emerging from a tradition-bound past. An uncomprehending peasantry must be converted into a modern farming population; a ragged corps of casual laborers must be made over into a disciplined work force; bazaar-minded traders must become production-minded entrepreneurs; nepotistic and corrupt state bureaucracies must change into reliable civil servants. Until these changes begin, economic development will wait. But to put these into effect is, in fact, to overthrow a whole way of life—and very often, to overthrow a government and a social order wedded to that way of life.

Hence the process of economic and social and political change tends to be a long-drawn-out and turbulent affair. If it could be done quickly, that would be one thing. But, unfortunately, this is not the prospect that the logistics of development offer. It is a painfully slow task for nations that are barely staying alive to accumulate the capital goods by which the great escape from poverty can be made. It takes years for a nation which is still striving to achieve widespread literacy to acquire the pool of skills and knowledge which is a requisite for economic growth. Nothing can be done overnight to relieve the dependence of many poor nations on the single crop they export to the unpredictable markets of the world. And meanwhile, to lengthen the timetable still more, a torrent of population growth washes away the small gains in production under a deluge of births—Malthus' specter come to life.

The situation is not that black in every underdeveloped nation. There is a spectrum of conditions (and hopes) for the backward lands at least as great as or greater than that among the industrially advanced nations. But in general the implication is plain. Economic development is not a smooth evolutionary process. It tends, on the contrary, to be a disruptive revolutionary process. It is not a healing and annealing climb, but a fearful ascent, in which old and stagnant regimes perish, and new—and very likely, ruthless—regimes achieve power. It is not a time of general contentment, but a time of wild aspirations and equally black despairs, of fierce resentments, of terrible sacrifices—imposed as well as freely borne.

In a word, economic development does not hold out the easy hope that it will encourage the rise of democratically orientated, economically free societies. More likely is the prospect of authoritarian politics, strong-man governments, mild or not-so-mild dictatorships, combined with authoritarian economics, strong-arm economic measures, mild or not-so-mild collectivisms.

Thus in the great contest among economic systems in the underdeveloped areas, capitalism does not enjoy a favored position—at least not in many nations. Indeed, a realistic appraisal of the obstacles and possibilities leads us to the unwelcome conclusion that communism may well be the *direction*—although not necessarily the final destination—toward which these countries swing.

For regardless of the ulterior quality of its motives or the perversion of its purposes, communism does have one article in its export kit which we do not: a technique for vastly accelerating the rate of growth of the impoverished nations of the world. This technique is collectivism—often an iron collectivism which finds its most stark expression in the barrack-communes of the Chinese. What collectivism does—and very likely does more effectively than a free or "mixed" economy—is to mobilize the resources, material and human, of an underdeveloped economy, and to direct them with massive impact upon the problem of building the capital needed for sustained growth.

From our point of view, the cost of this collectivism is fearfully high. Not only does it often dispense summarily with the political liberties which are the treasured and delicate achievement of the West, but it deliberately denies the economic freedom which is no less a hard-won and precious Western achievement. Collectivism does not await the slow, often wasteful, growth-producing ways of the market. It simply puts men where they are needed, whether their acquisitive impulses would put them there or not. It is the method of the stick rather than the carrot—the method of ruthless force rather than voluntary choice.

Such a system is naturally repugnant to Western eyes. Yet it need not be so to many Eastern and Southern eyes. The harsh discipline of collectivism is much less noticeable at the margin of existence where life is already horribly disciplined. The loss of liberty is hardly a loss to men who have never known liberty. Such a method of achieving growth would be unsupportable for people who have already benefited from a long history of past growth. But to a people who now exist in conditions of misery and despair, it may offer the only means of escaping rapidly from the insupportable present into a better future.

In this contest of economic systems, it matters not whether our aims are ultimately more noble, more humanitarian, or more virtuous than the Communists'. Because we cannot easily encourage a revolutionary collectivism, we are very apt to appear in the eyes of a sweated Bolivian miner or a debt-ridden Brazilian tenant farmer as defenders of reaction, while the Russians play the role of Robin Hood. It is neither realistic nor necessarily advisable that we should attempt to steal the Communists' thunder. But this leaves us with the immeasurably more difficult and subtle task of persuading the world's dispossessed that we are just as concerned with their lot, just as eager to aid reform as the Russians—although our means and slogans are less dramatic and our promises less tinged with paradise than theirs. Perhaps it leaves us with the prior job of convincing ourselves that this is indeed the case.

Thus the great external problem facing capitalism is not economic at all. It is the political problem of establishing itself as the arsenal, not only of production, but also of hope and meaningful freedom to the anonymous hundreds of millions who may otherwise distrust us, fear us, and—if the awful day should ever come—take arms against us.

That is the external problem.

There is an internal one, too. For as we depart, little by little, from a philosophy of *laissez faire* and espouse a philosophy of active guidance, the question of social responsibility is inescapably thrust upon us. As long as the game of economics was played without fear of its consequences, indeed, in glad acceptance of them, the matter of responsibility lay in the background. It was not the business of business to worry about its social obligations, nor the concern of trade-unions to fret over the repercussions of their acts. Responsibility was purely a matter for the government; it was political rather than economic.

In the future that area of responsibility must vastly broaden. As long as our fate lay in the hands of an impersonal process, who could be called to task for whatever unpleasant consequences matured? But as our future becomes increasingly the object of our own selection, it is no longer possible to avoid the question of the kind of future we *want*. Do we want a more equal distribution of income or a less equal distribution? Do we want big business or little business? Do we want free labor unions or circumscribed labor unions? Do we want inflation or deflation? All these choices—and many others—lie within our own control.

Curiously the more successful our *economic* mechanism, the more pressing become these political—and moral—problems. Growth, as Professor Galbraith has pointed out, brings us more and more out of the old environment of want into a new environment of plenty, and in this increasingly affluent atmosphere the time-honored rationale which sanctified profit-oriented production begins to lose its self-evident purpose. There was a time when every act of production, by adding a needed bit to the skimpy pile of social wealth, justified itself without further question. But as our streets become clogged with traffic, as our refrigerators bulge with food and our closets with clothes, more and more of society's production takes on a "luxury" air—pleasant, but hardly comparable to the production of roads when there were no roads, of food when we were still hungry, of clothes when many people still wore rags. Worse, as we go on heaping up the items of a richer and richer life, those goods and services which fail to cater to the market demand of an affluent society lag behind. Our schools, our slums, our health, our recreational space, our cultural activities get short-changed; our "social balance" gets badly tipped. As Galbraith writes in *The Affluent Society*, "The family which takes its mauve and cerise, air-conditioned, power-steered and power-braked automobile out for a tour passes through cities that are badly paved, made hideous by litter, blighted buildings, billboards and posts for wires that should long since have been put underground. They pass on into a countryside that has been rendered invisible by commercial art. . . . They picnic on exquisitely packaged food from a portable icebox by a polluted stream and go on to spend the night at a park which is a menace to public health and morals. Just before dozing off on an air mattress, beneath a nylon tent, amid the stench of decaying refuse, they may reflect vaguely on the curious unevenness of their blessings. Is this, indeed, the American genius?"

Affluence, and its uses and misuses, are not problems which government alone can resolve. Rather, they make vivid and inescapable the fact that the political supervision over the economic process becomes more and more a problem for the entire electorate. The more we desire to intervene into the automatic working of the market system, the more profoundly we wish to reshape the economic complexion of society, the more does the electorate itself become its own guardian, its own counselor for good and evil, the director of its own destiny. A government may impose its will on a monopoly, on a credit splurge, on a gold crisis. But only a whole people can vote a change in the texture and social balance of its basic economic efforts.

And hence, curiously, economics takes on a new significance in a world in which "pure" economic society is on the wane. "Men cannot live without an economic theology," Galbraith wrote in 1952, and never was that truer than when men must themselves determine the course of their own society and elect what destination they wish to steer it toward. In the past, when economics was only an aggregative, mass process, the great economists could stand aside from the flow of events and shed their light on history purely as commentators, as analysts, or as disinterested prophets. In the present, as economics becomes entangled in the political decision-making process, that aloofness is no longer justified. There is no longer only one possible conclusion for the economic drama, but many, and the economists must not only describe for us the course on which we are sailing but point out other courses, other destinations to which we may, if we wish, direct ourselves.

This is not to say, alas, that one finds economists in general today keenly aware of the historic responsibilities and implications of their task. The trend of economic thought in our time is not toward the "magnificent dynamics" of the future, but turns aside from such speculative social forecasting to a consideration of more "scientific" matters. Many economists build "models" which reveal very skillfully the relationships of an economy in growth, or concern themselves with complex quasi-engineering problems of labor inputs and commodity outputs. These are very useful studies, but they do not open our eyes to the full meaning of the economic futures they project. For in these edifices of theory there is usually left unexamined the question of how economic growth will affect social change, or of the relevance of purely quantitative considerations to a system which produces not only goods but attitudes, morale, morality.

Perhaps this prevalent disinterest in the long-run evolutionary portents of capitalism is merely the tacit expression of a quiet confidence that capitalism is here, if not forever and ever, at least for a good long stretch. Perhaps it is evidence of an unwillingness to peer too closely into the dangerous possibilities of a time of great historic stress.

But if the temper of most contemporary economists tends to be unadventuresome and academic, there is no lack of prophecy and persuasion to which we can turn. Only they are not new voices. They go back—all of them—to the arguments and architecture of the great economists themselves.

Thus at the extreme left stand the Marxists, whose prediction of the ultimate undoing of our system is little changed from the days of Karl Marx himself. Their prophecy we know; their persuasion is that we should line up on the side of history, as they see it. It is not a blueprint of the future which the Marxists try to sell us, but a sense of historical participation, of joining the winning team, of riding the "wave of the future." If Russia or China were not there as an object lesson in applied Marxism, their urgings might be a more formidable competitor for our belief. As things now stand, the rigors which are the price of rapid collectivist growth have an appeal only to the most miserable peoples in the world—those who have never known anything but a beggar's lot. Perhaps our task is to understand with genuine compassion the hard choice that history has enjoined on the poor—and to attempt in every way to facilitate their escape from poverty.

To the right of the Marxists are the socialists. Many of them are Marxian in their prognosis of capitalism's end, but they are not Marxian in their prediction of things to come. The Marxists extol the inevitability of history; the socialists extol the idea of liberty inherent in social change. The Marxists are not so much interested in What Comes Next—but this is the very heart and essence of the socialist persuaders. Whether the society of the future is to be centralized or built on old-fashioned guilds; whether it is to be entirely planned, or only partially so; the extent to which the consumer should have a voice, and the extent to which the producer should be heard—these are the burning questions of socialism—but not of communism. While the Marxists hold out the prospect of blindly and trustingly enlisting oneself with the inexorable process of history, the socialists ask us to join them in *shaping* history as they wish it.

Next on the spectrum of prophecy and persuasion are the advocates of managed capitalism. Unlike the socialists, they do not believe that capitalism must disappear, and unlike the socialists they do not want to displace the institution of private ownership with public ownership. Their central philosophy is something else again: they feel that capitalism can be maintained *if* we intervene sufficiently to make it viable. Left to itself, they say, capitalism may run off the rails—if not its economic rails, then its moral rails. Given a strong policy of guidance, it can continue to prosper. Hence we are asked to ensure our futures with a strong pillar of government investment, with active enforcement of antimonopoly laws, with the encouragement of public activity as well as private. This road to the future lies in *making* capitalism work—rather than in relying on its inner stability.

Not so, say the next group of public counselors, the protagonists of the Right-of-Center. Capitalism can work only in an atmosphere of hands-off. While liberal aims may be commendable, the liberal means are incompatible with the essence of a market economy itself. Let the system alone and it will fare well; try to patch it up and you will only succeed in hopelessly paralyzing it.

It is some such spectrum of prophecy and persuasion that we face.

As we listen to the debates which now surround us—and which will command our attention as long as our society survives—we can recognize the voices of the past. Adam Smith still speaks to us from the platform to the Right; Karl Marx seeks to enroll us in the legions of the Left. We can distinguish the voice of John Stuart Mill in the words of the socialists, and that of John Maynard Keynes in the arguments of the liberal capitalist reformers. The analytic insight of Ricardo, the gloomy presentiments of Malthus, the vision of the more utopian Utopians, the complacency of the Victorians, the disquietude of the underworld, the shrewd skepticism of Veblen—they are all there.

Much of the teaching of the great economists no longer quite applies. And yet, it has not gone entirely out of date. For the great economists gave men an understanding of the world which has become part of our everyday philosophy. What they taught us was that the world was not just an unrelated confusion but a concatenated process, not just happening but developing. They gave us an understanding of our environment so that we might profit by it more fully; they gave us an understanding of our past so that we might better comprehend the process which is sweeping us into the future.

We shall need their insight as we progress into the future. As the control of our destiny devolves increasingly upon ourselves, we shall have to make choices—desperately important ones—among the counsels of the present. It is from the scope and wisdom of the economists of the past that we must reap the knowledge with which to face the future.

ACKNOWLEDGMENTS

THIS BOOK, more than most, owes its existence to others than the author. The economic treatises of the last two centuries would fill a fair-sized warehouse, and someone who presumed to rummage in that warehouse without a pretty fair idea of its contents would soon be overwhelmed.

Certainly I could never have undertaken such a project unless I knew what I was searching for, and therefore it is my guides— my teachers—to whom I should like to express my indebtedness. But while my guides led me to the warehouse and told me what was in it, they cannot be held responsible for the selection of ideas which I have exhumed. My purpose has been to illustrate great flowerings of thought and not to document them, to rouse the interest of the curious reader and not to drown it, and therefore my selection of material may dismay a scholar. Some men of justly great fame to the professional economist have been cavalierly dismissed with a line or two or not mentioned at all; others of minor importance may merit several pages. It is admittedly an arbitrary rearrangement of the Hall of Fame, but I must ask the scholar to recognize that many great economic ideas are interesting only to a professional, and that many minor figures in the history of economics have at least propounded interesting mistakes.

My deepest appreciation must go to Dr. Adolph Lowe of the New School for Social Research, whose help and advice I have had on every page. In particular I am indebted to him for an understanding of Adam Smith and David Ricardo, although he cannot be held to blame for whatever damage I have done his teaching. Even more than that, I am grateful to him for his warm, inquiring, and passionately human conception of economics, not as an intellectual plaything, but as a vehicle for social betterment.

To many others at the New School I also owe a debt of thanks: to Drs. Hans Neisser and Eduard Heimann for the instruction I have received at their hands, and particularly to Dr. Henry Aubrey whose many concrete suggestions and criticisms were invaluable. To my teachers at Harvard goes a belated tribute, above all to my tutor, Dr. Seymour Harris, who was the source of an enthusiasm that has lasted many years.

A special note of thanks is due my friend Peter Bernstein for his frequent and valuable counsel. And my most heartfelt appreciation goes to my wife, who has patiently endured the ups and downs of writing with superhuman good nature, who has given generously of her aid, and who has contributed most of all by steadfastly believing that the book would one day, after all, be done.

Finally, I wish gratefully to acknowledge permission to quote from Roy Harrod's *Life of John Maynard Keynes* and from John Maynard Keynes's *Economic Consequences of the Peace*.

ROBERT L. HEILBRONER

New York

A GUIDE TO FURTHER READING

ECONOMIC reading, by popular hearsay, is a veritable desert of dusty prose. In all honesty, much of it is: the student of economics must be prepared for long journeys without a single refreshing sentence; it takes the endurance of a camel and the patience of a saint to finish some of the great texts.

But not all economics falls into this category. There is much that is alive, provocative, and stimulating even to the novice, and much more that is sufficiently interesting, persuasive, or important to warrant a certain amount of heavy going. These are the books I am recommending here. They are by no means an exploration of all of economics—no short list could possibly do that. These are merely good jumping-off points from which to reconnoiter one area of the whole field. There are difficult books here, but no impossible ones and no unrewarding ones. For one reason or another I enjoyed or profited from them all. And incidentally, many of the books mentioned below are available in paperback.*

The reader might want to begin by taking a chance on an economic textbook to see what economics is really "about." It is well worth a try, provided he is prepared to go through it at his leisure, with education rather than entertainment as his aim. Out of a dozen good texts, I would suggest these two: *Economics, An Introductory Analysis* by Paul A. Samuelson (McGraw-Hill Book Co., Inc., New York, 1966), and *Economics: Principles and Policy* by Royall Brandis (Richard D. Irwin, Inc., Homewood, Illinois, 1962).

It is less simple to suggest reading in the history of economic doctrines —to suggest, that is, a book which covers the scope of this one, but in greater detail and with more attention to the full range of economic ideas. The standard is Gide and Rist, *A History of Economic Doctrines*

* Paperback reprints appear so fast it is hard to keep up with them. I have put an asterisk next to all titles that I know about in paperback editions.

(G. G. Hamp & Co., London, 1948), which is thorough and full of interesting side lights. Deeper and more critical is Eduard Heimann's *History of Economic Doctrines* (Oxford University Press, Toronto, 1945), but it requires a considerable degree of familiarity with the field. Better, perhaps, is a mimeographed two-volume set published by August Kelley in 1949: *Lecture Notes on Types of Economic Theory*. This is the actual transcript of the classroom lectures delivered by Wesley Clair Mitchell, one of America's great economists, just before his death. Mitchell delves into biography, social history, and economic ideas all at once and with great skill and charm. The two short books (together they are only five hundred-odd pages) will more than repay the concentration they justly ask, and the fact that they were originally lectures gives them an easy lightness in style which greatly simplifies the task. They even contain questions asked by pupils in the classroom.

A reader who wishes *excerpts* from most of the great economists might look into Robert Lekachman's *Varieties of Economics** (Meridian, New York, 1962). There is a short textual comment, and brief passages give one the pith of a wide range of thinkers. And finally, Joseph Schumpeter's posthumous *History of Economic Analysis* (Oxford University Press, New York, 1954) is a masterpiece of its kind, a truly encyclopedic survey of economic analysis, as brilliant and as opinionated as its author. It is apt to be pretty rough going for the non-professional; I suspect that most academic economists have never read it through.

The subject of the rise of capitalism itself has been fascinatingly dealt with in Karl Polanyi's *The Great Transformation** (Farrar and Rinehart, New York, 1944). Polanyi's book is mainly a study of the difficulty of imposing the market idea in the eighteenth century on a nonmarket-oriented world, but it also deals with contemporary aspects of this same problem. I found it wholly absorbing. On much the same subject, but focused on a different aspect of the rise of capitalism, R. H. Tawney's *Religion and the Rise of Capitalism** (New York, 1937, recently reissued by Harcourt, Brace & Co.) is in a class by itself. It is a profound work written in an unsurpassable style by a great historian. Max Weber, *The Protestant Ethic and the Spirit of Capitalism** (G. Allen and Unwin, London, 1930) is another classic in the field but somewhat more demanding of the reader. The person who wants a less specialized overview of the history of capitalist evolution might look into my own *The Making of Economic Society** (Prentice-Hall, New York, 1962).

For further historical background, the reader might turn to H. Pirenne, *Economic and Social History of Medieval Europe** (Harcourt, Brace & Co., New York, 1937) or the heavy but definitive two volumes by Eli Heckscher, *Mercantilism* (G. Allen and Unwin, London, 1935). Both are texts, not casual reading. Or there is the *Cambridge Economic History of Europe* in two volumes with many first-rate and fascinating essays by various economic historians (Cambridge University Press, London, 1952). For enjoyment I would suggest *England in 1815,* the first volume of a *History of the English People in the Nineteenth Century* by Eli Halévy (E. Benn, London, 1949) or Paul Mantoux, *The Industrial Revolution in the Eighteenth Century* (Harcourt, Brace & Co., New York, 1928), one of the best books in economic history that I know. Another excellent introduction is Phyllis Deane's *The First Industrial Revolution** (Cambridge University Press, Cambridge, 1965), lucid and fascinating.

I know of no biography of Adam Smith which I would recommend for pleasure. *The Wealth of Nations* (Modern Library, Inc., New York, 1937) has an introduction by Max Lerner which is instructive and the book is, of course, in a class by itself. It cannot easily be read through, cover to cover, but it can be wandered through with pleasure and profit.

As with Adam Smith, so with Malthus and Ricardo. The non-professional reader has slim pickings. Keynes has written a nice short sketch of Malthus in his *Essays in Biography* (Horizon Press, New York, 1951) and Mitchell's treatment of Ricardo in the aforementioned *Lecture Notes* is wholly absorbing. The whole of Ricardo's writing is now available in a multivolume edition edited under the scrupulous eye of Mr. Piero Sraffa, *Works of David Ricardo* (Cambridge University Press, London, 1951) and the last volume contains a good deal of not terribly interesting biographical material. But the reader is not advised to hurl himself into Ricardo unless he is prepared for intellectual bruises: it is all abstract argument and no easy going at all. If curious, nonetheless, try the second volume of Sraffa's work, in which Malthus' *Principles* is reproduced with Ricardo's annihilatory comments affixed to every paragraph. Here are the two friendly adversaries at their best. And for Malthus proper and the population dilemma, read *On Population* (Modern Library, Random House, New York, 1960), with a most interesting introduction by Gertrude Himmelfarb. Better yet, any one of a number of modern books on the population problem.

There is no use trying to read the Utopians. Try instead Alexander Gray's *The Socialist Tradition* (Longmans, Green & Co., Inc., London, 1946) on which I have leaned heavily for Saint-Simon and Fourier. The style is a trifle arch, but some of the quainter figures can bear this, and the book is heavily and avowedly biased in favor of Utopian as opposed to "scientific" socialism. If the immersion takes, the library will give one access to the originals: warning, however—they are all intolerably verbose. There is a nice old-fashioned biography of *Robert Owen* by F. Podmore (Appleton, New York, 1907) and a more factual but less readable one by G. D. H. Cole (E. Benn, London, 1925). Neither, however, does adequate justice to this astounding man: perhaps his own story, *The Life of Robert Owen* (Alfred A. Knopf, Inc., New York, 1920) is best for that.

Personally I prefer John Stuart Mill to any of these, and strongly recommend his *Autobiography* (latest edition, Columbia University Press, New York, 1944), a classic in itself. There is also an excellent biography by Michael Packe (Macmillan, 1954). If Mill interests one, Dr. Friedrich A. Hayek has recently published the correspondence between Mill and Harriet Taylor, *John Stuart Mill and Harriet Taylor* (University of Chicago Press, Chicago, 1951) which sheds a new light on the man himself. And as far as economics is concerned, Mill repays the effort. *Principles of Political Economy* (Longmans, Green & Co., Inc., New York, 1909) is beautifully written and still full of interest to the modern reader.

The literature on Marx is voluminous. The reader might tackle a good straightforward biography by F. Mehring, *Karl Marx: The Story of His Life** (Ann Arbor Paper Books, University of Michigan), but I would suggest a book by Edmund Wilson, *To The Finland Station** (Harcourt, Brace & Co., New York, 1940). This is, among other things, a biography of Marx and Engels, a review of their work, and a critique of historical writing in general, the excellence of all of which is enhanced by a superlative style. It is like reading a novel.

However, Edmund Wilson is not much interested in Marx's economic analysis of capitalism, and the reader who wishes to learn more of that might turn to Paul M. Sweezy, *The Theory of Capitalist Development* (Oxford University Press, New York, 1942). This is difficult thinking, but not difficult reading, and it is the best explanation of Marx's economic doctrines that I know. *Contemporary Capitalism* (Random House, New York, 1956) by John Strachey is more chatty and rather shallow, but does serve to spoon-feed the basic ideas of Marxian analysis to the general reader. It is also an interesting "second-thoughts" book by a somewhat skeptical Marxist. *Das Kapital* itself can be tackled in a one-volume Modern Library edition, or one can sample *Marx on Economics,** edited by Robert Freedman (Harvest Book, Harcourt, Brace, New York, 1961). Still better is the *Handbook of Marxism* (Random House, New York, 1935). This is a selection of the best of Marx's writings including his superb historical sketches and bits of *Das Kapital* itself. Also included are important works by Engels and Lenin and a smattering of Stalin. It is a good compendium of Marxist thinking, interesting both as historical masterpieces and as an acid comment on the level to which most Marxist writing has currently degenerated.

There is no volume on the Victorians themselves. Again Mitchell's *Lecture Notes* or Gide and Rist's *History* will be of some help. The reader might wish to look at Alfred Marshall's *Principles of Economics* (recently reissued by The Macmillan Co., New York, 1948). It is ponderous but not difficult; the obstacle is the amount of patience, not the amount of knowledge needed. Keynes, by the way, has a nice biographical bit on both Marshall and Edgeworth in his *Essays in Biography*.

The underworld makes for more enjoyable reading. Henry George is out of date, but his *Progress and Poverty* (Doubleday & Co., Inc., New York, 1926) retains an emotional appeal and is written in a rich—often overrich—journalistic style. Hobson is more serious and more absorbing. *Imperialism* (G. Allen and Unwin, London, 1938) is still to the point and enormously interesting, more so than Lenin's famous pamphlet by the same name.

Veblen himself makes magnificent reading, if you take to his style.
Not everyone does, but *aficionados* go about quoting his gems. *The
Theory of the Leisure Class** (Modern Library, Inc., New York, 1934),
is his best known work, but I would suggest *The Portable Veblen* (The
Viking Press, New York, 1950) with a brilliant introduction by Max
Lerner which projects the man himself and his basic ideas with great
clarity. The book itself covers a wide variety of Veblen's work. For
Veblen's life, one can turn to the definitive biography by Joseph Dorf-
man, *Thorstein Veblen and His America* (The Viking Press, New York,
1947), which is, unfortunately, a bit pedestrian. The times themselves
are both trenchantly and rollickingly illustrated in a superb book by
Matthew Josephson, *The Robber Barons** (Harcourt, Brace & Co., New
York, 1934).

There is only one biography of Keynes: the comprehensive but somewhat pompous *Life of John Maynard Keynes* by Roy Harrod (Harcourt,
Brace & Co., New York, 1951). Better to meet the man himself directly
through his sparkling and lucid prose, and for this the *Economic Consequences of the Peace* (Harcourt, Brace & Co., New York, 1920) and
Essays in Persuasion (Harcourt, Brace & Co., New York, 1951) are both
excellent. *The General Theory of Employment, Interest, and Money**
(Harcourt, Brace & Co., New York, 1964) is very difficult going; the
Treatise on Money (Harcourt, Brace & Co., New York, 1930) is a better
first reader, although none too easy. The meat of Keynes has been put
forth in many popularized versions, of which the best-known is Robert
Lekachman's *The Age of Keynes* (Random House, New York, 1966).

The issues of the last chapters have been compellingly discussed in
many books aimed at the general reader. It is worth while to refer to
Berle and Mean's *The Modern Corporation and Private Property* (The
Macmillan Co., New York, 1933) and to Berle's *Twentieth Century
Capitalist Revolution** (Harcourt, Brace & Co., New York, 1954). A
wittier and more iconoclastic view of corporations can be found in
Thurman Arnold's urbane *Folklore of Capitalism** (Yale University
Press, New Haven, 1937). Along the same line, James Burnham's *The
Managerial Revolution** (The John Day Co., New York, 1941) is gen-
eral enough to offer no obstacle to the nonprofessional and is a pro-
vocative—sometimes provoking—book. One might also consult a highly
readable book by John K. Galbraith, *American Capitalism, The Concept of Countervailing Power** (Houghton Mifflin Co., Boston, 1952) or
his well-known *The Affluent Society** (Houghton Mifflin Co., Boston,
1958). And do not overlook the tough but fascinating volume by Joseph
Schumpeter, *Capitalism, Socialism, and Democracy** (Harper & Bros.,
New York, 1947). In somewhat the same vein, Hayek's *Road to Serfdom**
(Chicago University Press, Chicago, 1944) is engrossing, and for a less
frightening view of the future one might look into my own *The Limits
of American Capitalism** (Harper Torchbooks, New York, 1966).

Finally the great problems of the developing nations are discussed in
a number of accessible books: W. W. Rostow's *Stages of Economic*

*Growth** (Cambridge University Press, New York, 1960) is very well known and warrants the reading. *The Strategy of Economic Development** by Albert Hirschman (Yale University Press, New Haven, 1958) is more technical but very interesting. C. E. Black's *The Dynamics of Modernization* (Harper & Row, New York, 1966) is a sweeping survey that puts the developmental process into sharp focus. And for a last, somewhat controversial view, let me again immodestly put forward my own book, *The Great Ascent** (Harper Torchbooks, New York, 1963).

INDEX

ABOUT THE AUTHOR

ROBERT L. HEILBRONER has been studying the great economists ever since he was introduced to them in Harvard University in 1936. He was graduated *summa cum laude* and Phi Beta Kappa and went on to practice economics in government and business and then to complete his graduate studies at the New School for Social Research. *The Worldly Philosophers,* his first book, achieved an immediate success with its publication in 1953 and has, with the publication of this edition, been translated into a dozen languages and become a standard introduction to economics in scores of colleges and universities. Subsequent books— in particular *The Future as History* (1959), *The Making of Economic Society* (1962), and *The Great Ascent* (1963)—have also reached a wide public, both academic and general. Dr. Heilbroner is Adjunct Professor of Economics at the New School, where he teaches, and has lectured before the National War College and many business, government and university audiences. He is married and lives in New York City and Martha's Vineyard.